When BAD things happen in GOOD bikinis

LIFE AFTER DEATH AND A DOG CALLED BORIS

Helen Bailey

BLINK

bringing you closer

Published by Blink Publishing
107-109 The Plaza,
535 King's Road,
Chelsea Harbour,
London SW10 0SZ

www.blinkpublishing.co.uk
facebook.com/blinkpublishing
twitter.com/blinkpublishing

978-1-910536-12-4

Design by Blink Publishing
Printed and bound by Clays Ltd, St Ives Plc

3 5 7 9 10 8 6 4 2

Papers used by Blink Publishing are natural, recyclable products made from
wood grown in sustainable forests. The manufacturing processes conform to
the environmental regulations of the country of origin.

Every reasonable effort has been made to trace copyright holders of
material reproduced in this book, but if any have been inadvertently
overlooked the publishers would be glad to hear from them.

Blink Publishing is an imprint of the Bonnier Publishing Group
www.bonnierpublishing.co.uk

When BAD
things happen
in GOOD
bikinis

To know the road ahead, ask those coming back.

Chinese Proverb

A PROMISE

If you are reading this book because you have suffered loss, there is only one thing I want you to know: however you feel right now, however bleak your life is, however much despair you are in, you won't always feel this way; on my dog's life, I *promise* you.

I hope that you will read the entire book, but if you are at the stage when your mind is so wired you have the attention span of a hyperactive grasshopper and the energy of a banana slug*, put the book to one side, use it as a doorstop or a fly swat, but hold on to one thing: you *will* emerge from this tunnel of grief to live, laugh and, possibly, love again. Trust me.

You won't believe me when I tell you that your life will be good again in ways that you could never have imagined. I didn't believe it either. I had to live it to believe it. So if you are grieving right now and can't see a way forward, hang on in there, it will all be OK in the end. Trust me, because I've been there, done that and bought the coffin. Trust me, because, like you, I've known what it's like to have a mind so warped with grief and despair that I've screamed at the sky, prayed to spontaneously combust in M&S, and walked out into the traffic, tempting fate, only to be sworn at by a swerving cyclist.

When our world is ripped apart, we have to start again from scratch. Think of it as learning to ride a bike, a bike with a bent frame, flat tyres and dodgy brakes, across unfamiliar stony ground. Good friends, perhaps family and those who know first-hand the

---

* The banana slug is said to be the slowest mollusc in the world with an average speed of approximately 0.000023 metres/second, making a tortoise look like Usain Bolt in comparison.

pain of bereavement will be beside you, encouraging you when you think you can't do it, supporting you when you wobble, picking you up when you fall and steering you in the right direction when you veer off course. One day, you'll realise that you are peddling on your own; you'll look back and see a crowd waving and cheering as you speed off into the distance. The bike will never be perfect, but it will get you to where you need to go.

This is the story of my learning to ride that broken bike across the alien terrain of Planet Grief. If I can do it, so can you. I promise you.

Love,

Helen

BACK THEN

*On August 11, I was walking with my supremely fit and healthy partner of eleven years to the scan of our first child, when he said he felt dizzy and collapsed. They tried for an hour to bring him back, but couldn't. The ten weeks since then have been a horrific blur, and everything you all say resonates so profoundly. It has been so comforting to hear your stories, people that know and understand. At thirty-two I am widowed (and pregnant) before my friends are married, and though my friends are being so kind at the moment, I am aware that they will inevitably stop asking, as life for everyone else carries on, whilst I am trapped in that horrific day when my world and the life of my beloved boy ended. ~ **Sam***

On Thursday 17th February 2011, I stood on the stage in the dining hall at Dover Grammar School for Girls in Kent, to give a talk about my life as a writer of young adult fiction. I enjoyed giving speeches and running workshops, and the audience in Dover was a particularly good crowd of girls eager to learn more about the life of a writer.

I've always loved writing. Throughout my childhood and teenage years I kept a diary, wrote stories and poems for magazines, and entered writing competitions. I never yearned to become a writer because there was never any doubt in my mind that I wouldn't be. Quite how I ended up doing science to degree level and beyond is still a mystery. After a short and rather wretched spell in academia where I experimented on ferrets, a strange choice of research project for someone who sobs when she sees a one-legged pigeon, I stumbled into advertising and marketing. Later, I wrote children's books and young adult fiction, and have now written or collaborated on 22 published titles.

To me, writing has always been as natural and necessary as breathing; getting words out of my head and onto paper has not only been a life-long pleasure, but a safety valve in times of distress. I have written my way out of anxiety and upset, diffused anger, soothed hurt and put difficulties into perspective.

One of the recurring themes of the emails and letters I have received from readers of my books was, 'Where do you get your inspiration from?' and so I always covered this in my talks. I would read out an entry from one of my teenage diaries: the same day of the same month, but written three decades ago. The girls loved giggling over my anguished prose (mostly about boys), but as I read them out, I still found some of those entries painful to recall. I used my diaries as an example of how I turned my real-life experiences into inspiration for my books. I told the girls that material is everywhere you look, everything you hear and anything you've been through, and also of something the writer, actress and comedian Meera Syal had said. I'm paraphrasing – and probably wildly misquoting – but the gist of it is that, as a writer, terrible things can be happening to you or around you, but there is always this little voice inside your head that is whispering, 'One day you will use this in your writing. *This* is good material.' Or, to quote the writer Nora Ephron's mother, Phoebe, 'Everything is copy.'

On Sunday 27th February 2011, ten days after this talk, a few days into a holiday in Barbados, and against my advice, my husband, John Sinfield, known as JS, went for a swim in the sea. As he got off his sun lounger I shouted after him, 'Be careful! I mean it!' and wagged my finger at him. I felt embarrassed that I sounded such a heckling wife, but I was sufficiently uneasy to get up and sit on the wall to watch him leave. He walked across the beach and stood in the water, pulled up his swimming shorts and flexed his shoulders before plunging in. The shimmering, turquoise-blue Caribbean water was deceptively calm; within minutes he was swept away from the shoreline by strong currents. Alerted by tourists further down the beach, I heard him call for help and saw him waving his arms until he fell forward, face down into the sea. Bravery by other hotel guests and a passing jet ski rider brought him back to the beach, but despite attempts to resuscitate him on the sand and on the way to the hospital, he had drowned. And instead of a little voice whispering, 'One day you will use this in your writing. *This* is good material,' I could hear myself parroting, 'But I'm wearing a bikini! But I'm wearing a bikini!' as if bad things couldn't happen in good bikinis.

Almost as soon as I landed back in the UK, the Friday after the accident, people said to me, 'You'll be writing about this of course.' I wanted to. I needed to. I couldn't. For months I couldn't write anything. Internet bereavement groups and chat rooms were filled with accounts of other widows journaling their grief or writing letters to their dead husbands, but here I was, a professional writer used to churning out hundreds of thousands of words, yet completely and utterly blocked through shock.

I tried to keep a gratitude journal, in which each night I intended to write down five things that I was grateful for. Night after night I wrote only two entries: The Hound (my dachshund, Boris) and PG Tips instant tea.

There were three things that had supported me through difficult times in my life: my writing, my sense of humour and, for 22 years, my husband. All of these vanished. I can't begin to describe how terrifying that felt. I'd never believed in writer's block: juggling a full-time career in marketing and running a small business of my own whilst writing professionally meant there was no time for being blocked. On days when I suffered from a bit of 'keyboard constipation', taking The Hound for a walk usually moved things along, often just as I was bending down to 'scoop the poop'.

Physically and emotionally, I couldn't write, but instinctively I knew that unless I did, I'd never begin to heal, and so I set myself the goal of starting a blog to coincide with JS's birthday on 14th June 2011.

You might be wondering why I wanted to blog, why I didn't just quietly write in a journal or pen private letters? The answer is: I have no idea; it just felt right. I had started a blog some years previously about my feelings of not being a mother. It was a private blog, not even my husband knew about it, but after a couple of entries I decided that bloggers were introspective navel-gazers who needed to stop battering their keyboard, and get out and get a life. Little did I realise that years later, blogging would help give me *back* my life.

The name of the blog – *Planet Grief* – took no time to think up. People used to say to me, 'You must feel as if your entire world has been turned upside down.' Irritated, I'd tell them that, no, an upside-down world implied that the UK and Australia had swapped places. This was no upside-down world; this was as if I was living on an entirely different planet, Planet Grief, because *nothing* was recognisable to me, not even the sight of my own hands on the computer's keyboard. I was wearing a wedding ring, but I had no husband.

For that first entry, I remember staring at the white screen, feeling physically sick with fear over what emotions writing about my grief might unleash. All writers suffer from the terror of the white page at the beginning of a new project, but this took terror to a whole new level. But once I started tapping away and the words flowed from the end of my fingers and appeared on the screen in front of me, I felt a growing sense of relief. I knew that I was never going to get my husband back, but for the first time since JS died almost four months before, I realised that my sense of humour and my ability to write had survived the most terrible event imaginable. It was the first sign of any sort of normality in my life, although there were many dreadful days and calls to the Samaritans to come.

I began to write about the little things that shook me: the loneliness of buying a single Scotch egg; the pain of tearfully dragging the wheelie bin onto the street and thinking, 'Is this it? Is my life going to be an endless and lonely battle with the bin?' And when I wrote those posts about everyday life on *Planet Grief*, the comments and private messages flooded in from others who were in the same situation, men and women who had also been sobbing over the rubbish and the shopping. There became a feeling of solidarity in grief, a sense that we were all stumbling along as best we could, together. My writing style is naturally chatty – I used to tell 'my' schoolgirls to write as if they were telling their best friend a story – and that is how I wrote the blog, as though it were a conversation between two friends. One of the most touching and memorable comments I received was when a widow wrote to me to say that when she opened her laptop and read a post on *Planet Grief*, it was as if I was sitting at her kitchen table, talking to her.

The blog became a lifeline to me and I soon realised a comfort to many. I've sobbed as I typed, pouring my heart out and opening wounds that I thought would never heal. I've wept with and for my tribe of fellow widows and widowers. I've written late into the night and first thing in the morning. I've received many intensely personal thoughts and experiences, stories that will always remain confidential. I've often written after too much alcohol, but always had the good sense to wait until the next day before posting. I've taken my revenge in print, slamming out words about those who have hurt me, but been thankful for the 'Delete' key once I've calmed down. I've tried to be absolutely honest about my life and my grief, whilst endeavouring not to hurt or expose those close to me. I've retreated, exhausted, and popped back up to cheers and encouragement from 'my' tribe of fellow widows.

Planet Grief was never started with an audience in mind, it was started to prove to myself that I could write again, and that by writing, I could begin to heal. That *Planet Grief* had such a following encouraged me to keep writing. I never thought of it as 'my' blog: my role was as a facilitator, to throw out a topic for discussion based on my own experiences and let others run with it. And run with it they did.

What follows is my journey through grief, interspersed with the thoughts and experiences from other widows and widowers who took that journey with me. I make no apologies for the illogical and at times completely bonkers nature of my writing: one moment I was never going to move house, the next I was planning to shove the keys through the letterbox and move to Ireland to drink Guinness in a bar. My husband could be recalled as a saint one minute, capable of doing no wrong, only to be lambasted in print for his selfishness the next. I can quite see why those widowed longer than me told me not to make any life-changing decisions for a least a year after JS died – though the temptation to jack it all in and escape from my grief to a Greek island with a twenty-year-old, olive-skinned, long-limbed waiter was intense. If I hadn't had Boris to consider, who knows where I might have ended up? So don't expect any consistency in what follows. Grief does not follow a straight course, and nor does my writing.

Let's go.

UP UP AND AWAY

*It's the silliness I miss. I now change light bulbs, dig out tree stumps and do all sorts of stuff, but there is no one to put cream oven gloves on their head and pretending to be a judge solemnly announce, 'I declare that dinner is ready!' or put a pair of underpants on their head and pretend to be a racing driver in one of those fire masks they wear under their helmets. JS wasn't a crazy man prone to being daft; he was very controlled and could be very serious. I was a bit crazy and not serious at all, so we tempered each other. I brought out his fun side and he made my slightly eccentric side acceptable. If we were at a party and I started telling a story (with all the actions), I could look across at him and see he was giving me a look that told me that I was in danger of going into orbit. He wouldn't have minded, but he knew that later, I would. ~ **Helen B***

During one of my regular 2am trawls through an American bereavement site, and dismissing other ideas such as getting plastered on champagne, listening to James Taylor, crying my eyes out over photos or just staying in bed with The Hound and watching endless re-runs of *Two and a Half Men*, I finally decided how I wanted to celebrate JS's birthday without him: a helium balloon released on Hampstead Heath in north London.

I mentioned my plan to my friend Hat, a fellow recent inhabitant of Planet Grief. Hat thought it such a good idea, she decided to do the same for her husband's birthday, which fell a few days before JS's, and in a touching gesture, bought a second balloon for JS.

Being somewhat remote from a Clinton Card shop and gas canister, Hat procured her balloons in advance, in hindsight a tactical error. By the time she took them up the Welsh hillside for the big launch, they had deflated and defiantly refused to take off, cue sobby trek back down the hill clutching a couple of wilting airbags. Life is hard enough without your balloons deflating.

Based in central London rather than rural Wales, I was able to get my balloons (£2.50 each from Chapel Market in Islington) on the day: a burgundy heart for JS, and a pale pink star for Hat's husband. The cheery lady on the stall put them in a big plastic bag, I took them home, wrote a message on each tag and in the late afternoon June sunshine, took balloon bag, messages, scissors, camera and The Hound to the Heath for the grand send off.

As I walked along, the balloons were bobbing up and down in the bag, threatening to escape like a buxom woman's boobs in a too tight bra. As The Hound and a German pointer stopped for a mutual bum sniffing session, its owner said, 'Balloons! How lovely! Are you having a party?' I'm still prone to terrible bouts of verbal Death Diarrhoea, i.e. telling complete strangers what has happened, even if they have just asked me the time at the bus stop, so I told this man in great detail why I was letting off the balloons, and then, seeing his shocked face, wished I hadn't. I need some sort of Imodium for the brain-mouth connection.

By the time we get to the venue for the big send-up, it's windy. I wrestle the balloons out of the bag, stand on the ribbons and the shiny things go mental, weaving in and out of each other like some crazy, ecstasy-fuelled Maypole dance.

I still have to get the tags on the balloons, which, because of the constant ducking and diving proves impossible, so I implement Plan B: shortening the ribbons by kneeling on them whilst I try to attach the messages of love and hope. The Hound decides this is a game and launches himself at the balloons, jumping on them and barking. Laughing, I push him away, increasing his excitement and turning him from dachshund to demented collie as he tries to 'round up' the balloons and kill them. If there is anything worse than a deflated balloon, it's a punctured one, so I go back to Plan A. I stand on the ribbons whilst being constantly head-butted by a couple of foil shapes and watched by the Heath Police (who have parked up behind me), and accompanied by the sound of frenzied barking, I manage to tie the messages on, but give up trying to separate the balloons whose pink and white ribbons are now bound tightly together.

Then I get my scissors, cut the strings, say what I want to say and watch as the balloons soar gently up into the blue, cloud-dotted sky. There is a brief panic when a small plane appears to cross their path – not unexpected as there are more planes in the London sky than sparrows – and I have a flash of terror at the thought of my balloon being sucked into a jet engine, the plane plummeting over London and my being responsible for hundreds of new inhabitants of Planet Grief; but then the balloons continue their gentle flight, at first familiar and recognisable, then just dots and then – nothing.

As I search the sky with teary eyes, I think to myself, 'I know they're out there.' Only moments ago, I was holding them. I could feel their form and energy. I could see them and they were bright and shiny and fun. Even when I let them go, for a while I could watch them. But now, however hard I look, however carefully I scan every inch of the skyline, I can't see them. They may have gone from my sight and my touch, they may soon be punctured and in a change of shape, end up hanging in a tree or be swept up and binned, but I know that in some form, they're still out there.

And I'm not just talking about balloons.

EGGS AND THE CITY

I just can't bring myself to cook for myself. I feel like we had such fun cooking together, what is the point on my own? I look round the supermarket thinking, 'Just buy anything that you fancy,' but I don't fancy anything, so I come home with tins of beans. ~ **Linz**

It's June 2011, and after a meeting in town, I find myself wandering along Marylebone High Street. JS and I once fantasised about moving to this fabulously stylish area a stone's throw from Selfridges, but a world away from the hustle and bustle of Oxford Street, until we realised we were hopelessly out of touch with the housing market, and prices had shot up after Waitrose moved in. It's now très fashionable with a wonderful mix of independent stores, nationwide chains, cafés and specialist food shops. I used to see Caroline Quentin in Waitrose. She always looked stressed.

Living on Planet Grief, I find I am no longer interested in stylish boutiques (those familiar with my wardrobe will be gasping at such a bold statement) or Chi Chi home accessory emporiums. Where once I would be in The White Company salivating over zillion-count Egyptian cotton sheets (before going home to John Lewis non-iron poly-cotton), I now shun such fripperies. The Emma Bridgewater shop no longer beckons me like a mermaid on a rock, and I haven't the attention span to be interested in the tomes on the shelves of Daunt Books. In any case, I already have a huge and mostly unread collection of books about grief, the afterlife and how to live frugally on a small income. (Chickens and churn your own butter, apparently.)

But, sometimes it's sunny and you're stumbling along and your brain is on autopilot, and like scores of times over the years, you find yourself walking through the doors of Divertimenti, a wonderful Aladdin's cave of super-stylish cookware. And then you stand there surrounded by things which only weeks ago would have had you eager to rush home, don a pinny and get cooking before you remember, 'It's just me! What's the point? Why am I even *in* here?'

Before my unexpected trip to Planet Grief, I loved to cook. The merest sniff of a get together and I'd take Jamie, Nigella, Gary, Rick and Gordon to bed with me, along with a pile of fluorescent Post-it notes and start to plan the menu. The duvet flattened by hardbacks, I'd constantly interrupt my husband's reading by asking him what he fancied (in a culinary sense), pushing recipes under his nose for inspection and late-night discussion.

But now those cookbooks taunt me. Like a eunuch surrounded by pornography, I have a vague memory of the urge, but little desire to do anything about it. I no longer cook. I pierce, I open, I assemble, but I don't cook, and nothing in this cuisine-barren landscape makes me feel more like flinging a Le Creuset family-sized casserole at the wall than my ancient copy of Delia Smith's *One is Fun!* right down to its perky exclamation mark. The sight of Delia's dreamy stare on the cover as she presides over a table set for one: a candle, flowers, wine, a white linen place mat and a platter of fruit, as opposed to the bleak, drained stare of the recently bereaved facing an empty kitchen, night after ruddy lonely night, had me banishing Delia from my bookshelf within weeks of JS's death.

Rejecting the delights of Divermenti, I stumbled out and, trying not to sink to my knees in the street, turned into a side alley to pull myself together, only to find I was standing outside The Ginger Pig.

The Ginger Pig is a wonderful butcher's shop selling rare-breed meat and mouth-watering charcuterie. Once, I nearly had to be given mouth-to-mouth resuscitation by the butcher when he told me how much four lamb loin chops were, but as I have the appetite of an anorexic gnat at the moment, I thought that something tasty from The Ginger Pig's deli counter might tempt my comatose taste buds back to life.

I stand behind a couple that are choosing what they want. They'll have a little bit of this and some of that and how about two of those, and, 'Oh! They look wonderful, don't they darling? Shall I get four? Two for today and two for the freezer?'

Other than the fact that the man is a porker and the woman has a shockingly obvious facelift, it could be JS and me deciding what delicacies to purchase. We loved food shopping, though before you have visions of us as a modern Johnny and Fanny Craddock, I should point out that JS rarely cooked anything beyond scrambled eggs and lamb chops, and that was always a palaver. But still.

And then an assistant asks me what I would like, and I look at the array of produce and say bleakly, 'A Scotch egg, please.'

'Just the one?' Her tongs quiver over the tray of meat-blanketed oeufs.

'Just the one,' I confirm.

She bags up the solitary golden orb.

'Will there be anything else?' she enquires, handing me the bag, the contents of which fit perfectly into the palm of my hand.

I shake my head, hand over some coins, scuttle out and, dizzy with grief and oblivious to those around me, steady myself on a waste bin and howl in pain at the searing loneliness of buying one Scotch egg.

Still, it was delicious.

GROOGLING THE NIGHT AWAY

*I wish I lived in Spain and could just put on the 'Widow' black so that everyone would know and therefore not ask or expect anything from me. ~ **Deena***

I'm sure that I'm not alone in surfing the internet for something I shouldn't, only to stumble across something I wish I hadn't. I'm not talking about naked ladies posing suggestively with tropical fruit, or the time when needing a picture for a presentation I innocently typed 'Nuts' into Google Images, and found an alarming montage of human meat and two veg. No, I'm referring to something potentially much more damaging: egosurfing, the practice of putting your name into a search engine to see what comes up.

My career means I'm named on various internet sites across the World Wide Web. I've long since learnt that tapping my name into Google after a couple of sherries late at night is a recipe for disaster: 20 great reviews are meaningless compared to one where the author slates what I've written and holds me entirely responsible for everything they believe is wrong with the youth of today, from teenage pregnancy to thinking Jordan's humungous breast implants are something to aim for. Fizzing with tears and/or anger, I'd burst from my study waving a printout of the offending article and thrust it towards my husband, irrespective of whether he was watching TV, snoozing or having a shower. And because JS was a calm, thoughtful and measured man (unless someone blocked our garage, when he'd make John McEnroe's 1981 Wimbledon outburst look wussy), he'd soothe my angst, put it all into perspective, remind me I'd feel better in the morning, and only later admit that he was seriously tempted to track down the reviewer and wreak terrible and lasting revenge in retaliation for hurting his wife.

But I have discovered there is one thing worse than egosurfing, and I discovered it on a dark and rainy Saturday: Grief Googling, or as it shall be known henceforth, Groogling.

It all started innocently enough. I was sitting at the computer, trying to work out if keeping the heating on low constantly is more economical than firing it up twice a day (the jury is still out according to *Money Saving Expert*), when I found myself Groogling: typing my late husband's name into Google and pressing 'Search'.

Up came the industry obituaries and the notice in *The Times*.

As my heart was already banging away in my chest at the sight of JS's name on the screen, I should have stopped there, gone back to Martin Lewis and the central heating conundrum, but no, like a moth to a flame or a Page Three model to a footballer, I clicked on 'Images'.

And there was the picture I can't look at, the photograph displayed on the lid of my husband's coffin at his funeral, an image taken at a wedding in Australia in 2008. JS hated having his photo taken and usually adopted his stern 'photo face', but catching JS off-guard, the professional photographer had captured the essence of the man I love and have lost: smiling, a twinkle in his eye, kind, fun, decent, caring. My soulmate for almost half my life.

The pain felt as if someone was pouring boiling water over my already scarred body. When it wouldn't go away and my grief reached such a point I felt scared for my own safety, I rang Aussie Jo, a friend who isn't afraid of my tears and my terror, and who will always put her busy life on hold to help me. Aussie Jo did what JS used to do: she listened, she soothed, she consoled, until scores of damp tissues later, I calmed down.

She was and is marvellous.

But there was one thing JS used to say to me that Aussie Jo couldn't. 'You'll feel better in the morning.'

Because when morning comes, even if I am not always outwardly convulsed with tears, I don't feel better, not even a little bit.

ON THE COUCH: COUNSELLING PART ONE

I saw a counsellor who had not experienced what I have. We failed to hit it off at the point where she thought it appropriate to mention the 'and you're so young' thing. I decided leaving was better than punching her ruddy lights out. ~ **Nancy**

Ten years ago, whilst sitting in the stalls at the London Palladium watching Dennis Waterman belt out *Get Me to the Church on Time* as Alfred P Doolittle in *My Fair Lady*, I had a heart attack. At least, I *thought* it was a heart attack; the crushing pain in my chest, the dizziness, the feeling that I was going to pass out at any moment certainly felt like I imaged a heart attack might. Drenched in sweat, I fled the auditorium in terror, stumbling over and stamping on the feet of those next to me. Strangely, my heart attack stopped the moment I was out of the theatre. Instead of calling for an ambulance, I flagged down a black cab and, frightened and bewildered, sobbed all the way home to be met on the doorstep by a less than sympathetic JS. The following morning, on my way to work and still rattled by the events of the night before, I was hit by a tsunami of the same terrifying symptoms the moment I opened the front gate and stepped out into the street. I made it into the car, but 20 minutes later, sitting in the outside lane of three lanes of traffic at a red light on the Holloway Road in north London, I had a strong urge to jump out of the car and run into the road. I didn't, but only because JS shouted at me and locked the car from the inside. I really thought that I was seriously ill.

I was due to fly to New York a few days later, and, as I didn't fancy being the reason for the broadcast at 33,000 feet of 'If there is a medical doctor on board, please could he make himself known to a member of the cabin crew,' I trotted off to my GP who diagnosed something much less dramatic than a dickey ticker: a panic attack. He sent me away with a prescription for beta-blockers, and a suggestion that if nothing improved, I might consider counselling. I wasn't keen on counsellors or counselling. Some years earlier, I'd become embroiled in a 'situation' and one of the people involved wanted everyone to see a psychotherapist. I sat for three hours being assessed by a fat, wheezy man who at the end of the session told me that despite my emotionally chaotic childhood, rarely had he come across someone more quietly confident, grounded, balanced and secure as me. I remember thinking that he probably wasn't a very good psychotherapist, but still.

Despite my reservations, one Wednesday evening and several panic attacks later, I find myself opposite a bearded gnome of a man who's wearing black leather motorbike trousers and a tight grey T-shirt, a garment which accentuates his impressive man boobs. It occurs to me that if I were a woman with body-image issues, specifically lack of 'va va voom' in the bap department, it would be disheartening to find my male therapist sported bigger baps than me. The weirdest thing was that whilst *I* perched on a hard-backed chair, *he* reclined on a couch in a pose reminiscent of a Roman emperor dangling grapes over his mouth.

Beardy-Weirdy boasts that he's such a brilliant therapist he has celebrity clients who have stuck with him for years (er…) and angrily accuses me of taking the mick when in answer to his question, 'What is your coke intake?' I reply innocently and truthfully, 'I don't like either Coke or Pepsi. Fizzy drinks make me burp.'

It doesn't take long to realise Beardy-Weirdy isn't for me.

I tell him.

He maintains that without him I will *never* recover. I will be *forever* damaged.

I decide he's a fruit loop and go to leave.

'Take care,' I say at the front door.

'You don't mean that,' he spits. 'You don't really care about me, do you?'

'Thinking about it, I don't,' I reply sarcastically.

He tells me that I am superficial, a phoney. Insincerity is at the root of my problem.

I tell him to f-off and go home.

I'm not upset or angry; the whole thing is so absurd. Over a glass of wine, my husband and I laugh about my confusing cocaine with carbonated drinks, and conclude there is nothing wrong with me other than not taking enough time off, a consequence of running several businesses. I vaguely wonder if I should report Beardy-Weirdy to someone, but then forget about it.

Years later, I am alerted to an article in the *Daily Mail*. Beardy-Weirdy has been struck off the UK Council for Psychotherapy for gross malpractice, including (alleged) sexual harassment, swearing and drug taking in therapy sessions. There's also mention of encouraging clients to dance naked in front of him.

I swear blind that I will never *ever* seek any sort of counselling *ever* again.

THE TISSUE ISSUE: COUNSELLING PART TWO

During out of control crying episodes, as much fluid seems to escape my mouth as it does my eyes. Weird. And Messy. ~ **Emma A**

I was offered counselling seconds after my husband died and whilst still wearing that wretched Bikini of Death. Ushered out of the hospital side room where my husband lay – navy blue, stone-cold and dead on a trolley in his blue Burberry swimming shorts – I was approached by someone with a leaflet in their hand who asked me if I wanted counselling. 'When?' I asked. 'Now,' she said. 'I just want to go home,' I said. 'Someone will run you back to the hotel,' I was told. 'No,' I said. 'I want to go home, *now*. I want to get on a plane and go home.' 'That's not possible,' they said. No one mentioned counselling again. I found the leaflet when I was packing up the hotel room five days later to finally go home: it was a prayer card. Looking back, it reminds me of when my friend gave birth to a whopper of a baby girl, and the midwife asked the new and still sore mother what contraception she intended to use: well meant, but terrible timing.

Back in the UK, despite my Fat Man and Beardy-Weirdy-induced distrust of therapists, including another attempt to resolve my panic attacks, this time with a woman who seemed more obsessed with picking the flaky skin off her scabby spots and examining it between her fingers than listening to me, it became clear that I was going to need professional help. You expect to come home from holiday with a tan and a bottle of the local grog, not an interim Death Certificate and an unused airline ticket.

Grief literature provided by the Foreign Office suggested I contact my GP who would be able to 'outline the range of services in your borough', which in my area of north London turned out to be a six-month waiting list for NHS counselling, and no immediate help from volunteer-strapped Cruse*. My only option was to go private.

The trauma psychotherapist my GP recommended came straight out of Central Casting. Small, bespectacled and grey-haired with a penchant for purple clothes and ethnic jewellery, she reminded me of the American Jewish Sex Therapist, Doctor Ruth, except my Doktor R (as Hat christened her) was from north London rather than New York via Germany.

Each session with Doktor R followed the same pattern. Twice a week, we'd face each other in wing-backed chairs as with a sad smile she'd enquire, 'How has it been?' my cue to sob and snot not just for England and St George, but for widows everywhere. After forty-five minutes, Doktor R would leave the room to 'think', whilst I sat in her fire-hazard of a study doing my own thinking, which was usually along the lines of wondering whether she was an obsessive compulsive hoarder which stopped her throwing anything out. Then she'd return to trot out such gems as, 'You're coping remarkably well,' or, 'I am impressed by your resilience,' after which I would hand her cash, book another appointment and drive to the nearest Rymans to buy box files and envelopes in an attempt to deal with the mounting pile of 'deadmin': paperwork relating to JS's death and its aftermath.

At first it was a relief to sit and sob with a professional who I assumed would try and pull me back if I became suicidal and ran out into the traffic, something I had done several times as part of my death wish. She also gave me one very good piece of advice: 'Never

---

* Cruse Bereavement Care offers support after the death of someone close.

underestimate the healing power of the mundane,' something that saw me furiously hosing out the stinky wheelie bin in the hope of snaffling extra healing points.

But after a few sessions, it all went horribly wrong.

Doktor R kept a box of tissues strategically placed to my right. During each session I went through these like a dose of salts, something not helped by the fact they were of the scratchy, thin, 'budget' variety. One sob-and-snot-wipe combo and they dissolved into damp shreds, leaving my nose sore and raw. About to leave the house for another Doktor R sobfest, I grabbed a bunch of my own tissues – Kleenex Ultra man-sized with a touch of balm – and bunged them in my bag.

I sit in front of Doktor R and before she can give me her regulation, 'How has it been?' intro, I pull out the wad of quality tissues, wave them in the air and announce that I have brought my own supplies.

45 minutes of sobbing later, Doktor R gives me her analysis of the session.

'I see you have brought your own tissues,' she smiles.

'Um, yes,' I say.

'I'm wondering if this is your attempt to take some control over your own grief?' she ponders.

This is barmy. I tell her it is nothing to do with trying to control my own grief, just that her tissues are thin and scratchy and exfoliate my nose, whereas mine are man-sized with a hint of comforting balm.

Doktor R appears not to agree with my simple, practical explanation.

I point out that surely other clients bring their own tissues?

She cocks her head, first left, then right and tells me that some do and some don't but – she straightens her gaze – she feels it's significant that I am the only one to have ANNOUNCED that I have brought my own tissues.

I become wickedly obsessed with paper products to take to my next session. If I whip out toilet roll, will this signify that I don't value myself? What if it's quilted, premium bog roll? Coloured? Recycled? The shiny Izal stuff we had at school that smeared rather than absorbed? Would using kitchen roll send Doktor R into psychotherapy orbit, particularly if it had a Winnie the Pooh pattern on it? Would cartoon paper products lead her to believe that I was reverting to my childhood, rather than the real reason – they were on offer in Poundland?

It occurs to me that if I am spending more time trying to wind my therapist up than sorting my problems out, it's time to call it a day.

So I did.

But I still needed help.

Desperately.

ONE GREEN BOTTLE

At seven and a bit months, I found myself trying to garden last week and just having to sit on the lawn and sob my heart out loudly to the daisies, who just nodded knowingly. It just creeps up on me sometimes, and I have no idea when it will strike. He should be here and he isn't and it's wrong. ~ **Lauren**

In the early nineties, my husband joined a gym. Because he loved me and was a generous soul, he gave me a year's membership. It was a swanky gym with a big pool and an indoor running track, and whilst JS did his thing, I did mine – a quick sprint round the track whilst holding my tummy in then off to the bar for wine and crisps. Eventually I gave up this rigorous workout regime to stay home and watch *Coronation Street*.

The following year saw JS still in love, but not so generous on the gym membership front. As he pointed out, my cost per visit had actually gone *up* if you factored in the bar bill. 'I'll show you!' I thought. 'I'll pay for my own gym membership!' the logic being that I was quite prepared to waste his money, but not my own. Of course all that happened was that when I didn't want to go, or I did go but didn't want to stay, I'd think, 'It's my money! I'll do what I like!'

Year three and JS is still keeping fit, whilst I am blobbing at home watching the Holy Quadruple of Soaps: *Corrie*, *EastEnders*, *Emmerdale* and *Brookside*. It's not that I don't want to keep fit, I just don't want to leave our flat to do it.

But then I see an advert for a NordicTrack Ski Machine, a contraption that promises to not only tone and trim my bod, its silent glide mechanism means I can watch telly *and* keep fit. It's made for small spaces too: the foxy chick in the advert demonstrates that with just one finger it will fold up to store neatly against a wall or under the bed. My husband is sceptical and refuses to pay. I am enthusiastic and happy to. It's the perfect solution! Whilst he is schlepping to the gym in all weathers, I will be at home, gliding along, toning my abs whilst keeping abreast of Ken and Deirdre's shenanigans.

I hated it.

It wasn't silent, and instead of folding up with one finger, I had to beat and kick it into submission. Invariably I left it up, resulting in one or other of us tripping over it so it still got a kicking.

My dear friend and colleague, Karen, mentioned that her boyfriend (later husband) wanted a ski machine, but couldn't afford one. I *begged* her to take it away. I didn't want money; I just wanted it gone. In exchange, they gave us a bottle of champagne: 1989 Bollinger, an extraordinarily generous gesture given the state of their finances at the time.

Years passed and the champagne remained unopened. JS would sometimes slide it from the wine rack and I'd shake my head. 'Let's wait,' I'd say. 'For a special occasion.'

Then, tragically, Karen died within days of being admitted to hospital with excruciating back pains and uncontrollable vomiting following a miscarriage. It was undiagnosed cancer, a malignant melanoma that had spread like wildfire from a mole on her shoulder through her body to her brain. She was 33 and had worked with JS and me since she was 19. We were devastated.

Karen's champagne became even more symbolic. For me, no occasion was ever special enough to pop its cork.

And then JS died.

After my husband's death, I wept buckets over that unopened bottle of Bolly. JS was the type of man who would have opened it because it was Friday or sunny or because Arsenal had won. Why couldn't I have seen that just being alive and with JS was the only reason I *ever* needed to open it? I had been waiting for some big flashy occasion to come along, when in fact life with him *was* the big occasion. And now we would never be able to drink Karen's champagne together; that opportunity had been lost forever.

A couple of weeks ago saw a significant family birthday. I decided to take the champagne. It seemed right that it would be opened amongst people he loved and loved him. I also hoped it would chase the Regret Monster away.

Wrapped in a tea towel and with great ceremony, the bottle was opened, the contents poured.

Instead of straw-coloured fizz, it looked dark and cloudy, like urine from someone with a kidney infection. It smelt rank and tasted foul. We poured it down the sink.

Karen would laugh and say we should have opened it just because we could.

JS would be annoyed that it was a waste of what was once an excellent bottle of champagne.

But they are both gone. I hope that they are together, somewhere, looking out for each other.

I'm the one left weeping over the empty bottle as the Regret Monster digs its claws in ever deeper.

BEREAVEMENT BLING

After Mark's suicide, I had to go and identify his body. I made sure I was in an outfit that Mark had always said was his favourite. The funeral was a woodland burial (neither of us are of religious) and was just going to be twelve of us around the grave drinking champagne and telling stories, no officials to oversee things, just Mark's trusted circle. In preparation of the funeral, I went out with a friend and I bought the loveliest dress: floor length and bright colours and a teal cardigan to go with it. It was important that it wasn't black and that Mark would have approved – it was his mission to get me out of black. We do these things to cope and get through. Who cares what they are and who cares what other people say. ~ **Emma S**

In May 2007, I was in a beauty salon in east Kent having a pedicure. It's the type of salon where people drop in not just for a Brazilian, but a gossip. That Saturday, instead of the usual small-town tittle-tattle, there was only one subject on everyone's lips: the disappearance of little Madeleine McCann from the villa in which she was sleeping, whilst on holiday in Portugal with her family.

The unanimous verdict of the women around me was that Kate McCann was undoubtedly involved in the disappearance of her daughter.

The evidence of Mrs McCann's guilt was overwhelming and based on two counts: firstly, she had gone out running whilst her daughter was still missing, and secondly, she had changed her earrings.

What sort of a woman could find the energy to keep fit not knowing whether her daughter was dead or alive? How could she even *think* about putting on jewellery or brushing her hair at a time like that?

None of them had lost a child, but if they had, they knew for a fact that they would be in bed under sedation, not careering around the Algarve in running shorts. They certainly wouldn't be bothered about their appearance.

Guilty! Guilty! Guilty!

I was reminded of this recently because I bought Kate McCann's book, *Madeleine*; I had read an extract of the book in a newspaper where the McCanns talked about how valuable they found trauma counselling, and I wanted to read more about their experience. Kate McCann doesn't write about her earrings, but she does talk about going running as a way of coping. But even if she had changed her jewellery, what did that prove?

In my experience, absolutely nothing.

The Monday after my husband's Sunday morning accident, I went back to the hospital to register his death. The day before I had been wearing a bikini, flip flops and carrying a beach bag. I couldn't help my outfit, but it all felt so wrong, so undignified. JS was an elegantly understated man who looked good in casual clothes, but was really more at home in the formality of a jacket and tie. Dead or alive, he deserved dressing up for. I put on a short, flippy dress that I had brought to wear to dinner, all the jewellery I had with me, some blusher; a slick of Bobbi Brown 'Buff' lipgloss and my pretty patent-leather ballet pumps.

With shaky legs and accompanied by the undertaker, I walked along those hot sticky corridors of the administration wing in the Queen Elizabeth Hospital in Bridgetown, towards the woman sitting at the desk who needed my signature confirming my husband had died. My world had ended. My life felt over. My heart was shattered. But to anyone looking at me, blinged-up and made-up, I probably looked as if I was ready for a good time.

Those women judging Kate McCann's innocence or guilt on how she behaved and what she wore hadn't got a clue. I suspected that the days when Mrs McCann was so physically sick and drained she couldn't even get in the shower or change her clothes were yet to come, as they were yet to come for me.

CHAKRAS AND CARROT CAKE: COUNSELLING PART THREE

I went to one Mindfulness-based therapist who told me if I would only breathe and be present in the moment, I would realise that death was alright. Oh, how hard it was not to put my hand on his arm and tell him his lovely wife would not ever come home again, that she was at this very moment dead, and then ask him how serene his moment felt.
~ Megan Devine

So here I am, desperately needing help, but after my encounter with the Fat Man, Beardy-Weirdy, Flaky Face and Doktor R, distrustful of conventional psychotherapy. I consider relying on my small band of loyal friends and ditching counselling altogether, but Doktor R had tossed a phrase into one of our sessions – 'sympathy fatigue' – and I begin to worry that there is only so much weeping and wailing normal people with full-time jobs can stand.

Somewhere on my travels, I'd picked up a leaflet for a 'Soul Therapist'. I dig it out. This sounds *exactly* what I need, a counsellor who practises healing and spiritual enlightenment.

After an exchange of emails outlining what has happened, I book an appointment for Thursday afternoon at two.

The day arrives; it's unseasonably warm. Full of hope that Soul Therapy is the way forward, I put on my manky but comfortable trainers, and walk from my home in north London, down the hill to the therapist's practice. I'm early – way too early.

Aimlessly mooching around the area to kill time, I wander into a delicatessen. Displayed on the counter is a single fat slab of carrot cake smothered in cream cheese icing. The cake looks tempting, but because of the heat, I delay its purchase. The last thing I need is a sad greasy puddle of icing by the time I get home. The plan is, if I'm still hungry after my session, I'll go back and get it.

The woman who greets me at the therapy rooms reminds me of Lady Penelope from *Thunderbirds*, right down to the slightly puppetish nodding of her head. She gives me a smile, the type of smile with which I am now depressingly familiar – tight and sad and full of pity – this time from a mouth painted in an alarming shade of orangey-red lipstick. I know within seconds that Lady Penelope is kind, but not for me.

She asks me to tell her again about the accident, so, sobbing, I recount that fateful morning. She suggests that before we move on to other areas, we use this first session to do some healing to replenish my energy levels. She talks about chakras, points me towards the couch, and as I am about to swing my legs onto the pristine covering, I clock my shoes: dirty and battered. I go to take them off and, apologising for their disgusting state, explain that I walked here. She sounds surprised that I have made the trek. I assure her that in this heat I will get the bus back up the hill.

I lie down and close my eyes, aware of her hands hovering over my body.

Within seconds, my stomach starts to rumble.

I apologise.

Lady P tells me that the rumbling is a sign my chakras are opening; energy is moving around my body. I have a degree in Physiology, and whilst I haven't used it for 25 years, I'm pretty certain the curriculum didn't cover chakras as a reason for digestive disturbance.

The rumbling gets worse and I begin to stress that I might fart.

I wonder if Lady P will explain it as my chakras exploding.

I tense my bum and start obsessing about the carrot cake. I should have bought it before the session and not worried about the icing. What if it's gone? It's the only thing that's whetted my appetite for ages and now someone else – someone who isn't grief-stricken, just greedy – might have bought it. The more I think about the carrot cake, the more my stomach rumbles. I mentally walk into the shop: I can see the cake and – Oh! – there were sausage rolls too. I could have a sausage roll *and* a slice of carrot cake. But what if they have *both* gone?

The session is over. Lady P asks me if I have seen any lights, felt any warmth, experienced any tingling?

I tell her the truth and say I felt nothing, withholding my feelings of anxiety over carrot cake and my rumbling gut.

She says she has a strong sense that my emotional energy is very weak, but that my physical energy is surprisingly strong. As I lace up my trainers, I cynically reflect that anyone could have deduced this from my walking/sobbing combo.

Lady P is kind, sincere and means well, but as I hand over my money, we both know I won't be back.

I'm in the deli. Oh! Happy! Happy! Joy! Joy! The carrot cake is still there, along with an 'artisan' sausage roll. The girl behind the counter puts them in a bag and then squashes them with my impulse purchases – some cheese and a pork pie – but I don't realise this until I get home.

I'm annoyed that I have spent more money on quackery, disappointed and tearful that yet another avenue of therapy has failed me. I'm still lost, frightened and grieving my husband.

24 hours pass. On Friday evening, sitting in the garden, I reflect on the day. To my surprise, I realise that it has been the calmest day

since the accident, *almost* peaceful with minimal tears. Perhaps it was just the calm before the next storm as the feeling didn't last, but weeks later, the day after my Soul Therapy session still stands out as the calmest I have felt in the last four months.

I haven't been back to Lady Penelope – there was no connection – but as for healing being a waste of time? Now, I'm not so sure.

LONELINESS AND THE LATE NIGHT GARAGE

*Our world has been smashed into millions of tiny shards and that is extremely disorientating. I didn't return home for months after Phil died suddenly, and before I did come back, my parents had to redecorate and box up Phil's things for me. The razor on the sink, shoes on the mat, laundry in the basket and coat on the hook eviscerated my soul to the point of screaming madness. I returned once, to choose the clothes we were burying him in. That was and will always be the hardest thing I will ever do. The colossal weight of the grief, shock, loss was so immense as I took out some carefully folded underwear and his favourite well-worn jeans, I really thought it might kill me. ~ **Sam***

One evening, a long time ago (two decades) in a land far away (Northumberland), my best friend's father jumped up to answer the phone and died of a heart attack. I'd come across death before, but only in the old or very ill. Mr P was fun, feisty and barely into his fifties, a larger-than-life character whom I adored; it seemed impossible that he was here one minute and gone the next.

During a trip home, I visited his widow. 'What have you been doing?' I enquired with all the finesse of a young elephant. Much to my surprise, instead of sobbing, 'Nothing,' whilst clutching a tissue and swigging Harvey's Bristol Cream straight from the bottle, Mrs P gave me a run down of what she had been up to: going here, going there, doing this, doing that; a veritable social whirl.

'It's great you're going out!' I trilled, relieved that she *appeared* to be getting over her husband's death so quickly.

Even before JS died, I still remember the bleak look in her eyes and the bitter edge in her voice as she said, 'Oh, it's not the going out that's the problem – it's the coming in.'

Now, with painful clarity, I understand what she meant.

Explaining to a friend the searing loneliness of coming in through the front gate to the front door after an evening out, he suggested I used the garage door as part of trying to establish a 'new normal'. I'll try anything other than potholing once, so one night as the minicab drove off before I even had my key in the lock of the gate, I decide to give it a go.

I press the 'dibber' on my key ring, and in the deserted street, wait for the garage door to chug open. It occurs to me that if someone wants to mug me, now would be an ideal time. 'Bring it on!' I think defiantly, imagining myself overpowering any mugger who dares to even glance at my wedding rings. I feel bolshy, ballsy: I've been out! I'm coming in! I'm establishing a new routine and I'm not crumbling in a heap of tears and yelling into the silence at the unfairness of it all! I can do this!

The garage door opens, and the security light flicks on, illuminating the interior with harsh cold light.

Any hint of bravado I was feeling drains away.

I'm like a rabbit caught in the glare of car headlights, trapped and transfixed in horror by the scene spread out before me.

Right by the door are my husband's golf clubs with their furry animal covers. Next to them, his bike jostles for space with his golf trolley. I spot the bit of carpet he'd stuck on the wall to stop me scraping my car door on the concrete; I must have seen it hundreds of times, but only now do I appreciate his kindness. His Black and Decker workmate is folded up against the wall. There's tins of paint and wood stain and preserver and battered old jars and packets for jobs around the house, which only he did, and which I know nothing about. Gardening equipment hangs neatly around the walls. There are bits of wood which JS always kept 'just in case', wood he'd now never use. I feel overwhelmingly sad at seeing his golf shoes sitting on a shelf, just where he left them after his last game.

Tears sting my eyes and I look up to stop them falling. Hanging across the roof is a black plastic package. It looks like a small wrapped body, but it's the fake Christmas tree we put up in the kitchen; alongside it, the stand for the giant real Christmas tree we always have in the front room. My heart breaks at the thought of Christmases past and those yet to come without him. And then there are the ladders: folding, extending, step. There are so many questions I long to ask my husband, but right now, 'What's with all the ladders, JS?' is first on the list.

I press the switch on the wall and the garage door shuts. I sidle past my car to the side door whilst realising I'm not alone: every giant spider in north London is partying around me.

I unlock the door to the garden and closing it behind me, pick my way through an orgy of slugs.

Finally, I get to the front door. The Hound is on full alert having heard the garage open, and he greets me with noisy excitement. It's lovely to see him, but we missed the class at Puppy School where they taught him how to flick the kettle on. He has lots to say, but even if I could translate his barks, I doubt he'd be asking, 'How was your evening?'

I decide that I won't come in through the garage again, but it doesn't matter anymore because I've solved the problem of coming in at night.

I no longer go out.

THE VELVET ROPE

*I recently had cause to think of my grandmother, who died of stomach cancer in 1975. She was in a ward with flowers (long before flowers carried MRSA, etc.) and was adamant that a 'man' brought her flowers each night and sat with her. She smiled a knowing smile, and that of course had to be my grandfather, or so I wish to believe. ~ **Deena***

The Grim Reaper chose the wrong person on 27th February 2011, for so many reasons, one of which was that whilst JS avoided talking about what he wanted should he die before me (he promised me he'd live to be 100), I had my funeral all sorted out: a plumed horse-drawn glass hearse (you have to know me to appreciate the irony of the ostentation – even bows on ballet flats are too OTT for me); a wreath in the shape of a dachshund; a Keynote presentation featuring photos of my life and dogs and three tunes: Blue Öyster Cult's 'Don't Fear the Reaper', all nine minutes and six seconds of Lynard Skynard's 'Freebird' and 'Help' by The Beatles. And in case you think this was all said tongue-in-cheek, it wasn't and JS knew it.

But the one area of my funeral JS couldn't agree with was that I wanted my body to be left to medical science. 'Not if you go before me!' he'd protest indignantly. 'I wouldn't want someone messing around with you.' I'd come over all sanctimonious and respond primly, 'The body is just an overcoat for the soul. What happens to it after death is immaterial.' And I meant it, I really did, and something I witnessed years ago seemed to further underline my position.

One busy Sunday summer afternoon on the seafront in Broadstairs on the east Kent coast, an elderly woman collapsed. She was smartly dressed and on her own, and because there was an event happening in the town, an ambulance crew arrived on the scene within moments. As the paramedics worked on her, I had a very strong sense that her 'soul' had departed. I wish I could tell you that I saw a white light or some ghostly form float away, but there was nothing other than a powerful feeling that some essence of her had left her body, which was being frantically pummelled and shocked and injected in an attempt to bring it back to life. Shortly after I 'felt' her 'soul' leave, the ambulance crew stopped their efforts, exchanged glances and pulled a blanket over her body. JS commented that it was a wonderful way to go – quickly and in the sunshine. I slightly disagreed: the lady's skirt had hitched up in the commotion. I would have liked to push past the paramedics and pull it down to preserve her modesty.

Not only did I plan my own funeral, I didn't fear death. I feared the *process* of dying should it involve pain or suffering, but as to what happened beyond death, after Karen died I can honestly say that death held no fear for me. I used to say to JS that if there was something on the other side then it meant I would see Karen again, but if there was nothing, if death meant the end of everything including consciousness, then I wouldn't know anything about it anyway. It seemed, at the time, a win-win situation.

But JS didn't live to be 100 – the Grim Reaper came on holiday with us and saw to that – and whilst the terrible circus surrounding my husband's death on the beach meant there was no chance to coolly observe what was happening as I did that afternoon in Kent, I still believe that consciousness survives the body.

On that basis, was it possible that Karen and JS were together?

It was this very thought that floated into my mind one sobby morning as I was making a list of things to buy at Sainsbury's: bleach; bog roll; Mr Kipling Almond Slices (again). One of the things I'm desperate (but unlikely) to know is that JS is OK. I'd read in one of my many 'Life after Death' books that the souls of those who die suddenly and unexpectedly are in turmoil for a while, the thought of which puts *me* in turmoil, and so the circle of turmoil tightens. If Karen could be there (where?) for JS in some way (how?), guiding him through his new form, I'd find it comforting, but by that 'logic', if JS *is* with Karen, who else might be with him, easing his journey?

I abandon the bleach and the bog roll and start making a list of people JS was close to who have died: friends, family, work colleagues. The list is long. I miss some of those people too; some of them I ache to see again, to laugh with, to share a drink with, to reminisce with, though none so much as my husband.

I survey my list – it looks fantastic – full of interesting, witty and warm people, some I've never met but heard about and would like to have known. I imagine JS being welcomed by those he lost and has now found: catching up on publishing news with John B, Michael and Don; swapping family gossip with Kay and Aunt Emmeline; discussing cricket with Robert and Lance; embracing his parents; telling Ernest that his children and grandchildren are a family to be proud of; laughing with Barry; telling Karen that I miss her, still, every day, maybe even seeing our old dog, Rufus.

I look around the soulless silent kitchen. 'No wonder JS hasn't sent me pennies from heaven or white feathers,' I think. 'He's too busy having a good time on the other side to give me signs.' I long for JS to be at peace, but what about me? I'm not at peace, I'm stuck here, heartbroken and lonely. Bizarrely, I feel as if I am behind one of those velvet ropes outside a nightclub, shivering in the cold, peering ahead, excluded. I haven't been to a club since I was in my twenties, but I can still remember the anxiety of inching closer to that rope, wondering if I looked cool enough or pretty enough to join the in-crowd.

This time, I know there is no way back through that rope, that it is a one-way invitation, but that doesn't stop me from wanting to be at the party. But of course, if I tried to push my way to the front of the queue, invite myself, there's a risk that they wouldn't let me in, or worse, that I finally discover there is no party after all…

ACCEPTING THE UNACCEPTABLE

I have accepted Jane's death from the moment it happened, but I haven't accepted my new life yet, and this will take a loooong time. ~ **Marieke**

One of the things I find heartening about internet bereavement groups is not only the support they offer, but the way in which people who feel shattered and flattened with grief still manage to summon up enough energy to participate in discussions. This is particularly the case when a subject sparks lively debate; we may *feel* we have no interest in life, but the indignant feelings some subjects provoke show me that there is still life in us, even if we don't like the life we now lead on Planet Grief.

One topic that recently piqued my interest was about acceptance, and whether it is ever possible to accept the death of our partners. I think it is fair to say that this subject divides the bereaved like Marmite. When a widow wrote on an internet bereavement forum that for her the only way forward was to accept the death of her husband, someone fired back, 'You're wrong. Acceptance is when you agree to something. I didn't want my partner to die hence I'm learning to live with it.'

The strength of the initial sentence, its assertion that this widow was wrong to advocate acceptance, had me looking up the definition of the word 'acceptance' in the Oxford English Dictionary: whilst acceptance *can* mean agreeing to something, there is another definition listed: 'Willingness to accept an unpleasant or difficult situation'.

From the very early days of my 'widowing', I was clear on two points:

1. Whilst my life would be forever shaped by what had happened, it would not be defined by it.
2. If I was to live any sort of meaningful life, as I couldn't change what had happened, I had to accept it.

For me, at not yet five months, both points are difficult to adhere to, and I believe that there are some for whom acceptance may always be too much to ask, such as those whose loved ones have died at the hands of others either through malice, negligence or ignorance.

Last night, during one of my daily trawls around the internet, torturing myself by putting the word 'drowned' into Google, I came across an article in *The Telegraph* about the death of Elspeth Thompson, the gardening expert who, suffering from depression, drowned herself in a manner reminiscent of the suicide of Virginia Woolf. In the article, Elspeth Thompson's husband, Frank Wilson, talks about how he and his young daughter are coping with the sudden death of his wife. It is moving and tragic. Reading it, one of Frank Wilson's comments resonated with me. Talking about advice his mother had given him he says, 'She taught me that one has to accept. Even if you can't understand.'

I'm holding on to those words.

PARTY POOPER

Just knowing he was there at parties gave me confidence and made me smile. Now, in a room full of people, I feel so alone. ~ **Linz**

There are at least a million things that I miss about my husband, one of them being the way we worked together to protect each other from difficult situations. I'm not talking about the time JS had to literally put his body between me and a woman who took offence to my suggestion she bogged off and had her roots done (she'd blocked our garage and was snottily unrepentant), or the countless times I'd answer the phone whilst he frantically pointed towards the front door, relieved when I finally said to the unwanted caller, 'No, he's out walking the dog,' at which point he'd have to grab The Hound's muzzle for fear of the dog woofing and giving the game away.

No, I'm referring to the way in which, together, we could defend ourselves from the hell of the surprise invitation. I'm sure you know the sort of thing I mean, the moment when someone asks, 'What are you up to on Tuesday evening?' and flustered and unable to come up with something plausible you mutter, 'Er… nothing,' and find yourself invited to trek miles across town and country for a 'simple kitchen supper,' a phrase which usually means Mrs Smug doesn't just want you to sample her salmon coulibiac, but coo over her new dual-fuel Aga in the Farrow & Ball 'Elephant's Breath' painted kitchen. Yawn. Oh, and to me, an exiled Geordie, supper always means cheese, biscuits and a pickled onion before bed, whereas what southern folk mean by supper is actually tea, though my husband maintained tea was at four and included cake.

But I digress.

With two of you, it's easy to get out of an invitation as you can always toss in at the end of the phone call/random meeting in the street, 'I'll have to check with JS in case he's got something on,' which of course he has, even if he hasn't, hence the follow-up phone call to Mrs Smug: 'I'm *so* sorry, but we can't make Tuesday evening. JS forgot to mention his sister has just come back from competing in the Extreme Ironing World Championships; she wants to show us the silver iron she's won. Let's get together soon!'

But now I have no one to shield me from social invitations, so I say yes, go, am miserable, decide never to say yes ever again, and then become terrified that if I keep saying no, eventually people will stop asking me and I'll end up housebound and word-perfect for every one of the 177 episodes of *Two and a Half Men*. Anyway, under normal circumstances, I like meeting people, and if I want to try and claw back some sort of normality, however uncomfortable it is, I must try and socialise. So to start going out and about whilst minimising 'Social Stress', I draw up a list of my requirements.

1. Be back by 9pm at the latest (6pm during the winter months).
2. No dinner parties, to avoid Spare Part Syndrome.
3. Within easy reach of home.
4. Includes food, so limiting the amount of time spent in my own kitchen.

Points 1, 2 and 3 are non-negotiable, but at a pinch, I could accept an invitation without point 4, and just make some cheese on toast.

Recently, some good friends of ours rang to say that they had been invited to a bit of a do two roads along from my house, and having mentioned to the hosts I was local and what had happened, the invitation was kindly extended to include me.

It was on Sunday! At 5pm! Five minutes away! There would be food! A good mix of children, couples and singles! JS had never been there! You can tell by my shocking overuse of the exclamation mark that I was excited by the possibility of this party, indeed, it could be *the* perfect party for a shaky widow; it certainly ticked all the boxes on my list.

Sunday came and the first hurdle appeared: having lost a great deal of weight in the last five months on the Death Diet, nothing fits me, and the smart-yet-casual, stone-coloured chinos I intended to wear shot over my hips to my knees. Undeterred, I resorted to Plan B: to cinch the waistband of the trousers tightly with a belt. Whilst this has worked with some items in my wardrobe, for the chinos, the excess material resembled a rather large tumour underneath my white shirt, just below my tummy button. I changed into a pair of navy trousers that could be belted without the weird growth effect, strapped on my silver cork wedges and, with a spring in my step, set off.

I met my friends outside, we went in, the host and hostess were welcoming, the guacamole was delicious, the weather was lovely, we stood around in the garden and then, after about an hour, it all went *horribly* wrong.

I was talking to a man with such winged eyebrows and odd teeth, he resembled an owl. Bored of discussing house prices, I glanced across the garden at the assembled throng. It was a typical north London mix of writers, artists, a photographer, people who did something in the City, women with ethnic necklaces and low-slung boobs, the sort of gathering I've been to countless times before with varying degrees of enjoyment. But this time as I looked at them, a train of thought came into my head; not an Intercity 125 train, but one of those Japanese bullet trains, searing through my grey matter: *My husband is dead. I am alone. My husband is dead. I am alone.*

The thought-train gathered pace. I gulped my glass of white wine. *My husband is dead. I am alone.* I tried to concentrate on Owl Man who was by now hooting about his son moving back home at the age of 30, but the dreadful reality of my life wouldn't go away: *My husband's not here. He's not at home. My husband is dead. I'm all alone.* I gripped the stem of my glass as I realised that JS was never going to glance across a party at me and smile, or give me the look that says, 'Shall we go?' He's never going to come over and fill up my wine glass or get me another plate of food. I can't tell him all about Owl Man; dammit, he's never going to rescue me from Owl Man!

I stood there and tried desperately to follow the conversation, but I couldn't, because any sort of communication is hard when you've got such terrible thoughts careering around your skull, so I made my excuses and left. The party was in the garden and basement kitchen, so I climbed the stairs to the front door, and alone, let myself out. Whereas only an hour ago I had marched down the street in my sandals, full of hope, now I tottered home, sobbing.

A neighbour rang my mobile, heard my sobs, and as I passed her front door, she met me and ushered me inside.

As I sat in her sitting room convulsed with sobs and reeling in pain, I realised that the million things I miss about my husband boil down to only one: the man himself.

SEARCHING FOR CLUES

I search for signs all the time, willing Mark to show me he is here. A pinch of my behind would do me. I want to turn the page and reach a sense of calm. It has to be around the corner, right? ~ **Emma S**

For a brief time I was a scientist. I'd really love to tell you what I did, but in order to do what I did I had to sign the Official Secrets Act, and I'm not sure whether something I signed in 1986 still counts. I hope it doesn't, because after a few glasses of Merlot I usually start telling lurid tales of what went on in the Physiology department at St George's Hospital in Tooting. Anyway, with a 2:1 BSc Hons after my name and ambitions to upgrade to a PhD, I pretended to be a scientist, before eventually admitting I'd rather read *Cosmo* than *Nature*, and preferred dresses to a white coat that stank of the contents of a ferret's anal glands. A year and one nasty mammal bite later, I left and became a secretary.

I mention my science background, because in a recent Twitter storm, one of Professor Brian Cox's tweets appeared to mock people with a belief in the afterlife, describing them as (ahem) 'nobbers'. As the debate raged on social media sites, many sided with the sexy physicist: what sort of sane and rational person with an understanding of science could possibly buy into this ghost/ afterlife silliness?

Me!

I've always believed that after death, our loved ones are still around, it's just that we can't see them and ask them to help prise the lid off the jar of Doritos Hot Salsa Dip.

So, when JS died, I *was* certain that he would be with me, that I would feel his presence guiding me, comforting me.

The early signs looked promising. Back in London (but before his repatriation, which took two weeks; the funeral was almost a month after the accident), I had a 'vision'. JS's face appeared to me with such startling clarity, it was as if he was backlit in 3D high-definition. He didn't smile, speak or look directly at me, he was just there, in the bedroom doorway, suspended slightly above me and to my left. When I put my arms out to reach him, he dissolved. At the time, I didn't find it comforting; I found it profoundly distressing.

It's five months tomorrow since my husband drowned, and other than my vision, I haven't felt him with me or guide me. All I feel is shattered, disorientated and frightenly alone.

Did I scare him off by my reaction to his 'appearance'? Perhaps, despite my supposed open mind, I am too cynical to tune into clues that other widows seem to take as proof of a life after death. Have those early years examining evidence and making sure it was statistically viable left their mark? If my scalp crawled whilst watching TV, I'd think it was nits rather than JS stroking my head. I often find pennies lying around, but the dates are never significant. White feathers litter our lawn because of the pigeons that nick the bird seed intended for the blue tits, and we've always had robins in the garden. There was one bizarre incident involving photograph albums, an IKEA bookshelf and an army of flying ants, but would JS really send me a sign through insects? If so, then, as I sobbed my way through Sunday morning, brandishing the Hoover and fly spray, shaking ants out of photographs I wasn't yet ready to confront, I can only conclude that JS has developed a mean streak on the other side.

I constantly ask myself why others can sense their loved ones, yet I can't. I *long* to feel JS's presence. I cry out for signs, shouting at the sky. I stare at a tiny scrap of paper on my desk, urging him to make it quiver. Instead of crying, sometimes I get all stroppy and say defiantly, 'Right JS, now's your chance. Get that lamp to flicker!' only to sob in frustration when the beam of light remains strong and unwavering. I find myself sitting in a room, scanning it, my eyes flicking here and there, looking for clues as to where he might be and how he is. I read endless books on grief, the afterlife and the progression of souls, finding flaws and discrepancies in all of them. In one, a boy who had drowned tells his parents he has a girlfriend and is finishing college on the 'other side'; in another, I am told that earthly concerns such as status and education mean nothing. One book claims that we make a pact before we're born as to how we die. Am I really to believe that JS chose to drown and leave me stranded and heartbroken four thousand miles from home? I cherry-pick my mediums and their message: I watch Sally Morgan and sneer at (what I believe to be) her music-hall, cold-reading (informed guesswork) act, and yet I seriously consider flying to America to see John Edward, or to Scotland for a reading with Gordon the Psychic Barber. I nearly ring a psychic telephone line late one Saturday night, but pull back at the last minute. I might be desperate, but a woman called Angel on an 0906 number isn't for me or my Barclaycard. And what if I did have a reading and JS came through? What if I had a reading and he didn't? I'm too scared to confront either scenario. Sometimes I wish that I was like Prof Brian Cox and had no belief in an afterlife; I'd still be heartbroken but this searching for clues is exhausting.

'Talk to him,' friends urge. 'Tell him how you feel.' I do, every morning whilst making The Hound's breakfast. I cry and tell JS out loud that I can't bear another day without him, pleading with him to give me a sign to let me know he's OK. Then I wait, always hopeful, but every morning the silence in the room and in my head is deafening, the effect on my heart crushing. I'd hoped The Hound might sense his master, but even he's let me down. 'Do you know where your dad is?' I ask, and he runs to the front door wagging his tail. I get the same response if I ask him about the ginger cat next door, or where his squeaky ball is.

But perhaps there is hope for those of us who don't feel our loved ones walking with us through life. Towards the end of last year, a friend of ours died after a long and painful battle with cancer. He was an atheist who chose a humanist funeral, his wife was brought up as Jewish and neither of them believed in life after death. At six months, his widow was exhausted and depressed; seeing her and what lay ahead frightened me. It's now just over eight months since her husband died, and I had champagne and lemon drizzle cake with her recently. She didn't look exhausted or depressed, she looked like she always used to: poised, fun and with light in her eyes. She said that one day she was feeling desperate, and then suddenly it was as if a page had turned and she felt an overwhelming sense of calm. Shortly after, and for the first time, she felt her husband was with her.

Prof Cox might be an expert on the Hadron Collider, but he's no more of an expert on life after death than any one of us. As for me, that page-turn moment can't come quickly enough.

MOVING STORIES

*The best role model, and the image that I still cling to in the depths of my grief on really bad days, is a lady I know who lost her husband eighteen years ago. For the first two years she was in such a state and so frightened by life without her man, even leaving her house was a big ordeal. At the time she was in her early forties with four young children. Eventually she returned to her job and now she is a busy, vibrant, motivated and strong lady with a very full social life and four grown-up kids. She says that she will always, ALWAYS love and miss her husband, but she is now strong and has been able to be happy again, just in a different way. She is living proof that it can be done, and she is the person I aspire to be like one day. ~ **Angela***

When I was seventeen, I travelled up and down the country wearing an emerald-green woollen suit and a tomato-red blouse in an attempt to decide what I was going to do at university, and where I was going to do it. There were workshops and open days and interviews, but, in the end, it was all a waste of time and money because I flunked my A-levels and went (without an interview) to the only place that would have me: Thames Polytechnic. But before my fall from academic grace, armed with my student railcard, I hopped on trains in search of my future. On one of these journeys (Newcastle to Leeds), I got chatting to a woman who subsequently became so distressed, she threatened to throw herself off the train.

As I teenager, I could drone on for hours to anyone who would listen about whether AC/DC could continue once Bon Scott died and which Led Zep song was the greatest, but it wasn't my heavy-rock rambles that caused this woman to lose the will to live as she sat next to me. The reason she threatened to end her life on the East Coast Main Line was because she'd been widowed.

I can't remember who started the conversation or how old the woman was – at 17 someone of 46 is ancient – but I vividly remember her story. She'd recently lost her husband, and, lonely and desperate, had acted on her sister's suggestion that she sold up and moved south. In theory, it was the ideal arrangement: the two of them could be near each other, her brother-in-law would be around to help out with odd jobs, she could downsize to a smaller, more manageable property and there was a ready-made social life waiting for her. In practice, the move was a disaster. Not only did she miss her husband, she missed her house, her beloved garden and the memories that went with living there together. The fact that her sister's husband was still very much alive and kicking highlighted that hers wasn't, as did her sister's social life that revolved around couples.

The woman became more and more hysterical as the story unfolded. She felt she'd lost everything; she couldn't go on; she didn't want to go on, what's more, she had nothing to go on for. She might as well throw herself off the train, in fact, she *was* going to throw herself off the train, right *now*. In 1981, the old slam-door type carriages meant that this was a real possibility.

I don't know what I said, but at 17, I suspect I wasn't much use. I do remember looking around the carriage for a grown-up to help me (and her), but everyone had their noses stuck in books or newspapers. Someone must have been listening in, as eventually a passenger turned up with the guard, and they led the distressed woman away. Perhaps they took her to the dining car and gave her a stiff drink and let her cry. Perhaps they took her to the guard's van and sat on her until we reached the next station. I'm ashamed to say that at the time I didn't find the incident upsetting – I found it rather exciting.

I've never forgotten the conversation, but of course now it resonates with me, particularly because one of the first rules of widowhood everyone trots out is: make no major decisions for the first year.

Three weeks after JS drowned and about a week before his funeral, I trudged up our road, in the dark, with The Hound. Our house is on a corner and I could see it ahead of me: the lights were on, but there was no one home. In the street, my husband's car was parked where he'd left it before we went on holiday. It was at that point that, with startling clarity and conviction, I made a decision: I was going to move house.

Actually, I wasn't going to move; I was going to leave, put my keys through the letterbox and run away. Others could sort everything out in the way that I was having to. My husband had disappeared, and so would I.

But where to?

Marbella? I'd never been, but last year I'd met a lovely woman at a party who'd lost her husband, moved from London to Marbella and loved it. Slight location problem: Marbella is by the sea, a no-go at the mo.

Australia? Perfect! I *love* Australia. I've got family in Sydney, friends in Perth and an ex-boyfriend in Melbourne. Damn! They're all by the sea too. But Oz isn't all Bondi and buff bodies. I could relocate to somewhere in the outback and, if it all got too much, make a Lady Gaga-style dress out of kangaroo meat and let the dingoes cart me away. Knowing my luck, a passing dingo would just sniff me, cock his leg against mine and trot off, leaving me stinking of rotting joey and dingo pee. I decide to scrap Australia, plus, I couldn't put The Hound in quarantine.

Ireland? Ideal! The Irish accent is *so* soothing. I could reinvent myself as a mysterious and tragic figure and sit alone, in a bar, tracing initials (JS) in the foam of my Guinness. People would approach me, but I'd give them a glacial stare, and they'd back off muttering about what dark secrets I held: Murder? Tax evasion? A communicable disease? This was a non-starter: I don't like Guinness, I'm by nature a talker and it's hard to look mysterious with a glass of Merlot and a dachshund who wags his tail at anyone who looks his way.

I'd like to point out that this train of thought took place roughly between the 'Give Way' sign and my front door, and by the time I got in, I didn't want to move. And even though I no longer have such sudden and fleeting bouts of clarity about the future, I still lunge from being so desperate to stay here I'll live in one room and eat pickled herrings from Lidl all winter in order to be able to afford to run it, to playing estate agent roulette: plugging random places into *PrimeLocation* and seeing what comes up. Last week it was Leicester, last night the Cotswolds. I suspect that even if I did move, I'd still be living on Planet Grief. It seems to me that however fast you run from The Grief Monster, however far you travel, you can never really hide or outwit it.

So, all in all, I think that the first rule of widowhood is a good one to stick to, *if* you can. There are some business decisions I've had to make which I would have preferred to have left for a while, but couldn't, and JS's beloved car was sold days before the funeral. When he was around I never drove it, I couldn't park it, and the sight of The Hound rushing up to it and wagging his tail further shattered my heart.

I wonder what happened to the woman I met on the train 30 years ago, and how the rest of her life panned out. I hope she eventually met a widower at the local golf club and ended up happy and cherished, even if there was always darkness at the edge of the light. I'd like to think that although she never remarried, she and Golf Club Man bought a little bungalow together and she got her garden back. I'd like to think they had photographs on show – ones of her late husband, some of his late wife and others of the two of them together – acknowledging the past and the people they'll always love and never forget, but able to live in the present. Most of all, I hope she found some peace.

CRUSE CONTROL: COUNSELLING PART FOUR

At only four months in to my grief, most people don't want me to grieve anymore. They are tired of it, it's old news to them. If only they knew.
~ **Gaynor**

'I'm from your local branch of Cruse. Are you still looking for counselling?'

I was at the bus stop when I took the call, and I could have hugged the people in the queue next to me with relief. I'd contacted Cruse some time ago, only to be told that the waiting list in north London was long and their pool of volunteers small. I'd all but given up on them (and their daytime helpline which was constantly engaged), telling myself that I didn't want to sob in front of some do-gooding woman wearing a floral skirt and American-Tan popsocks anyway. But right now, I'd see anyone. I gushed down the phone that yes, I still needed help.

'I'm sorry, but I'm ringing to let you know that we still can't offer you anything for the foreseeable future.'

It was another kick in the gut. I'd reached a dead end with my attempts to get help: private counselling was expensive and hadn't been for me; the NHS had a long waiting list; my council had nothing to offer unless I was a drug user or an alcoholic, and although the local hospice was rumoured to provide wonderful support, I failed to qualify on two counts: JS didn't die under their care, and he died too quickly.

I felt *totally* abandoned.

But then, less than a week after this conversation, Cruse called unexpectedly to tell me that a slot had become free; the counsellor could visit me at home on Thursday evenings. It sounded ideal: I didn't have to travel and it filled up a lonely hour before *Coronation Street* kicked in and the Merlot came out.

Confirmation of my appointment arrived by post a few days later, together with the first name of my counsellor. It was an unusual name, so of course I Googlestalked her. When I began to write about my grief, I made a decision to conceal the identity of *everyone* I write about, unless they are happy to be 'outed' or deserve to be humiliated, so my code of conduct means that I can't tell you what I discovered in advance of our first session. With that in mind, let's just call my counsellor, Sister Mary…

At the agreed hour, Sister Mary arrived dressed head-to-toe in black, a middle-aged woman looking every inch like a Victorian child in mourning dress, from her ruffled, high-necked blouse to her lace-up ankle boots, skirt and thick tights.

As The Hound did back-flips with excitement over a visitor, Sister Mary and I shook hands.

I have a bit of a thing about handshakes – I'd rather my meta-carpals were crushed in a firm confident grip than my digits held in a limp dangle: Sister M's handshake was like grasping a fillet of raw halibut.

Sister Mary refused my offer of tea, coffee, wine, water, short-bread and Mr Kipling's finest, so I sat down and then thought, 'S*d it! Just because she isn't having anything, doesn't mean I can't,' so I got up and made myself a cuppa and sat down again waiting to start. But Sister Mary didn't speak, she just smiled at me in that sad, pitying way I have come to despise, even if it's meant kindly. And it was then that I noticed her teeth. I had never seen anyone other than Julia Roberts with so many teeth in one mouth – it was like being grinned at by a dolphin, and if you're already feeling disorientated, being counselled by Flipper wearing a black blouse and brooch whilst sitting at your kitchen table doesn't help.

Still Sister M didn't speak. Decades of running business meetings has given me the irritatingly high-handed habit of taking control if others fail to, so unable to stand it any longer I said, 'Perhaps you could tell me about your experience of bereavement?' As she began to talk about the training courses she'd been on, I realised I hadn't made myself clear. I clarified my question: How had bereavement touched *her* life?

The poor woman looked very uncomfortable: she shifted in her seat and wrung her flippers and twisted her mouth and kept saying, 'Um... er... um' at which point I thought I'd put her out of her misery. I told her that if she wasn't allowed to share her personal experiences, that was fine. I hadn't intended to put her on the spot. Finally, she said, 'If you're asking me if I've lost a partner, then no, I haven't. But I have lost my parents.'

And at that, the glass screen came down.

I had two sessions with Sister Mary before I called it a day. I know that Cruse has proved invaluable for thousands of people, and in no way would I wish to ignore the work that they do. Like so many things, your experience is only as good as the person you're dealing with, but for bereavement counselling, I feel strongly that counsellor and client have to connect at some level. Sister M believed (according to my internet 'research') that faith grows stronger if it is tested. I don't share her belief system, but even if I did, I'd wonder why JS's immediate family has been singled out from our wider circle to be subjected to such a brutal and searingly painful test. Not only that, I'd want to hunt God down and punch his ruddy lights out. I'm not belittling the loss of a parent, but to lose a parent when you're 'grown-up' with an independent life (as it transpired Sister M had done) cannot compare to losing your partner, and I challenge anyone to argue that it does. But more importantly than our differences of experience and faith, after each session with Sister Mary I felt more depressed than I did before she arrived. I am sure she is a kind person who meant well and would be wonderful for someone with a different personality to mine, but I needed someone with energy, flair and verve, with experience of losing a husband or wife or other catastrophic life event; someone I could look at as a role model for widowhood, someone who not only talked the talk but had walked the long and painful walk. I wanted to be able to sit across from someone and see not a smile of pity and sadness, but a look of compassion and understanding. I needed someone who knows first-hand the pain I feel, yet has built a new and richly fulfilling life from the ashes of their old one.

It took a while, but eventually I found just the person I was looking for.

THE TIES THAT BIND

The ties get me: James had so many, and such lovely ones. I have tried to give some of them away to people who knew him – I don't want some stranger who doesn't appreciate how lovely he was wearing his ties – although I think some people were slightly freaked out by my insistence that they have a tie. I did not get many acceptances so they are still there in the wardrobe, reminding me what I have lost. ~ **Linz**

It's been the most shockingly tearful start to August I've ever known, even worse than the time when my parents warned me in advance that I wouldn't be getting a pony for my twelfth birthday. I've sobbed the length of Oxford Street, at the bus stop and on the bus; all over a poor woman walking her dog on the Heath (I bet she wished she'd never asked how I was); on the phone, and in the changing rooms at Uniqlo whilst trying (without success) to find a pair of jeans to fit my depressingly flat butt.

At just over five months, I thought the days of the Widow's Wail had gone, but I was wrong. Along with feeling completely overwhelmed by the terrible past, my frightening present and a bleak, JS-less future, that uncontrollable guttural roar of grief and frustration returned to further knock me off my already unsteady Converse-clad feet.

On Friday lunchtime, I was in tears whilst frying some out-of-date halloumi cheese, when suddenly I couldn't stand at the stove for a nanosecond longer. I felt incredibly restless and anxious and began pacing the kitchen crying out, 'No! No! No!' clenching my fists. Then – 'WAAAAAAHHHH!' The noise was so loud, such a lion's roar, it sent The Hound ricocheting through his cat flap in a barking frenzy.

The Widow's Wail is perfectly acceptable (if horrible) at home, but a bit more difficult to deal with when out and about. I remember some months ago sitting on a loo in the toilets of John Lewis in Oxford Street, weeping, when one suddenly emerged. In an attempt to get myself under some sort of control, I tensed up only to realise that I was beating my thighs with my fists whilst making squeaking noises. To those washing their hands at the sinks on the other side of the door, it must have sounded as if a chimpanzee was using the cubicle.

As if life isn't hard enough at the moment, I've been having lots of problems with my BlackBerry: the touch-screen keeps freezing and the phone goes through a total reboot without warning, usually whilst I'm using it.

JS loved gadgets, and when my BlackBerry started playing up I fantasised that the unpredictable nature of the phone was due to his 'energy' interfering with the electronics. Then I faced up to the more mundane reality that it was a software, not a soul problem. I really should go back to the Orange shop, but I can't face explaining my problem to some eighteen-year-old, sinewy lad called De-Wayne who oozes with street cool and wears a diamond stud in his ear, the outcome of which will undoubtedly result in me being cut off, or emails going missing, or SIM cards not being recognised and lots of frantic calls to Orange and tears, because even in the best of times, that seems to always happen to me and my moby.

As a stop-gap, I keep taking the battery out and starting again, but I'm going to have to sort it out because the phone keeps randomly ringing the first name on my contact list: a woman who I don't want to speak to, though as she never rings me back, I suspect she doesn't want to speak to me either. I've tried to delete her contact but when I press on her name there's a delay, and instead of going to my address book it rings her, cue frantic battery action.

But on Saturday, as a break from Grief Googling, I looked up my BlackBerry problem on the internet. Just as I had no idea that there were so many grief-stricken widows and widowers out there, nor did I have any idea of the grief a frozen BlackBerry Torch screen can cause those who are addicted to their CrackBerries. It seemed that I could do some sort of re-install via my computer, IF I had the right lead. I have lots of leads – they lie entwined like a basket of snakes snoozing in the sun – but of course none of them were the right lead, so I went hunting for other places the lead might be lurking. I became quite manic on the lead-hunt, convinced that if I didn't do the back-up and re-install within the next few minutes my BlackBerry was going to die along with all my contacts, texts and random photos of The Hound looking cute. So determined was I to find this wretched lead, I rushed into the spare bedroom, opened a cupboard door, and then I saw them…

Ties.

Beautiful, shimmering silk ties.

Row upon row of them hanging on tie racks.

Though a quietly understated man in most areas of his life, JS did like a statement tie and I loved to buy them for him. He'd get a kick out of going somewhere and someone commenting on his tie, and I'd feel proud when he'd smile and say, 'Thank you. My wife bought it for me.' His ties were even mentioned in the eulogy at his funeral.

And there they were, a rainbow of colours, a reminder of events we'd been to, weddings we'd witnessed, business trips we'd been on, parties we'd enjoyed. The only tie I never liked was his MCC tie, the egg and bacon colours (or pus and blood as I used to sneer) worn by so many old buffers at Lord's cricket ground, but even this seemed a tragic tie. Just before he died, JS was looking forward to cutting back on work, spending more time doing the things he loved: watching cricket was one of them.

But the saddest tie of all was the one that he hadn't quite put away – the one looped casually over the front of the others. A Christian Lacroix, shimmering pink tie, undoubtedly the last tie he ever wore five-and-a-half months ago, left hanging, waiting to be worn again. It was the same tie he was wearing in the photograph that sat on his coffin in the crematorium.

I stared at it, and then I wept and wailed until I could no longer breathe.

And then I closed the wardrobe door and went and made a cup of tea.

DOGGONE

The morning my husband was killed, we were due to go away for the weekend. I was ironing and packing as he said goodbye. He was just 'popping along the road' being driven by a friend. He didn't come back. It happened one minute from home. I was ironing and he was dying and I DIDN'T KNOW. How can that be possible? ~ **Emma A**

I'm a list-maker. I make so many lists, sometimes I have to make a list of the lists I've made. Personally, I don't think list-making comes high on my list (ha!) of vices, but that was before I read an article which warned that women were becoming slaves to their lists, that instead of giving them control, the lists were controlling them in a vicious cycle of ticking things off and adding stuff on. 'Loosen up your lists!' the article advised. 'Renounce listmania!'

I gave it a whirl when we had friends round for a meal. Instead of instructions taped to the inside of a kitchen cupboard door (7:00pm: *Put oven on to 170*; 7:05pm: *Double check oven is on,* etc.), I went (list-wise) commando.

It was a disaster. Instead of wafting around the kitchen in a state of list-less bliss, I forgot to do pretty much everything but drink alcohol.

Making lists comes naturally to me. I find lists a way of keeping some control in my life, and never has my life been more out of control than it has been in the last 23 weeks. So, as bizarre as it now sounds, I decided to make a list of ways in which, pre-accident, I could have imagined losing my husband: cancer; car crash; heart attack; brain tumour; slipping on ice and banging his head on the kerb; carjack at gunpoint on the Holloway Road; some DIY disaster involving a ladder and electricity – dammit, even perishing by terrorist attack on the Northern Line made it onto the Death List. But walking into a calm, turquoise-blue sea whilst on holiday and drowning? It never once crossed my mind.

I ached to talk to JS about his death, to say, 'You know all those times I freaked out that I would lose you because [*insert Doomsday scenario here*]? Actually, this is how it all ended…' I couldn't imagine what he would say. It was so inconceivable; it was unimaginable.

I could imagine him rationalising other deaths:

Cancer: 'Well, we knew there was a lot of it in the family.'

Car crash: 'I'm surprised I didn't have a serious prang earlier.'

Terrorism: 'Even the tightest security can't stop a nutter stuffing Semtex up their jumper.'

Heart attack: 'So much for the expensive BUPA ECG test!'

But had I said to him one night, whilst sitting on the sofa watching *Top Gear*, 'I'm worried one day I'll be in my bikini on a beautiful beach and watch you drown,' he'd have felt my forehead and asked whether I was delirious or been at the cooking sherry.

A few months after the accident and in major self-pity mode, I trudged tearfully around Hampstead Heath with The Hound, wondering just how many people are unlucky enough to have lost both a husband and a beloved dog whilst on holiday. Yes, dear reader, a death *en vacance* has happened to me before, which is why I doubt I will ever need my (still packed) suitcase again, not that anyone will want to accompany me given that clearly the Grim Reaper sneaks into my luggage.

In early March 2008, I travelled with JS and our dachshund, Rufus, from London to Northumberland to spend a week in Embleton, a tiny village on the north-east coast. The weather was glorious when we arrived, so we unpacked the car and rushed straight to the beach. Rufus went wild with excitement, zooming over the sands and along the dunes. We laughed at him careering about. 'What a lucky dog he is!' I remember JS saying fondly.

A few hours later, back in the cottage, we heard the dog repeatedly sneezing in the kitchen. I went to investigate and found the room *covered* in blood, as if someone had been shot against the fridge-freezer. Rufus seemed fine: he was wagging his tail, excitedly licking blood off the floor. I was confused. Surely if he'd cut his paw he'd be in pain or licking the wound? Then he sneezed again, and blood splattered *everywhere*.

I rang the vet who told us to bring Rufus in. JS drove like the clappers in the dark through the country lanes to the surgery. The vet asked us to sit in a nearby pub for an hour whilst he examined the dog. I remember going to the loo and realising that my face, hands and clothes were covered in blood; JS was so distraught, he hadn't realised I was doing a Jackie Kennedy impression, but in jeans and a rugby shirt rather than a pink designer suit. We must have stood out like sore thumbs: it was Saturday Karaoke night, and all the Geordie lasses were in their pelmet skirts and plunging tops, belting out 'I Will Survive' whilst clutching luminous bottles of alcopops. I wanted a clear head, so had a cup of tea and a packet of cheese and onion crisps.

We went back to the surgery. The bleeding had worsened. The dog with the waggy tail was now sedated and kept in overnight. We were still wide-awake and rigid with anxiety in the early hours of Sunday morning when the vet rang with his diagnosis: the back of Rufus' throat – his soft palette – had completely ripped apart. The vet didn't know for sure, but it seemed likely that Rufus had an undetected tumour that had burst, probably by running on the beach. It was a bomb waiting to go off, and it went off on our holiday. As my husband wailed and paced the bedroom of the rented cottage, I made the only decision I could, to allow the vet to increase the sedation and put our beloved friend to sleep. Three of us had arrived on holiday a few hours before. Now we were two. I make no apologies for confessing that Rufus was our child substitute, that we had both poured an unhealthy amount of emotion and love into the little lad. And now he was gone.

We both wanted to go home immediately, but with no sleep we were too tired to drive the 300 miles back to London. On the Monday, instead of packing a rucksack with a picnic and heading off on a walk, we went back to the surgery to sign forms, pay the bill, get Rufus' red leather collar and arrange for him to be cremated. We spent days sitting in coffee shops, tearful, passing time, not wanting to go home, not wanting to stay. We barely ate; we couldn't sleep. We were both heartbroken, but I remember JS saying that as long as we had each other, we'd be OK. Together, we could get through *anything*.

Going home without Rufus was traumatic; walking through the front door without him rushing ahead of us, harrowing. Life felt empty, the house soulless. Even work was no escape: he had been an office dog since he was ten weeks old. Staff cried.

As I walked on the Heath with The Hound, the similarities to what had happened almost exactly two years apart felt profound, even down to the Sunday morning holiday deaths. As bizarre parallels swirled around my brain, I was amazed that I hadn't thought of them before.

And then I remembered what JS had said when people commiserated about how awful it must have been to lose Rufus on holiday. I remembered it as clearly as I could remember my own name, and it literally took my breath away. JS said, 'Oh, he had the most wonderful death. He had a great life and a fantastic last day on the beach. He didn't get ill or suffer. He went out with a bang. Wouldn't we all like to go like that?'

JS wouldn't have wanted his family to suffer and the timing was rotten, but I now know what my husband would say about his own death.

The problem is, back then JS was right when he said we could get through anything, together. But we're no longer together. I'm alone. And I haven't lost my dog. I've lost my husband.

SOPHIE'S STORY

Two months ago, I put my head under the water in the bath for the first time without totally freaking out. Last month, I swam across a (small) river in an obstacle race. After a brief panic, I realised I was going to just do it, and I did. One tiny step, word or breath at a time, whatever our circumstances. It's such a cliché, but it's true. ~ **Sophie Day**

Bereavement is tremendously isolating, which is why so many of us find comfort online, sharing our experiences, fears and tears, sometimes with a humour so black it can only be appreciated by those who have 'been there'.

I remember getting a list of members of the charity, WAY: Widow and Young, and instead of feeling comforted by the roll call of names and deaths, I felt even more alone, frightened and isolated. In those days, I didn't realise that whilst our individual journeys to Planet Grief might take different routes, the landscape was the same when we got there.

I read the causes of death on the list: cancer, cancer, heart attack, brain tumour, heart attack, cancer, RTA, cancer, RTA, brain tumour, cancer, cancer… I felt in a club of one until – blistering bikinis! – there *was* a woman on the list whose husband had died on holiday by drowning! I remember my heart lurching with a feeling not so much of hope, as some sort of solidarity. I wasn't alone! Someone else had been through a similar ordeal! If this poor woman could survive, so could I!

Hope turned to despair as I realised the 'poor woman' on the list was me.

I have spent countless hours (usually late at night) searching the internet for stories about people who have drowned. During those lonely nights with the laptop in bed, little did I know that there were others out there searching for exactly the same thing.

Firstly, I came across Julia Cho through her blog, *Dear Audrey*. Julia's husband, Daniel, a talented cellist living in New York, drowned in Lake Geneva on 6th July 2010, whilst in Montreux for the jazz festival. He was 33, his daughter, Audrey, not yet two. It felt like a lifeline.

But I wanted more. I wanted to find someone who was there when their husband drowned. I still felt completely alone in what I saw, what I felt, what I experienced.

Then Megan in Maine, USA, found my *Planet Grief* blog. In 2009, Megan had witnessed the drowning of her partner, Matt. She wrote in her own blog, *Not Even a Wren*: 'I somehow landed on this blog [*Planet Grief*] and was stunned to read that she was widowed by drowning. That she was there when it happened. There are a couple of other similarities between she and I, but enough to say – wow.'

Megan posted a comment on my blog. I was amazed, thrilled and relieved. I emailed her. This is the opening paragraph of that first email:

Dear Megan, I was both sorry and yet 'glad' to see you arrive on my *Planet Grief* blog – I am sure you understand the strangeness of that first comment. One of the things that I have been saying over and over is that even after searching on the internet and all the stories people have told me, I haven't come across one person who was there when their loved one drowned. Until now. I'd like to find someone who saw their other half drown whilst they were thousands of miles away on holiday, but that might be too much to ask!

Megan replied. She said she knew of a person in the same situation, a woman from the UK who was on holiday in Egypt. Rightfully, she kept most of the details confidential, but gave me just enough facts for a Google search.

Up popped an article in *The Guardian* about Sophie Day titled: 'My husband died on our honeymoon'. Sophie and her husband, Luke, were on honeymoon in Egypt when, on the first night of a three-day trip along the river Nile, the boat they were in overturned and sank, trapping them in a pitch-black cabin that rapidly filled with water. Despite a fractured skull, Sophie found her way to the surface, but Luke was missing. His body was recovered a few hours later. With no money, no passport and no help, Sophie eventually made it to a cruise ship and called her father, who contacted the British embassy.

Stunned at what I read, I immediately emailed *The Guardian*'s features desk, who passed the details of *Planet Grief* on to Sophie, who then read the blog. In the meantime, Megan forwarded Sophie my contact details and Sophie got in touch. I asked Sophie whether she was happy that I share her story on my blog and generously she wrote back: 'Yes please. That is why I did it – if anyone can find a glimmer of hope I want them to.'

Sophie, thank you. I found more than a glimmer of hope. In you and your story, I found a beacon lighting the possibility of a life worth living. I would say that you will never know how grateful I am, but of course, you do.

Postscript: It is difficult to convey the effect on my grieving that Sophie's story had on me. It was a turning point. To read, 'I returned to Britain on my own. It felt like I had been torn in half,' finally made me feel less isolated. Over the years, I have come across many widows and widowers who lost their partners whilst on holiday, but back then, Sophie was my role model; if she could make it, so could I. I remain in touch with all three widows. Sophie Day now has a partner and a young daughter. Julia Cho is a talented writer and blogger at *Studies in Hope*, her prose about living and parenting after loss as beautiful as ever. Megan Devine has used her experience and qualifications to become a respected grief counsellor, writer on bereavement and founder of *RefugeinGrief.com*.

Sophie, Julia and Megan. Three women whose lives were shattered by drowning, but who have not only survived, but thrived.

Ladies, I'm proud of you.

THEY SHOOT HORSES, DON'T THEY?

If I'd been told in my teenage years that contrary to my conviction and heart's desire I was not going to marry Donny Osmond, I would have been devastated. If I had then been told that I would in fact marry someone ten times better than Donny Osmond, but he would die and leave me a widow at fifty, I would have spent the whole of my married life terrified with this knowledge and every year of bliss would have been horribly marred. Thank goodness we don't know what lies ahead.
~ Angela

Nowadays, my standard response to the question, 'How are you doing?' is a simple, 'Oh, you know, plodding along.'

For a while I had a more comprehensive reply: 'I'm doing whatever I can to get through the day to cope with what's happened,' but after trotting this out a few times, I realised that most people who ask you how you're doing are terrified that you'll tell them the unvarnished truth.

Imagine the scene, let's say an encounter in a local shop, perhaps the chemist where I've gone to get a further supply of herbal Nytol to help me sleep.

Concerned person with tight smile and cocked head: 'So, how *are* you doing?'

Moi, a red-eyed string bean with a sunken blotchy face: 'Oh, you know, very little sleep, then waking up in floods of tears, anxiety vomming into the flower bed when I let The Hound out for his morning wee, going back to bed with my mobile and ringing the Samaritans, fantasising about getting my will up-to-date before climbing over the banister and strangling myself with the dog's lead...'

Not really on, is it?

But equally, I feel a fraud if I give them a cheery, 'Fine! OK!' because I'm not fine much of the time, and I'm never really OK. 'Plodding along,' is a good compromise, plus, I like the word 'plodding'. Not as much as I like the word 'Chanel', but still. Plod is an onomatopoeia: plod – plod – plod – the very word sounds like heavy footsteps moving slowly forward. And when I say I am plodding along, I can remind myself that although my progress might be slow and heavy, I am moving forward.

The problem is that I'm not a plodding-along sort of chick. I am more of a galloper.

Twenty-odd years ago, JS and I went to a beach in Dorset. He said much later that he knew he couldn't live without me when he saw me clamber out of the car, dash to the sands and skip along the beach in the wind. I knew for certain that he was the man for me when in a nearby gift shop he bought me a large toy dachshund that we christened 'Tuckton', and seemed unfazed that I sat in a coffee shop and included the stuffed mutt in our conversation.

Years after the Dorset dash, I was on a course with a woman called Diane who gave me a blow-by-blow account of her meno-pausal symptoms, bred Irish setters and was heavily into alternative therapies. She claimed that there were broadly two sorts of people: racehorses and carthorses, and identified me as a perfect example of a racehorse. She wasn't meaning that I had tremendously long legs, a muscle-packed butt and a glorious mane (though back then, perhaps I did), but that my energy came in wild hyperactive bursts. A carthorse type was more of a strong, steady plodder – just like my husband.

I raced home and told JS this equine-based theory, delighted to be thought of as a highly-strung fabulous filly. He dryly pointed out that at the slightest injury racehorses are shot because they can never recover, whereas a carthorse is patched up and on it slowly goes: plod – plod – plod.

I'm fed up of this grief stuff, of the tears, of the plans I make and break, of the face in the mirror haunted by the death I saw in front of me, of going to bed night after night with The Hound but without my husband, and the bleak mornings which arrive with depressing monotony. I want to gallop around like I once did, full of enthusiasm for life, even if such enthusiasm used to come in unpredictable bursts. Now, I have neither the energy nor the motivation to do anything other than plod – plod – plod.

Writing this, I realise that I not only miss my husband, I miss the girl on the beach in Dorset who careered about the sands – the racehorse with verve and energy and enthusiasm. A girl giddy with love not just for the man she was with, but for the life she was living.

HEAVENLY HANDS

I want to remember the feel of our hands together. What is it about that that is so special? The handholding? I knew I would marry my husband from the first time we shook hands. I still remember it vividly. When I was planning the wake, I told friends I had to hold his hand one more time, even if we weren't able to have an open casket or if I was too scared to look. They reminded me. 'It won't feel the same'. I touched it, didn't hold it. It didn't. Often in bed too, at night, I put out my hand.
~ Julia Cho

Growing up, we always had dogs, but after heartbreak with a young beagle and a bouncy Jack Russell who met his end under the wheels of a car whilst chasing a fox late one night, my mother declared: 'No more hounds.'

I longed for another dog more than I longed for Donny Osmond to sing *Puppy Love* to me, and I campaigned vigorously for a canine to be reinstated.

Determined to prove that I was capable of being the sole carer (I ignored the fact that I was at school during the day, presumably my dog would posses an iron bladder, be capable of crossing its legs or using a flushing toilet), I 'looked after' a toy dog, putting it to bed, feeding it and so on. I even took it for walks.

I may have been desperate for a dog, but not so desperate that I risked getting my head kicked in by the local hard girl when she saw me with a stuffed toy on a lead, but this didn't mean that whilst I was out and about I couldn't 'feel' my dog with me. I'd walk along the road and he'd trot beside me. I'd stop whilst he cocked his leg and whisper, 'Good boy!' when we passed another dog without any snarling or snapping. It sounds funny now, but my imaginary dog was incredibly real to me. I could feel him tug at the lead or hang back when a bus rattled towards us. I knew when he was frightened or having fun. What's more, my campaign worked: unable to live without a hound in the house, the parentals caved in and a new puppy arrived.

I tried something similar years later when I wanted a pony, but a teenager in jodhpurs and a riding hat careering around the garden whilst whinnying and neighing and slapping her thighs with a riding crop isn't cute – it's creepy – and I never got my pony.

Sometime after JS died, I was walking The Hound on Hampstead Heath when I inadvertently caught sight of my left arm and hand sticking out from my body, as if I was walking around holding hands with someone. It gave me a shock. I wondered how long I had been doing it. I carried on walking and after a while, slid my eyes to the left. There it was again, my arm outstretched, the fingers of my hand slightly curled as if I was holding onto something – or someone. I reined my hand in, but again it drifted away from my body. I seemed to have no control over my limbs.

Perhaps I was suffering from Anarchic Hand Syndrome? My husband and I once saw a programme about this condition and (rather meanly) practically wet ourselves watching perfectly normal people being unable to control their hand. We'd (OK, mainly me) sometimes act out Anarchic Hand Syndrome, combining it with Restless Leg Syndrome and finishing off this cruel little vignette with narcolepsy. One vivid memory of JS is seeing him sitting on the sofa, crying with laughter, watching a programme where a committee of narcoleptics tried to take meeting notes.

That day on the Heath, I gave up trying to control my left hand. I walked around holding thin air and yet the air wasn't thin:

I could feel my husband's hand in mine, I could feel its warmth and the roughness of his knuckles. His hand felt more familiar than my own.

Was it a sign? Was he walking beside me as I sobbed? I'd like to think so, but experience with my imaginary dog 40 years before tells me otherwise. JS's hand felt real to me, but so did the dog on the lead, and unlike my husband, that dog never existed. What conjured up the dog was my imagination and my intense longing for him to exist. I hardly need point out the parallels.

But there is a difference.

As a child, I could will my dog to 'exist' on cue. Now, however much I long for JS to be here, however much I try to imagine him walking beside me, other than that one brief time on Hampstead Heath, my hand has never again reached out on its own.

BIRTHDAY BLUES

For years our presents to each other would consist of 'fence panels' or 'new carpet', just stuff we needed for the house. Just as we reached the stage where we could actually start to buy real, thoughtful presents, whoosh, Mr G Reaper had to butt in and put a stop to it all. The bastard. ~ **Sue G**

Yesterday was my birthday. It was a day of tears, tantrums, laughter and terrible nightwear, and the first birthday in over two decades where JS hasn't woken me up with a cup of tea, a smile and a pile of birthday cards and presents.

The day started with tears, but that's standard issue nowadays, so I can't claim that the morning sob-fest was particularly birthday related, or that there was an increase in sobbing intensity because of the date. Anyway, at that stage I was still implementing my cunning plan, a two-part plan so cunning, even Baldrick from *Blackadder* would be in awe of its cunningness.

Part One of my plan was to totally ignore my birthday.

After breakfast, The Hound and I went for a walk on Hampstead Heath. It was a lovely morning, and although there was rumoured to be a flasher on the loose, we took a little detour off the main path through the woods. I was swinging the bright blue ball-launcher, scooping up the tennis ball and hurling it for The Hound, when I came across a fallen tree. This tree was totally inoffensive: it didn't trip me up or cause me to step in a pile of dog poo; it didn't have love hearts carved into its trunk or have a couple of cooing doves perched in its branches, but for reasons unknown to me, I began to beat the hell out of it with the ball launcher whilst yelling, 'I have had enough of this! I'm warning you – this can't go on! I am at the end of my tether! I can't stand it any longer! Day after day after bloody day!'

As I had my tantrum, I realised that I was doing an excellent impression of Basil Fawlty punishing his car by manically whipping it with branches, when it refused to start outside Fawlty Towers. I stopped, apologised to The Hound who was standing next to me with a day-glo yellow ball in his mouth, and carried on as if nothing had happened. I think we were both wondering whether I'd finally lost it, though on the plus side, thrashing a dead tree with a plastic stick whilst screaming would deter even the perviest flasher.

The second part of my cunning plan involved arranging a lunch in town with my editor, aka The Grammar Gestapo. I wanted to see her because we needed to get together to talk about work things, she didn't know it was my birthday, but mostly because she is bright, beautiful, warm and tremendous fun to be with. She's a little younger than me, and has been trying out internet dating. I would love her to find Mr Right or even just Mr Good for a Date or Three, but at the same time, I hope Cupid's aim isn't that great for a few more months, as her tales of the difference between the witty grammatically perfect men she meets online, and the arrogant weirdoes they turn out to be in real life are hilarious.

We went to The Riding House Café. Very nice, lots of gossip, a little work, some book recommendations to check out. A lovely lunch.

The Grammar Gestapo went back to her day job of policing inappropriate use of commas and exclamation marks.

I went to Primark on Oxford Street.

Now, in hindsight, going to a giant Primark during the school holidays at the height of the tourist season in a prime tourist area, when you're already feeling somewhat wobbly and vulnerable, was always going to be a bad move. The thing was, I had decided that in an attempt to comfort myself on those long, lonely evenings on the sofa, I couldn't live without a fleecy, all-in-one sleepsuit, the sort of garment that would have JS turning in his urn. I'm also concerned about energy prices and how much it will cost to heat this open-plan house, so I thought that I could keep the heating down if I was better wrapped up. My first attempt at tracking a onesie down led me to a *very* strange internet site run by a woman who claimed to be a nurse, but far from finding something snuggly, I was confronted by adult nappies and disturbing pictures of grown men in Babygros lying in cots sucking dummies. I refined my search terms, and discovered that Primark did a range of fleece all-in-ones, *with* feet.

After fighting my way through tourists who seemed to be buying armfuls of £1 T-shirts as if they didn't have clothes in their own country, I found the fleeces: pink ones and zebra-striped ones and something brown that resembled the pelt of a shot teddy bear. I grabbed a pink one and headed to the tills, the queue for which was longer than the immigration queue at JFK airport in New York when an Air India 747 has just landed on a Sunday afternoon. Sounding like Margo Leadbetter from *The Good Life*, I berated a passing assistant: 'This is ridiculous! Aren't there more tills?' Unfortunately, my snotty voice alerted others to the reply, which was that they had just opened some new ones further down. I almost got knocked over in the ensuing stampede.

I stood there and thought, 'What the hell am I doing, a forty-seven-year-old woman buying a £10 pink-and-white polka dot fleece Babygro with a cupcake on the front?' And then I remembered what I was doing. I was buying it because I am worried about heating the house in the winter. I wanted it because I thought it might feel nice to snuggle into now that I have no one to snuggle up to. I was desperate for some comfort in my life. But, standing in a discount clothes shop on my birthday it hit me: nothing that can be bought will provide the comfort I crave.

I dumped the pink monstrosity and fled, disheartened and disorientated.

I got to the bus stop. The driver hadn't pulled away, but he'd closed the doors. I knocked on them. He shook his head and flicked his hand dismissively at me. I pointed a finger at him and shouted, 'I'll see YOU at the next stop!' and began to run along Oxford Street, dodging the crowds on the pavement, darting in and out of the road. Oxford Street is *always* nose-to-tail with traffic, but this time the road was entirely clear and the bus accelerated past me. I watched it go, and for a moment reverted to my usual modus operandi in such situations, which is to phone JS and tell him indignantly what had happened. But of course I couldn't, and I could sense The Grief Monster lurking behind me, about to throw its black cloak over my head as it called out, 'Oi! Lonely widow on your birthday! Who's there for you now?' It was one of those moments when even though you're in a crowd, you long to sink to your knees, cover your head with your arms and block out the world.

I didn't scrape my knees on London concrete. I saw a cab with its light on, hailed it and jumped in. Of course now I wish I'd said to the cabbie, 'Follow that 390!' so that I could have caught up with the bus and carried out my threat of confronting the dismissive driver at the next stop. Instead I just said, 'Highgate Village, please,' slumped in the back and cried. The taxi fare ended up being twice the price of the foul fleece, which was enough to make me sob in itself.

I got home, walked The Hound, spoke to a couple of friends, had a glass of wine and a lasagne for one, watched *Coronation Street*, took a bath whilst listening to the football on the radio, and felt sorry for myself as I remembered the meal out we had a year ago in a local gastro pub, the same pub that hosted my husband's wake.

Just like all Baldrick's cunning plans, mine failed miserably, but I suspect that I won't learn, that I'll still be trying to dodge the evil clutches of The Grief Monster who didn't even give me a break on my birthday.

SIX, PACKED

*The first six months after IT has happened are the ideal time to get major dental work done. You don't care what they do, you even welcome the pain as it's so much milder than the other sort you're experiencing. Yeah, bring it on killer driller… ~ **Sue Ab***

Six months.

Ugh.

Actually, despite howling like an unneutered dog living next door to a bitch on heat (not *just* grief-related: my friend went back to Newcastle on Sunday and Arsenal were thrashed by Manchester United 8-2), I'm hoping that my six-month low came at five months, although of course The Grief Monster could yet hiss in my ear, 'Thought you'd got the six-month low out of the way early? You stupid, stupid woman!' before rugby tackling me to the ground and kicking me when I'm already down.

Still.

Six months!

Despite usually being pretty upfront about the accident, today, I can barely bring myself to write: 'It's been six months since JS…' Let's just say it's been six months since I wore The Bikini of Death.

Clearly, I am no swimwear model. On the internet, the bikini is modelled by a blonde poppet, but I'm told it looks fabulous on someone with olive skin and dark hair, someone exactly like me in fact, or at least that's what my husband said when he saw me wearing it standing on the stairs in the hall one February evening, bathed in artificial light and with no slap on, rather than on a beach with a team of make-up artists and photographic experts. I laughed and told him he needed new glasses or we needed new lights, but secretly I was thrilled that upping my Pilates sessions (since abandoned) had paid off. I remember thinking that, at 46, perhaps this was the last holiday when I could wear a bikini without looking mutton. I didn't want people on the beach making baaa-ing noises as I strolled to the water, barely able to breathe for holding my stomach in. Italian women might be able to pull off a two-piece with panache in their sixties, but they're brought up to look stylish in swimwear. My early beach life was spent behind a windbreak at Whitley Bay, my teeth chattering with the cold. I don't think I've ever seen my mother in a swimsuit. I'm sure she had one, but she never took her coat off, not just because of the cold, but because she was too busy handing round tea and soup from a range of different-sized Thermos flasks.

I shall never wear a bikini again – perhaps a stylish one-piece around a pool nowhere near the sea – but never a bikini. The word 'bikini' is branded into my brain along with 'CPR', 'ambulance', 'siren', 'blue' and 'dead'.

Six months.

Unbelievable!

It seems like yesterday and yet a lifetime ago.

I suspect that had I been in any fit state to think ahead on that dreadful Sunday morning, I might have guessed that six months down the line I would still be grieving, tearful and so on, but I doubt that I would have had any idea that amongst the constant sadness there would still be bouts of grief so searing, they take my breath away and leave me curled up in pain, or that I would still feel disorientated and disconnected. It seems to me the first few months were about surviving. Now they are about existing.

On 27th February, I had no idea what was in store for me. Six months later, these are just some of the things that I have discovered:

That I can be blotchy-faced, red-eyed, gaunt and with zits so large they need their own postcode, yet people will still proclaim, 'You're looking really well!'

That I have just enough self-restraint not to punch someone straight in the mouth when they trill, 'You'll find someone else and build a new life,' but not if they add the word 'soon' to that sentence.

That I still don't believe people – even other widows or widowers – who tell me that one day I'll feel happy again, not unless it's drug-induced, straightjacket-wearing, manic happy.

That God doesn't make bargains with people who plead: 'Please let me die in the night and let someone who wants to live survive.'

That it's easy to forget that I've put soup on the stove or started to run a bath, but impossible to dim the memory of my husband walking away from me into the sea.

That a dog is truly man's best friend.

That Arsenal losing is even more dismal without someone special to discuss it with.

That finding my purse in the fridge and a can of dog food in my bag is perplexing, but as old walnut face sings, it's not unusual.

That people who know where and how JS died will still say, 'Perhaps going on holiday would do you good?'

That even if every fibre of my being wishes that I could spontaneously combust in Tesco, I never end up a pile of ashes in the chilled meal aisle, just a wreck of a woman clutching a chicken-korma-and-rice meal for one.

That so many of the jobs around the house that JS did and I worried about can be fixed by putting an advert on *mybuilder.com* – in exchange for a heart-stopping bill.

That strangers can be unbelievably kind.

That friends can be breathtakingly crass.

That strangers can become friends.

That widows can be incredibly competitive.

That it really wasn't necessary to get the roof fixed, the windows cleaned, the Virgin engineer round, a woman to tidy the house *and* invite a friend for tea, all on the same day so soon after the funeral.

That when I sobbed as a teenager to Janis Ian's 'At Seventeen', I would be sobbing to it at 47, but feeling a million times lonelier than I did back then.

That you can't get away from watery metaphors about death and grieving: waves of emotion; tidal wave of grief; all at sea; drowning in a sea of grief; pulled under, etc. etc. etc, but that it can be quite amusing to see the horrified face of someone who realises they've just said, 'I suppose you've either got to sink or swim at a time like this.'

That when Catherine Deneuve said after the age of 40 a woman must choose between her face or her figure, *she* had a choice. The Grim Reaper has taken that choice away from me.

How to change halogen lightbulbs.

That my cunning plan of committing a crime and being locked up in prison so that I could run away from my responsibilities, failed to take into account that I found the violence and sex scenes on ITV's *Bad Girls* unsettling, or that MacBooks are banned in cells.

That 98% of my wardrobe either no longer fits or feels appropriate for my new life.

Just how much paperwork is involved when someone dies.

That often after laughing, I burst into tears, but rarely do I laugh after crying.

That QVC makes excellent wallpaper TV.

That playing Kamikaze Pedestrian doesn't kill you, it just pisses off cyclists who have to swerve to avoid you.

That call centres in India are the invention of the devil.

That cooking for one is only fun if you know that you won't be doing it night after lonely night.

The price of gas and electricity.

That when I go out I want to come home.

That when I'm home I want to go out.

That when friends are round, sometimes I want them to leave.

That when they leave, I want them to come back.

That I still can't look at recent photographs of JS without feeling my heart is being ripped out without an anaesthetic.

That drinking alone isn't sad, it's vital.

That I don't have as many true friends as I thought I had, but the ones I have I can never thank enough for their love and loyalty.

That if I meet someone in the street who looks like they have constipation, it's almost certainly caused by their embarrassment at bumping in to me.

That I know JS would want me to be happy again, I just don't know how to go about it.

That the number of condolence cards and offers of help bears no relation to the number of people still around now.

That if there are too many messages on the answerphone I feel hassled, but if there are none, I feel abandoned.

That life without my husband is hard, but it would be so much harder without the internet and the wonderful men and women I have met through it.

That looking at the photograph of The Hound sitting in my suitcase the night before we left for Barbados, still makes me unbelievably sad.

That I still can't bear to unpack either of our suitcases.

That life goes on, and that orphan Annie was right when she screeched that the sun will still come out tomorrow, but the sun shines less brightly even on those days when it does shine, and I'm scared my life will always be this dark and cold.

But most of all, at this six-month mark, that I love and miss my husband, the man who thought I looked better in a bikini than a blonde, professional swimwear model.

HOWLING AND HOUNDS

Oh my god, I remember the wailing, the body shaking, the face pulling, the noise. I said to a fellow widow friend, 'I seem to have developed this ridiculous cry' and she said, 'Yes, me too.' ~ **Sue Smith**

I was going to write about 'Courage' today. I knew exactly what I wanted to write, and I'm a super speedy typist so it wouldn't have taken long, but, annoyingly, work got in the way. So, instead of sitting at my iMac fiddling about on Facebook, sending or replying to emails or writing a post for my blog, I've had to buckle down and do some 'professional' writing. It wasn't a great deal of prose, just a letter to go in the front of my next book and some answers to questions that the marketing department want to include in the back, but as I've been majorly 'Bleurgh!' since my birthday, I've either been putting it off or genuinely forgetting to do it. But yesterday, The Grammar Gestapo sent me one of her 'I don't want to chase you but…' emails, which means that she doesn't want to chase me, but she has to. So this morning, I buckled down to the task.

Mornings aren't good for me. Actually, neither are evenings, afternoons, lunchtimes or bedtimes. There is a reasonable two-minute period when I come back from taking The Hound for a walk and put the kettle on, but I wouldn't get much done in two minutes, especially as I am an expert at tidying my desk, polishing the monitor screen, shaking crumbs from the keyboard, adjusting the blinds and so on before putting words on the screen, at which point I'm off like a ferret down a trouser leg, my fingers a mere blur over the keys. But starting anything new is always difficult, which is perhaps just one of the reasons why I find the start of a new day so difficult. Or it may be entirely down to the fact that my husband died.

Whatever the reason, it doesn't absolve me from having to do some work.

I sat at my desk and felt my heart banging away in my chest. The old cardiac muscle was racing faster than Usain Bolt when he's not disqualified for a false start, and I felt anxious, *very* anxious. Not anxious about writing or what bills the postman will bring, or whether I'm going to get any more vitriolic emails from people claiming that I'm claiming my grief is worse than theirs, just generally anxious. I thought about taking The Hound out and then writing like a maniac for two hours when I got back, but I knew I had to get some words on the screen before doing my daily 'Sad Mad Woman with Dog' impression, or The Grammar Gestapo would need to notch up the tone of her emails, and I don't want to be thought of as a typically unreliable author working to elastic deadlines.

For inspiration, I dug out copies of my books to see what I'd written before and I came across these two questions and my answers, which appeared in the back of my last teenage novel.

Describe your teenage self in five words. Anxious. Anxious. Anxious. Anxious. Anxious.

If you could give your teenage self one piece of advice, what would it be? Relax. It will all turn out OK in the end, I promise you.

And reading it, I wept. I wept for the anxious teenager I was, and I wept for the anxious widow I am now.

But most of all I wept because in a sense it *had* all turned out OK. The difficult issues I faced in my childhood were decades ago. I'd moved forward, used the angst of my youth constructively and creatively, and though life as an adult wasn't always hearts and flowers, it *was* good. But now, now life isn't OK. Far from it.

As I sobbed, I wondered whether if I'm still around in thirty years (which in itself turned the Sobometer up several notches), what advice I'd give the anxious widow weeping over her keyboard. Will I look back and say to her, 'Relax, it will all turn out OK in the end, I promise you'?

Right now, it seems impossible that I will ever be able to say that, but I doubt the fourteen-year-old me would have believed it either, and yet beyond my teenage years it was *more* than OK.

And then I pulled myself together and got writing.

SHELLEY: COUNSELLING PART FIVE

My own counsellor had the irritating habit of ending every utterance with the word Sue (it IS my name of course, but I don't need to hear it so often as I am still capable of identifying myself). I met her every Friday on the top floor of a disused vicarage, the panelled staircase lined with paintings of deceased parsons. In my mind she was Morticia Addams, and it took me weeks to get out of her dusty grip. Recently, I had another bit of counselling through the NHS with a cheery gay guy who made me think about stuff, and reminded me of my strengths rather than the dire situation I was in. Proof that counselling can be good, but don't make the mistake I made of thinking you've got to stick with the first one you're given. ~ **Sue Ab**

I have a very poor track record of getting on with counsellors. Prior to JS's death I had been to counselling three times: I'd encountered an enormously fat psychotherapist who wheezed so loudly I couldn't concentrate on my problems for wondering if he would make it through our session, a beardy-weirdy who turned out to be a pervert and a woman who picked her zits and flicked the dried scabs onto the floor. After JS died, I failed to bond with the strange woman in black from Cruse, the trauma psychotherapist Doktor R, and the woo-woo chakra-balancing woman who looked like *Thunderbirds'* Lady Penelope. Six counsellors, and I don't have a good word to say about any of them, although I have much more affection for Doktor R now than I did then.

Perhaps it's not them. Perhaps it's me and my, 'You can't tell me anything I don't know attitude,' that has clouded my ability to pick a decent one.

Four months after JS died, I was bemoaning my counselling misfortune to a friend who had been both divorced and widowed. H, a feisty Northerner who whilst of the same 'Get on with it' school of life as me, acknowledged that what had happened was so huge I needed some professional support. My friends were wonderful, but I was aware that some of them were suffering from sympathy burnout, and I didn't blame them. I'm finding it hard to be around me too. H felt that what I really needed was coaching, not counselling, and mentioned that an old industry colleague of ours – Claire D – had recently set up a life coaching business. Perhaps I should get in touch with her? I barely knew Claire, but what I knew I liked: she had formed and run a successful character licensing agency, sold it, started up a restaurant in Hammersmith and was now coaching. She had always come across as bright, straightforward, kind and no-nonsense, and, what's more, I knew that JS liked and admired her. I was convinced that Claire was the key to my getting my life back on track.

I Googled her and found her website. The words she used were *exactly* what I needed: her coaching was about setting goals and forming strategies to thrive, not just survive. The problem was Claire wasn't a life coach, she was a business coach. I was devastated. H suggested that I still contact Claire, but I couldn't imagine turning up to meet this admired business powerhouse clutching a wad of snotty tissues sobbing, 'JS is dead. Help me!' But H was right: perhaps it was decades spent in business or just my personality, but what I needed wasn't endless navel-gazing and introspection, but goals to strive for and strategies to put in place. I didn't just want to survive. I intended to thrive. So I put those exact words into the Google search engine along with 'coaching', 'grief' and 'bereavement'. The one word I deliberately missed out was 'counselling'. And up popped the website of a woman called Shelley. I had no idea where in the world Shelley was, but, immediately, I emailed her. Her email bounced back, but I was on a mission. I tracked her down on Facebook and sent her a message. She sent me her phone number and suggested I call her. I rang her and her first words, delivered in a clipped but warm South African accent, were, 'Darling, it's all going to be OK. I promise you.'

Shelley explained that she had been widowed (which I liked, because I felt she was one of 'us') and remarried (which I didn't, because I couldn't imagine ever wanting to be with anyone else but JS ever again), and that we should meet up for a chat. I am a firm believer that people come into your life just as you need them, and as it turned out, Shelley lived only a few miles from me, just past St Marylebone Crematorium in East Finchley, where my husband's ashes were still sitting on a shelf.

I know that Doktor R's code of conduct prevented her from becoming too involved with her clients, and I understand that (though I remember her looking pained and, just as I was about to leave, saying, '*Please* eat some breakfast every day,' which I found oddly touching), but when Shelley opened the door of her house and immediately gave me a hug, it was *exactly* what I needed. We sat in her office – a snug sanctuary – where I wept and wailed and drank tea and ate biscuits as her dogs snored next to me. When I left her house several hours later, I felt the first glimmer of hope for the future.

The approach that Shelley takes is, 'Yes, what has happened is terrible, but it *has* happened so what are you going to do about it?' This is bereavement coaching, *not* counselling. It's a practical, no-nonsense approach that resonates with me. During each session she allows me to weep and wail, but then we put in place a plan for the week. In the early days it was something as simple as aiming to eat breakfast every day (are they *all* obsessed with breakfast?) or making an appointment to massage my tension-packed shoulders and sticking to it. She's had me watching films on DVD (*The Bucket List!*) and then discussing them, or making a goal to deal with paperwork I find frightening. These small steps and practical measures have gradually made me feel as if I am regaining some control in a life which otherwise feels chaotic. The weight of grief is so intense, it's been a relief for someone to say to me at the end of our session, 'Right, this is what you are going to do this week...' This 'homework' gives the week a purpose, if only to be able to go back for the next session and say, 'I ate breakfast six days out of seven!' Just call me 'teacher's pet'.

I don't always agree with Shelley's methods: I'm not a believer in healing crystals for instance, though I keep the one on my desk I bought on her recommendation, and there have been times when I felt I was veering off in to a woo-woo world that doesn't sit comfortably with me. And yet, even with my scepticism of affirmations and meditation and feng shui and burning sage to cleanse a space, Shelley's practical plan to grieving is helping me to put my battered little soul back onto life's tracks to continue its journey.

I'm the first to admit that this approach is not for everyone. I've been very scathing about the counsellors that I have met, but the key, I think, is to keep searching until you find someone you feel fits your grief, and grief, like counsellors, is not a 'one size fits all' emotion. Some people don't need or don't want counselling, or get it on a more informal basis through family and friends, and if that works for them, good. Some people want to spend an hour a week rehashing the past and sobbing, and if they come away feeling better, then great! Traditional counselling didn't work for me, because the reason I was falling apart wasn't because my mother threatened to give my prized patent-leather shoes to poor children unless I behaved (Doktor R's 'Tell me about your childhood' approach), just as it wasn't the reason I was bolting from the queue in M&S with panic long before JS died (Beardy-Weirdy and Flaky Face). The reason I am in despair is because I have watched my husband drown.

But just as there are different counsellors for different people, perhaps we need different counsellors for different stages of our grief. I was so shocked and traumatised in those early weeks, perhaps I needed to just cry and shred tissues as I did with Doktor R. I became so angry about the hand that life had dealt me, I'd have sneered with contempt at anyone who sat at my kitchen table and trotted out stock sympathy phrases whilst cocking their head, not just the strange woman in black from Cruse. I hope there will soon come a time when I won't need Shelley to give me my tasks for the week, at which point I'm sure she will be delighted that I feel strong enough to set out on my own.

The Chakra woman? She was just bonkers.

PILLOW TALK

Many, many nights I picked myself off the floor, having flashbacks, and made pie, because I had to do something. I couldn't eat it, and never wanted to, but I had to do something. ~ **Megan Devine**

As summer comes to an end, I'm looking for ways to make things better in the bedroom.

I'm not talking about strange internet sites, late-night, subscription-only TV channels or the address of Fettered Pleasures, which I already know, because JS and I used to sit in a traffic jam outside the shop twice a day and giggle at the window displays which altered each season. One highlight was a spring tableau featuring a woman dressed as a bee cavorting amongst daffodils, a scene that brought a whole new meaning to the phrase, 'Sting in the tail'.

But as usual, I digress.

No, I'm talking about the thing in the bedroom that I long for, don't get enough of, think about for much of the day and hope will happen spontaneously once I get to bed, leaving me feeling refreshed and relaxed.

Sleep.

In the first few months after the funeral, although it often took me until the early hours of the morning to nod off, with the help of American over-the-counter sleeping tablets procured from a friend, I did sleep *and* I slept in. Even if I didn't get to sleep until three in the morning, dozing until nine or ten still gave me a good run of zzzzs. I used to read posts on grief forums about sleep-deprived widows and seriously wonder if I could have loved JS as much as these insomniacs loved their partners, guilty that whilst they were tossing and turning, watching the hours tick by until dawn, I was out like a baby stuffed full of Calpol.

It's now September and, oh, how things have changed.

I am now one of those widows I used to read about, awake at all hours, unable to get to sleep or stay asleep. I've tried hot baths with smelly oils, herbal sleeping tablets, which didn't work, and the once 'magic' American sleeping tablets now make me feel drunk in the morning. I bought an electric blanket to try and make the bed more inviting, but lying with wires down the side and a controller on the bedside table reminded me of a hospital bed. I flirted with Horlicks, but sitting in my 'hospital' bed under the electric blanket in my Snoopy nightie, drinking Horlicks with The Hound by my side, on his back with his plums in the air, I felt ready to be carted off to the sort of nursing home where the telly is too loud and everywhere smells of wee. So I stay up and look at strange internet sites and late-night TV channels, but these are grief forums and QVC, and I'm so exhausted that even if Alastair Campbell appeared at the end of my bed swinging a bag from Fettered Pleasures with a *come hither* look in his eyes, I'd be too weary to pour myself into a bee outfit, and anyway, I'd be worried the electric blanket would melt the PVC.

I do listen to the radio, but even that is fraught with danger. A piece on camping which seemed totally safe listening (the only tent I'll go into is one serving Pimms) had me tearfully reminiscing about a cottage in Northumberland we stayed in, right next to a camping site. A phone-in on what makes a long and happy marriage resulted in me shouting into the dark, 'Not dying helps!' As to the phone-in on widowhood, it was grimly fascinating listening to the Welsh fireman who coped by sleeping with every available female; I presume his uniform was the pull – it certainly wasn't his personality. Marieke, a widow I know, rang in and came over brilliantly, but then straight after her, the radio host said, 'And now we have a caller from Barbados...' Even The Hound looked sorry for me when I sighed, 'Can someone, please, just give me a break?'

I try to read, but I can't finish a book. Magazines seem to be full of articles featuring smug marrieds and advice about improving your sex life, or recipes that feed two or four or six.

And when I finally fall asleep, night after night there are the dreams; terrible, anxious dreams where I am desperately searching for JS. I'm in a taxi with him, but when the car stops, he's disappeared and the taxi driver denies all knowledge of a second passenger. I go to our office and a strange man screams that there is no one there by the name of John Sinfield and demands I leave. When I finally get through to JS's mobile, someone else answers and says he's never heard of my husband. I plead with him not to put the phone down, to try and remember how and where he got it from. Then, at the weekend, the dreams took a new turn: JS had run off with someone else, left me for another woman. My bereavement coach, Shelley, says this is good, that I am processing JS's death on every level. I tell her that I am exhausted.

The thing is, I'll be upfront and say that for the last six months of our 22 years together, JS and I had started to have a problem in the bedroom.

He'd begun to snore.

He'd always snored after a late-night curry and a few too many drinks and that was fine – a dig in the ribs would have him snorting and turning over – but the combination of carrying a bit of extra weight and a few winter colds had recently taken their toll on his nasal passages and my sleep. What I could never understand is why he could hear me growling, 'Stop snoring,' but he couldn't hear *himself* snore. My complaints in the morning were met with protestations that he couldn't *possibly* be as loud as I made out.

So, I formulated a cunning plan. Next time he snored so badly that it was like lying next to a truffle pig with bronchitis, I was going to use my mobile phone to record his snoring and then play it back the following morning to *prove* how loud it was.

I didn't have to wait long.

The snoring started.

In the dark, I tried to get the record feature on my BlackBerry to work, but instead managed to load just about every app except the media feature. Eventually, I thought I'd found it, so, leaning over, I held the phone by his face, pressed the button and turned on the flashlight, *right* into his eyes, causing him to wake with a start, The Hound to jump up and bark, and me having to explain why I was holding my phone over my husband's head in the middle of the night. JS loved my eccentricities, but that night and with an early morning meeting on the cards for him, there was a strong possibility that I could have ended up a divorcee rather than a widow.

But now, as I lie in the dark, I would give *anything* to hear my husband snore again. If he came back and still snored, after a while it would probably still annoy me, and I can't pretend I wouldn't dig him in the ribs or try and record his snores again. But, oh, how I would rather be kept awake by the sound of my husband snoring than by the image of him drowning.

LIGHTS, CAMERA, NO ACTION

My husband and son both played in a brass band. One month after John died, I was asked to attend a concert where my son (aged 14) was to be given the Bandsman of the Year award. For my son's sake, I dragged myself along, sat alone in the middle of a row about six rows from the front. Then, to my horror, the conductor began a tribute to John before presenting my son with his award. Totally unprepared and totally overwhelmed, I began to sob uncontrollably with the eyes of both the audience and the band upon me. I don't even remember what happened next, but somehow I made it through the end of the concert and scuttled off home to the safety of my familiar four walls.
~ Gaynor

During the last seven months on Planet Grief, I've discovered that it's not only the best-laid plans of mice and men that go awry. A widow's plans are subject to change, or at least, they are for this particular widow.

This is what I am wearing right now as I hammer my keyboard: red and grey tartan pyjama bottoms; grey t-shirt; grey zipped hoodie; lip balm and a vitamin A serum which promises to make my skin glow. (Still waiting…)

This is what I *intended* to wear this evening: black, knife-pleat, v-necked vintage dress; wide, black, suede belt with diamante round buckle; high, strappy, black, patent-leather sandals; selection of suitably sparkly jewellery; and subtle yet feature-enhancing make-up.

The former outfit would never feature in a *Vogue* double-spread as to what the woman about Highgate should wear, but it's appropriate for typing this at ten o'clock at night.

The thing is, I wasn't supposed to be at my desk tonight. I was supposed to be sipping cocktails at The Grosvenor House Hotel in Mayfair, before attending a reception in the ballroom along with 1,300 representatives of the industry JS and I worked in. I was supposed to eat dinner, laugh at comedian Greg Davies performing his stand-up routine, clap enthusiastically at the winner of the 'Best use of a cartoon character on a lunchbox award', and then, at the end of the evening, listen to a touching speech about my late husband against a photo backdrop. To applause, I intended to glide up onto the stage in my spiked trotters, graciously accept the award on behalf of JS from amazingly tall Greg, give a short yet witty speech (opening line: 'There must be easier ways to meet one of your comedy heroes than your husband dying…') before having my photo taken with Big Greg. I imagined posting said photo on my blog alongside a breathless commentary about how difficult the evening had been, but how glad I was that I did it, yada yada yada.

The dog-sitter was booked, as was the hair appointment and the Addison Lee cab. My pedicure (Jessica's 'Some Like It Hot' red) was immaculate, the outfit on the hanger ready to go and my speech polished to perfection courtesy of walking over the Heath for the last few days telling The Hound, 'My husband was a quietly understated man, nevertheless, I know that he would have been thrilled…'

There was even a cunning plan in place should I faint on stage with the horror of it all. My friend, Big Bird, has the serious hots for Mr D and wanted to meet him, but not being the recipient of a prize for Hello Kitty three-pack knickers or the widow of an industry grande fromage, it was arranged that as I crumpled to the floor in a heap of black pleats and bling, she would race on to the stage on the pretext of helping me, whilst actually stepping over me to push her phone number into Greg's undoubtedly large mitt.

On The Hound's life, I really and truly intended to go.

And then I woke up this morning and thought: 'I don't want to go.'

Not, 'I can't face it' or 'I can't do it,' but, 'I don't want to go.'

I texted Big Bird, who suggested that I had a weep, walk The Hound (my morning routine) and see how I felt. It was good advice, because Big Bird knows that even if I am nervous before giving a major speech or presentation, once I'm made-up and dressed-up and stand up with a microphone, on a good day I can make Joan Rivers look shy and boring.

So, I had a sob and walked The Hound and spoke to a couple of people and *still* I didn't want to go.

Sitting quietly on a bench on the Heath overlooking a pond, I realised it wasn't accepting the award or speaking in front of well over a thousand people that worried me – most of them would be so plastered by the time JS's award came around, they wouldn't notice if SpongeBob was given a lifetime achievement gong. I dreaded going out on my own with no one to tell me that I'd scrubbed up well, it saddened me that there would be no looks across a crowded room which signalled with just a small eye movement: 'Let's get the hell out of here and go home', and the thought of slumping into a cab, alone, at the end of the evening, was dire. But I'm going to have to get used to those things if I'm to live any sort of reasonable life, and none of those things was the real reason I didn't want to go.

What I couldn't bear was the thought of being amongst so many people who would be (understandably) hell-bent on having a good time in their black ties and ball gowns, people who still live the sort of professional life I once relished. We used to have a bustling, three-storey office with a showroom and lots of staff, but now there is just me stuffed into a tiny, one-woman room, winding-down the company, organising boxes to go into storage, sifting through decades of material collected over the working lifetime of my husband: *ET* clocks; *Miami Vice* cars; *Thundercats* action figurines; *Snoopy* toys; *Rugrats* activity sets; Nintendo comics; *Garfield* socks. It's heartbreaking on so many levels, and going to the dinner tonight felt as if I was peeping back into a life I once had. Just as with photos, I'm not yet at the stage of remembering those times with a smile, only searing pain.

So this afternoon, I rang a friend in the business and asked her to put the contingency plan in place: a friend of JS's would accept the award on his behalf. I cancelled the dog-sitter and the hairdresser and the cab and told Big Bird that she'd have to chat up Greg without me. She said she'd gone off him anyway and that if they were meant to be together, they'd meet again.

Tonight, instead of cocktails and speeches, I fired up the little Fiat and spent the evening eating pizza with friends who loved JS too. It wasn't the evening I planned, but I felt it was the evening I wanted, and it felt right. But there is no denying that typing this in my PJs wasn't what I intended.

This was supposed to be how the day ended:

Beautifully dressed and sparkling under the lights of the Grand Ballroom, JS's elegant widow fights back emotion as she brandishes his award in the air and says:

'John, wherever you are my darling, this is for you. It's well deserved. Thank you.'

IT'S ALL RUBBISH

*My husband died 14 months ago. He always insisted the teaspoons had to be put in to the front of the little basket in the dishwasher, as he couldn't get them out of the other little sections. His hands were too big. For months I continued to do this, then suddenly it hit me: Why? I can get them out, why do I have to separate them? So you know what, I stopped. Well, I did for a week or so, then I felt guilty and went back to putting them in the front, but now I put the bl**dy things wherever I want. And yes, I do feel somewhat guilty that I am not carrying on the 'family tradition' of the correct way to stack a dishwasher. ~ **Cheral***

Fasten your bra straps and hold on to your hats, I have an announcement to make: I have made a minor step forward with this grief business.

OK, not minor, more minorette. I've rather bigged it up, which perhaps I shouldn't have done, because it's not in the same league as being able to look at recent photos of JS without feeling as if I have been stabbed, unpacking the wretched suitcases or even delving below the Linen Barricade: the line of pillowcases in the washing basket I have carefully set up, underneath which the shirts, socks and, yes, underpants which JS wore pre-holiday still lie, just as he left them. In all honesty, I must do something about them. Sometimes, after a few glasses of vino and feeling bereft, I dive head-first into the washing to sniff it; it doesn't smell of JS any longer, just stale clothes, not helped by the fact that The Hound always tries to climb in with me.

No, the breakthrough is all to do with rubbish, specifically the wheelie bin.

The wheelie bin caused quite a rumpus in our house when it arrived because it didn't fit in to the two bin stores that the previous owner had helpfully constructed. This offended my husband, who couldn't bear the fact that the grey monstrosity would be on show. JS was all for functionality, but if it was in his line of sight, functional also had to be stylish.

There was quite a lot of childish flouncing around over what the rest of us in the area thought was a progressive move, given that the urban fox regularly ripped open all the sacks and left a trail of soiled nappies and organic pizza boxes along the road. JS was having none of it. He threatened to boycott the bin and stick to black bags, refusing to believe that the dustmen would leave *our* rubbish uncollected, a position taken on account of the fact that he was once (summer holiday job) a bin man, so felt he had an affinity with the refuse collectors, tipping them generously at Christmas. Eventually JS calmed down and modified the bin store so that with a bit of careful manoeuvring of wheels and negotiation of tight angles, the bin could slide in and out and be kept out of sight.

The wheelie bin (and a little later the recycling bin) became a part of our lives, being put out on a Thursday evening for collection early on Friday morning. We even had a wheelie bin song. One of us would announce, 'It's wheelie bin day!' and we'd burst into The Wheelie Bin song. I sang it, just now, sitting here at my desk. It made me cry and I thought, yet again, how bizarre my life has become that I should be weeping over a song about a wheelie bin.

The accident happened on the Sunday, I arrived home on the Friday, so the following Thursday evening was the first time I was alone on wheelie bin duty. I remember struggling to get the bin out of the store and sobbing, thinking that this was it, this was my life *forever*. I was now the only person to put out the bins. This was strange, because it wasn't as if I *never* put out the bins. Sometimes I did, sometimes JS did, though on balance he did it more than me, especially in winter when *massive* slugs held orgies in the bin store. I recall a particularly traumatic episode when I grabbed the wheelie bin and felt something squish between palm and plastic. From the screams and the sight of me running up and down the pavement yelling and waving my arms in the air, JS thought I'd been attacked. Still, it felt ridiculously inappropriate that I was weeping over a ruddy bin when my husband was lying in a mortuary thousands of miles away.

But so it continued.

Every Thursday night when I put the bins out and Friday morning when I dragged them in, I went through the same, 'This is my sorry life' routine. I thought I was mad to become upset over something so trivial until I read the following paragraph in Elizabeth Turner's excellent book, *The Blue Skies of Autumn*. Elizabeth was seven months pregnant with her first child when her husband, Simon, died in the World Trade Center attacks of 9/11. When I bought the book, I assumed she was a US-based widow, but they were a British couple who lived a couple of miles away from me and who shopped and walked in the same neighbourhood.

Elizabeth Turner wrote:

> I pulled the wheelie bin out through the gate and onto the road. I did this job every Monday night... Simon was dead. He'd never pulled the bins out before he died so it was always my job, but now it felt like a burden because there was no chance of anyone other than me doing it. I was feeling very, very sad and alone that night and knowing that Simon wasn't close made it all feel worse. I went back inside and closed the door.

The wheelie bin made another starring appearance on Planet Grief when my early counsellor, Doktor R., told me never to under-estimate the healing power of the mundane, a phrase which had me frantically cleaning out the wheelie bin, putting it on its side and crawling in it to scrub it clean with Jeyes fluid in the hope of finding a quicker way through the pain.

Then the bin store door started sticking, and one day, unable to get it closed, I kicked it and the bottom fell off. The whack with my foot closed it, permanently, so I left the bins in the front garden, something that would have horrified JS and his attention to detail.

By now my weekly bin routine went something like this:

Bins out (sobby, resentful).

Bins in (resentful, fed up).

Bins left in front garden (guilty, JS would not have approved).

I am fast approaching the seven-month mark. On Friday afternoon, I was flicking the Flymo around the tiny lawn that passes for a garden in London, found the grass box was full, so unhooked it and trotted through to the front garden to stick the cuttings in the recycling bin. And then I realised something which to a non-widow(er) would be insignificant, but which to me felt like a milestone: I had put the bins out on Thursday night and brought them in on Friday morning without even remembering I'd done it. There was no sobbing or resentful kicking of the bin into place on the pavement feeling sorry for myself, no despair that I was a wheelie bin widow battling slugs and slime and the slight step on and off the pavement. And then I looked at the bins out on display (though hidden from the street), and instead of feeling guilty that JS wouldn't like them being out of the store I thought: 'He's not here, they're no longer his bins. If it's easier for me to leave them out here, then here they will stay.' There are many values JS had that I will uphold and things that he did for his family that I will continue to do for as long as I am able, but remaining true to his wheelie bin wishes is no longer one of them.

Bizarrely, for a short period of time I felt elated. It felt like a breakthrough. If I could put the bins out without stress, perhaps one day I can wake up without feeling the only reason to get up is to let The Hound out for a pee.

But of course, there is a downside, because there always is, and it's one that is tapping me on the shoulder more and more these days. With every small 'victory' against The Grief Monster comes the feeling that my husband is becoming more and more distant from me, more lost. This upsets and confuses me. I can see how easy, how comforting it would be to make my life a shrine to his, to keep everything just as he would have wanted it – as I *still* want it. For the first time in almost seven months, I had 48 hours without tears. I got caught up looking for a lost dog, and I was so busy leafleting and looking and comforting and telephoning, I realised that I hadn't cried. It felt odd. Bizarrely, I didn't like the fact that I hadn't cried. Irrational as I know it is, it felt disrespectful not to have sobbed for JS.

My bereavement coach says that however much we don't want our lives to change, life *does* drag us along with it, and I know instinctively that she is right. I get tiny glimpses into a life without JS that *might* include the possibility of new experiences and new opportunities. For a brief time I feel elated, almost dizzy with hope, then elation turns to fear, not just fear of the future, but fear of losing my grip on JS any further, and I scurry back to my own little world which doesn't feel safe, but feels safer than what might be waiting for me out there.

It's a new dawn, it's a new day and I'm feeling… scared.

DISCONNECTED

This is a little message just for reassurance. I am now at seven years. I hardly ever cry for A anymore and I don't miss him acutely, but I do still think of him at some point every day. The tears and grief stop, but the memories and thoughts don't. ~ ***Jules***

The Hound found a phone on Hampstead Heath last week. The two of us were mooching about in the grounds of Kenwood House when he started sniffing something under a bush. Usually such nasal activity is connected to another dog's poo, pee or passing bum, but this time it was a phone battery. Scattered nearby was the front and back of a new-looking HTC smart phone. I gathered up the pieces and put it back together, intending to find the number of the phone, ring the owner and reunite them, but my cunning plan failed immediately because I hadn't got my reading glasses with me, so the hi-tech keypad was just a blur of random colour, like a psychedelic seventies album cover.

Back at home and specced up, I found the list of recently called names and numbers. The first one I tried, Cate, went straight to answerphone.

I tried name two: Mitch.

After a few rings, a man barked, 'What?'

Actually, 'WOT?' would be a more accurate description of Mitch's first word. A stroppy, irritated, 'What the hell do you want now?'-type 'WOT?'

I launched into my little speech. 'Er, you're going to think this is very weird, but I found this phone on Hampstead Heath about half-an-hour ago, so I'm ringing your number because it was in a list of dialled numbers.'

Now, in the movies, the script would go something like this: *Grief-stricken recent widow with no intention of finding romance **ever**, let alone after only six months and three weeks (previous scene shows her investigating becoming a nun in a non-silent order, but only if the habit is black and white and relatively stylish), arranges to meet Stroppy Mitch to hand over found phone. Widow arrives at appointed rendezvous (Kenwood House again: if it was good enough for Hugh Grant and Julia Roberts, it will do for my movie) sans slap, haggard-faced, wearing a dog-walking jacket stuffed with black poo bags, to be confronted by six-foot dishevelled hunk with sad eyes (due to his own grief at losing his wife, not because he's been crying over losing his smart phone). There is an instant electric connection, but, both freaked-out by their feelings, they beetle away in different directions and the next two hours of the film are spent in a 'Will they? Won't they?' game. (Yes they do!)*

That was a nice little diversion, wasn't it? I'm thinking Sandra Bullock and Hugh Laurie for the lead roles. The Hound has asked to play himself and be paid in squeaky balls.

Of course, what actually happened was that Stroppy Mitch said in a voice that dripped with annoyance, 'It's my wife's phone; she'll have dropped it out jogging. I'll get her to ring you,' and we exchanged mobile numbers and landline numbers. Then his wife called and gushed about how honest I was (given that my BlackBerry is on its last legs, don't think that I didn't have a brief thought of pocketing it) and how I had saved her life because she was due to collect a new nanny from the airport later that night. And instead of my little fantasy of arranging to meet Mitch in front of Kenwood House, Mitch's wife arranged to meet me at my house later that afternoon which she knew because of the ruinously expensive private school opposite.

She turned up and was just as I imagined her to be, because living in this part of north London I am surrounded by women like her: honed, toned, glossy, accessorised, confident; shiny black 4x4 parked in the road, hazard lights flashing, causing an obstruction. Did I ever mention that the *Daily Mail* saw Gwyneth Paltrow hanging around outside my garage? OK, so the *Daily Mail* didn't *specifically* mention my garage, but I heard that she was standing over the road from the school gate that is *directly* opposite my garage. She was picking up the fruit-named child from the school with her chum, Beyoncé. It's like that round here, but if you're trying to outdo Gwynnie and Jay-Z's wife, you're on a loser to nothing. I don't even try to compete, but in any case, I suspect that the glossy posse of mums think I'm the hired dog-walker, *if* they even deign to glance their Botoxed faces in my direction.

Anyway, Glossy Mum thrust a bottle of Prosecco in my hands as thanks and rushed off. As I closed the door clutching my fizz I felt unbearably sad, not because I had no one to share the bottle with, but because Glossy Mum had her husband and I didn't, and her husband didn't sound pleased to see her name flash up, but I knew mine would have been. JS wouldn't have answered with an irritated, 'WOT?' Perhaps Mitch was having a rough day being an international banker, or maybe they'd had a row that morning because she'd warned him not to make a pass at the new nanny, which was why the last one left, or any number of reasons that usually loving couples are short with each other. We had a code: if JS couldn't speak because he was busy, he would either leave the phone to ring and I'd leave a message, or, answer it and say, 'Can I phone you back?' Perhaps some of those times he didn't answer or said, 'Can I phone you back?' was because he was irritated with me. I know I used the same tactic when I was irritated with him. But if he did answer and wasn't busy, he always sounded either pleased to hear from me, or, at the very least, interested in what I had to say.

Well, not always...

Twenty-plus years ago, JS went away on business. Instead of going back to my little pad in south-east London, I decided to stay at the flat he was renting in town, a swish place (compared to mine) entirely decorated in cream (sofas/carpets/walls/the works). I also decided (with his permission) to use his car (smart, very powerful Audi Quattro) as opposed to my car (Citroen AX 1.1, a motorised tin can: nought to 60 in 15 minutes). It was an icy February morning and I tried to take the Audi out of the car park at the flats, said car park having a steep ramp out on to the Gray's Inn Road. What I didn't realise was that to engage all four wheels I needed to press a little button. As I accelerated up the slope, the car slid sideways and slammed into a concrete pillar. Unfortunately, in trying to negotiate away from the pillar, I simply embedded the concrete further and further into the side of the car. I have trouble remembering my husband's voice from seven months ago, yet strangely the sound of concrete screeching on metal two decades after the incident is toe-curlingly familiar.

In floods of tears, I rang JS to tell him what had happened. Instead of his deep voice telling me everything would be OK, his first words were, 'What do you expect me to do about it?' I should point out that I was ringing him at his hotel in the middle the night (his time) in New York, but even so!

As another digression, that week was also the time when sitting on the cream sofa, which rested on the cream carpet in JS's rented flat, I jumped up to answer the phone, totally forgetting that I had a plate of haddock and chips and tomato sauce on my lap. Don't think I ever confessed that to him. Too late now...

Anyway, I felt immensely sad that JS would never again ring me and I would never ring him, and I wanted to phone Stroppy

Mitch and tell him to cherish his glossy wife because no one ever knows when the 'Until death us do part' stuff is going to kick in, and you don't fully realise the implications until it's too late and you're choosing coffins out of a flip book instead of flicking through holiday photographs.

I kept mulling over Mitch and his jogging, phone-losing wife and then 24 hours later when I was out and about, I got a call from Orange. I'd been having terrible trouble with Orange and, in the end, I sent a two-page letter to their head office listing my complaints, threatening to approach BBC's *Watchdog* if they didn't sort everything out. I'd been keeping JS's BlackBerry going because of business calls, but such was the hassle with Orange, I asked them to close JS's account for simplicity. The woman on the end of the phone agreed they hadn't treated me well, offered me a £50 discount off my next bill and then said, 'Your husband's account will be deleted in the next few minutes and his phone will be disconnected.'

It was what I had asked Orange to do. JS's phone was costing me money, I knew he would never ring me again, every time his phone rang it made me jump, emails were still coming through, as were Twitter feeds, and yet, as I walked home, the fact that somewhere someone was pressing a button cancelling JS's number floored me. I had to sit on a bench at a bus stop to get myself together.

As I sat there, I fished my husband's phone from my bag.

The screen already proclaimed: *Unregistered SIM*.

Little by little, JS is being pulled away from me; our life together is disconnecting and there's not a damn thing I can do about it.

Sitting on a bench on a busy street looking numbly at a dead mobile belonging to my dead husband was never supposed to be a scene in the movie of my life, whatever Sandy and Hugh end up doing in the script.

I demand a re-write.

BRAIN STORM

The day after my husband died, I went with my daughter to see him at the Chapel of rest thing at the hospital. [Because he died suddenly and unexpectedly she was at the other end of the country when it happened so had travelled up, poor wee soul, to say goodbye.] Anyway, it didn't look like him. We all know what I mean and she only stayed a second. But I remained behind to cut a lock of his hair and then I had a sudden urge to see his feet, so I unwrapped the shroud and there they were, big and flat and white and very cold, but then that's how they always were, as he tended to walk around the house barefoot. His feet looked just the same, his poor old feet. I kissed them. ~ **Sue Ab**

I want to make it clear from the start that I am the sanest person you will ever meet. All of the therapists I have seen over the years have confirmed this, which just makes me realise how bonkers most of *them* are.

JS and I were the total opposites when it came to sanity. On the surface he appeared Mr Cool and Calm, the sort of solid man you could rely on in a crisis, yet underneath he was a mass of endearing insecurities, anger and complications, a man who found it difficult to confront a major problem without suffering palpitations and sleepless nights. I am the opposite. I zoom around stressing over the most insignificant things, yet at my core, I am steely and composed, a 'What will be will be' type of person. I chanted that out loud as we had the terrifying blue-light run from beach to hospital: 'What will be will be. What will be will be.' I stopped chanting after a while and started screaming at the driver, a frightened manic version of what I used to say to my parents as a child the moment we pulled out of the drive before a long car journey: 'Are we nearly there yet?' Even a cool, calm person has their limits and trying to haul my almost certainly dead husband back on to the trolley in a speeding transit van was mine.

But when not wearing The Bikini of Death, I am supremely sane.

Am I telling you how sane I am or am I telling myself?

Hmmm.

In a recent email, someone wrote and told me that they felt that their mind was 'f*ck*d' with this whole grief business. I thought about their comment. My heart is broken and I am grief-stricken, my brain is forgetful and I'm tired, but *no*, I wrote back, I didn't feel mindf*ck*d, because, remember, I am the sanest person you will ever meet. A fat man with a framed certificate on his wall confirmed it.

They say a week is a long time in politics, but that is nothing compared to a week on Planet Grief.

It is seven months today, by the date, since I was chanting, 'What will be will be,' pleading with a God I don't believe exists to save JS's life. Life is still a scary rollercoaster, but the last couple of weeks have been more positive. Yes, there are still tears and my grip on my little perch is very wobbly, but I can feel some sun on my face, if only for short bursts. I even went out on Friday night with The Grammar Gestapo. We had some drinks and then dinner as the London skyline twinkled beside us. It was fun. I had heels on. I felt good. *Really* good. A sort of 'Watch out world!' type of feeling that striding across the floor of a lovely capital city rooftop bar on a Friday night in high heels can give you. I could feel a touch of the old me peeping through. Coming home was fine. Actually, coming home was good. I never thought I would say that phrase: 'Coming home was good.'

I still wake up crushed by the reality of my new JS-less life, but the days and the evenings are slowly getting better, they really are.

I've even strutted around the house to Lady Gaga's 'Just Dance'. How long this 'up' phase will last I don't know, but I'm clinging to small comforts for now.

But the nights?

I have written before about my dreams, dreams where I never see JS's face, even if he's in them: the searching dreams which exhausted me night after night, which made way for panicky dreams where I knew JS was dying or about to die, but there was nothing I could do to stop it. I don't pretend to have any idea of the fear that knowing my partner is going to die from a terminal illness would bring, but it did give me a minute glimpse into a different type of death, what it *might* be like to stand on the edge of the abyss knowing you are about to slide slowly towards hell, rather than be unceremoniously booted in barely dressed. My heart aches for those who have stood there.

The dreams changed to knowing JS was going to die, but instead of panicking, I was almost wistful, comforting him, stroking his hair, telling him it (him? me? life?) was all going to be OK. I could 'feel' his presence, but I never saw his face.

Then I had a dream where I got out of a car. JS was driving, I was the passenger. I leaned over, kissed him on his neck, said something and left. I was perfectly calm. At the time, I believed that subconsciously I was saying goodbye. My last words to him (in the dream) certainly seemed to indicate this.

For a short while, I had no odd dreams. I still don't sleep brilliantly, but the tigers weren't coming at night. I felt I had made a breakthrough.

But last week, the night monsters clawed through the bedroom door roaring and snarling.

I have thought long and hard about whether I should publish what you are about to read. I realise that the subject matter (sex and death) might make some people uncomfortable, which is fine, but I really don't want to be on the receiving end of any nasty emails. As I have said before, my writing will always preserve the anonymity of the people I care about and whilst I want this to be a truthful record of the first year of my life without JS, there are some details I will keep back. Upsetting readers is one thing. Upsetting JS's family is non-negotiable. The rest of this doesn't fit into that category, but still, it may not be for you. On the other hand, I suspect that there will be others reading this who will identify with what they read. We all think we are unique in this grief game, but we never are.

So, dear readers, if you are early on in your grief journey, have a touch of the Mary Whitehouse gene or just feel that you don't want to read on, I am about to give you an escape; a sort of *Planet Grief* ejector seat. Flip the page where you can read about make-up and we can discuss mascara and lipgloss. Oh, how I would love to *only* be concerned with such stuff, truly I would.

Brave enough or curious enough to be still around? You have been warned. Here is the dream I had last week:

I was with JS and doing what I think we should refer to as 'Wifely Things' that began at his feet. In reality, I would never have started Wifely Things there because he had such ticklish feet; I even tried to revive him on the beach by tickling them. Somewhere 'along the way' in another 'it would never have happened' moment, I began to discuss decorating the room we were in, which was papered in strange seventies wallpaper, the sort of pattern which used to be on Hornsey Pottery. I can still see it in my dream: peeling, shabby, orange! It felt like sleeping in George & Mildred Roper's bedroom. JS didn't seem the least bit interested in talking about interior design, but to be frank, what man cares about wallpaper patterns when a woman is crawling over him? But then I realised why he wasn't talking about decorating. For the first time since the 'vision'

I had a few days after I got back from Barbados, I saw JS's face in my dream.

And he was dead.

As dead as he was when I saw him in the little side room they led me into in the Queen Elizabeth II Hospital in Bridgetown.

His face was the face I saw for the last time on the 27th February 2011; the face of a man who had drowned.

I had been making love to my dead husband.

If that doesn't f*ck with your mind, I don't know what does.

But I am sane, truly I am. A fat man with a framed certificate on his wall told me 22 years ago, so it has to be true, doesn't it?

THE EYES HAVE IT

*When my husband was ill I found listening to friends discussing how they had gone on the waiting list for Chanel Particulière nail polish very difficult, and don't get me started on the false eyelashes. However, on his birthday this year a friend presented me with a bottle of the fancy Particulière nail polish and said, 'Even on a really bad day you can have great nails.' Do you know what, I want to have great nails and it reminded me to stop and find joy in little things. ~ **Bonnie***

When I was about 12, my best friend and I hurried along the disused railway track near our homes, girls on a mission. We had made a decision that comes to all young girls sooner or later and, having made it, we couldn't wait to put our plan into action: it was time to hand over our pocket money and purchase some make-up. The choice of cosmetics from the local chemist in what was then a small Northumberland village was limited, so we ended up with little sticks of Rimmel cream eyeshadow: mine was hyacinth blue, Jan chose lilac. Giggling and camouflaged by hawthorn bushes, we swept the coloured grease across our eyelids and felt like the mutt's nuts, even though the reality was that we probably looked like a dog's dinner.

Decades later, Jan is still my best friend, but, unlike me, she has gone on to become a walking encyclopaedia of make-up brands, a woman who can identify a shade of Mac lipstick at a glance and who didn't need to join the waiting list for Chanel's Rouge Noir nail varnish when it came out, because she's on first-name terms with the woman behind the Chanel counter at Fenwick's in Newcastle.

After my early experiment with Rimmel on the railway line, I spent pretty much the next ten years sticking to the look I perfected in my teens: pale pink pearly lipstick (Miners' Shrimp); Cornsilk powder; bright blue Max Factor eyeliner; a pot of gold Miss Selfridge 'Kiss and Make Up' eye glitter and mascara from a block that you had to spit on. Make-up to me has always been less about the end effect than the promise of what is to come. Typing this, glass of red wine beside me, iTunes on shuffle, the memories are flooding back of getting ready to go out as a teenager: the planning; the make-up; the squirt of Charlie perfume; lying on my bed trying to do up my skin-tight jeans whilst listening to AC/DC's 'Touch Too Much' or 10cc's 'I'm Not in Love', depending on my mood. The make-up was essential because in my early years it seemed to me that the girls who wore the war paint got the boys. When at 16 I began working at Fenwick's on Saturdays and Thursday evenings (behind the scenes in the banking department – some of the happiest days of my life) it fascinated me that the women behind the cosmetics counters, women caked in make-up worthy of a Drag Queen, often dated Newcastle United footballers. To anyone that has read my Electra Brown books and knows me in real life, it is obvious that in personality, the teenage Electra is me. It is no coincidence that Electra's nemesis at school, Claudia 'Tits Out' Barnes, is a girl who both fascinates and horrifies Electra with her tarty, artificial looks and dubious behaviour with boys. As a teenager, I always felt that if I could just get my eyeliner right, my love life would fall into place.

This belief that the right use of the right products would turn me from Girl Next Door to Sex Siren continued into my early twenties and was strengthened by my first 'grown up' flat share with P, a woman a little older than me who put a card in the window of the local launderette in south-east London, advertising a room in the maisonette she owned. P had a heart of gold, was great fun and worked as a PA for a finance firm in fabulously plush offices near Liverpool Street. It was 1986, the City was booming and there was a great deal of money, champagne and mobile phones the size of bricks being flashed about by young studs wearing sharp suits. After a day making ferrets vomit at a London teaching hospital, I'd peel off my white lab coat and head to City wine bars to meet my flatmate, who attracted these men like wasps to jam. No wonder! Her make-up was Polyfilla thick and immaculate. During a Malibu and milk (our cocktail of choice)-soaked evening, I remember asking her what her secret was. She suggested I used Lipcote, the stuff that came in a little glass tube and stung, but sealed your lippie in place. Rather than turn me into the sort of pouting temptress who could snog for hours and still emerge *lipsticus intacticus*, it made my lips dry and cracked. One night (wearing Lipcote) I went to a nightclub with P. I waited in the taxi queue in the early hours of the morning whilst she got our coats. She came back with not only two coats, but also two men (complete strangers) who she'd met in the cloakroom queue and had invited back for a coffee. At the flat, it didn't take long for me to realise that I was expected to provide 'coffee' for one of these men, a beverage I wasn't prepared to offer. I scooted up the stairs and stuck a chair under the handle of my bedroom door. The upshot of my desertion from the 'party' was that P turned into the hostess with the mostest with *both* her guests, and I realised that it wasn't the Lipcote that was the secret of her 'success'.

The strange thing is that whilst my observations of others led me to believe that if I made my peepers into 'Come hither' eyes men would fling themselves at my feet with lust, the opposite was true. For instance, in a very brief lumberjack phase, I took a shine to an Antipodean tree surgeon who worked at Kew Gardens. No meaningful glance in my direction was ever made despite my efforts to impress him with my artfully applied eyeshadow and my knowledge of all things arboreal. Then, streaming with cold and too stuffed up to care about make-up or men, I tottered to a darts match to keep a friend company, whereupon the Kiwi with the flashing chainsaw asked me out. (Only one date – gosh he was boring. The only interesting thing about him was how he looked in a checked shirt.) Some time later, that same friend forced me out of bed and dragged me to the pub for last orders as she fancied a guy there and she wanted me to see him. I stood at the bar, barefaced, my nightie under my coat and tucked into my jeans, met this man's cousin, an Irish electrician, who turned out to be one of the loveliest and most significant romances of my life.

JS always found it fascinating that I wore more make-up when I was going out with my girlfriends than I ever did with him and he disliked painted faces, but old thought patterns are hard to break and at times of uncertainty, those slight insecurities of youth bubble to the surface.

When I was 30 and slightly freaked by the thought of a change of decade (what a child I was in reality!), I booked myself a make-up lesson with a famous make-up artist known for magazine sessions with Christy, Linda, Cindy, Naomi et al.

Famous Make-up Artist studied my face and said, 'Have you ever thought about having the bags taken out from under your eyes?'

BAGS!

I didn't know I had bags – those little pockets of 'fat' that show up only when you smile. She told me that *all* the models had them taken out when they were young and that I might like to consider it when I was older. She did my make-up: all smoky, dark eyes, ironic really as now I can easily achieve the same effect for free by putting mascara on and crying. I got on the tube and ran my finger down my cheek: thick foundation collected under my nail. I hoped I wouldn't see anyone I knew, whilst at the same time wondering if they would recognise me if I did. When I arrived back at the office, Karen looked at me and said kindly, 'It's not really you, is it?'

I went to the loos and rubbed it all off with damp paper towels.

Later that day, I shoved my face in front of JS's and said, 'Do you think I should have the bags under my eyes done?'

He said, 'Jean Shrimpton had bags under her eyes and she was considered a great beauty.'

What a man!

After JS's accident, for weeks I couldn't look in the mirror. Not through vanity as such, but because the eyes looking back at me were the eyes of a woman felled by grief, by what she had seen, by what she was living through. At the hairdresser's the day before the funeral, I asked them to swing the chair around so that my back was to the mirror as they blow-dried my locks and that 'backs to the wall' position continued for a while. But, gradually and more recently, I started to care about how I looked again. I was fed up of looking rank: the sudden and dramatic weight loss has taken its toll on my face and the stress is reflected in my skin, so I decided I was going to treat myself to a make-up session, the sort where you take your own make-up with you and they go through it and either agree you keep it or suggest more flattering alternatives.

'What made you decide to come today?' the make-up artist asked when I sat down.

Determined not to cry and therefore wreck the session before it started by getting puffy eyes and a blotchy face, I gave a vague, 'Oh, I've had a bereavement and wanted to cheer myself up,' answer.

She said she understood grief only too well: she'd started comfort eating after losing her father 30 years ago as a teenager.

He'd fallen out of a plane.

Now, this isn't the sort of thing you expect to hear when you've gone to be pampered as a way of distracting yourself from the image of your husband drowning. As the make-up artist started prattling on about peach concealer for dark circles, I kept thinking: 'Just how do you fall out of a plane?' In the end, I couldn't help myself and asked her.

It turned out her father was an aerial photographer who tumbled over the edge trying to get a great shot. And then she said, '30 years, and Mum has never recovered from the shock of that phone call.' She went on to explain that there had been no future happiness for her mother; her life had been ruined by the death of her husband. I've heard similar stories: a neighbour's mother who turned to drink and is still drinking decades later; the neighbour who has never recovered from her husband dying on New Year's Eve over 30 years ago. Everywhere I turn, people give me examples of women who have made their lives a shrine to their dead husband. Are there similar stories about men and their dead wives? If there are, I never hear them. I only hear about men who have remarried in haste and repented in the divorce courts.

The make-up was fine: it was a pleasant diversion for an hour or so. She confirmed the conclusion I came to years ago, that I look better with practically no make-up, recommended an eyeliner called, appropriately, 'Fog', used a peach concealer to erase my dark shadows and, when she'd finished, I didn't look *that* different, which was better than looking like Lily Savage, but hardly surprising given that she used most of the stuff I'd brought with me, other than 'Fog' and 'Peach'.

I went home. Unlike 17 years ago, there was no Karen to comment and no JS to tell me that I was beautiful, eye-bags and all. They are both dead. There was just The Hound and me. I should have arranged to see a friend or gone out somewhere fabulous, but I didn't think ahead.

That night, I stood in front of the bathroom mirror and took off the gunk. With or without 'Fog', my eyes are still the eyes of a woman who has seen too much, eyes being the window to the soul and all that jazz. Standing under the harsh halogen light, I thought of the make-up artist's mother who has never recovered from her husband tumbling out of a plane 30 years before, and it scared me. I know people say that you never get over it, you just learn to live with it, but learning to live with it isn't good enough for me. I *have* to get over this, to use what has happened constructively in some way, even though I will never forget the terror of what unfolded in front of me that morning thousands of miles away from home, and how it robbed me of the wonderful man I loved for almost half my life and his two children their father. But the ones who tell you that you learn to live with it because you never get over it, are much further along the winding paths of Planet Grief than me. Perhaps they already know what I will eventually learn for myself.

For the last couple of weeks the storm clouds have occasionally parted. Having lived in darkness since the end of February, the sunlight is blinding, those small glimpses of joy intoxicating and yet terrifying. In some ways I long to be like that make-up artist's mother, living the rest of my life as public testament to the world just how much JS meant and continues to mean to me, and yet I know I'm never going to be that sort of widow, because I am not that sort of woman. The problem is that already widow and woman are clashing in my head, making uncomfortable and warring bedfellows.

That's something no amount of peachy concealer can erase, only time.

I hope.

MARRIAGE GUIDANCE

*I remember sobbing to my bereavement coach about how perfect JS was. This of course was plainly untrue because he was human: grief had blinded me to all the things that used to have me mentally packing a bag including always thinking he was right, an attitude which cost him his life. But still. At that stage, he was still St JS, an angel with a set of golf clubs and an electric golf trolley, 'Isn't there anything you would do differently another time?' my coach enquired. 'Any other quality you would look for in a new relationship?' The only thing I could think of was that they would have to cook, JS not being the slightest bit interested in donning an apron. ~ **Helen B***

I spent Saturday packing up the office and moving files into storage.

This painful process has been in stages: firstly a move from a large office to a small one, and then when I realised I was paying a huge amount of money just to race in, grab the post, gossip with whoever was manning reception and flee, I decided to keep the business address, but not the space.

Saturday wasn't about sorting through paperwork, just emptying filing cabinets and drawers into endless archive boxes. Nevertheless, occasionally I came across stuff that made me wistful. I've always been a 'tackle it head on' sort of gal, but sometimes the only way to cope is by bunging things into a box to deal with another day. I'm wondering whether I should take the still-packed suitcases to the storage place...

There was one document lying loose at the bottom of a filing cabinet that opened the floodgates: a copy of the Father of the Bride speech JS gave at his daughter's wedding.

My husband wasn't a natural public speaker; the run-up to any event which required him to entertain an audience turned the house into a pressure cooker of tension, but once on his feet, JS's speeches reflected the man: elegant, understated and full of humour and warmth.

I suspect that even the most accomplished orator feels the pressure on his daughter's wedding day, and months before the big event, JS began drafting his speech. He never hinted at what he intended to say. Like everyone else, I had to wait for the big reveal.

A week before the London wedding, the two of us were on holiday and sitting in one of our favourite pubs, The Packhorse Inn in Ellingham in Northumberland. I was flicking through a little pamphlet left on the table. It was mainly lists of rotas for the local church (flowers, coffee, playgroup, etc.) and an update on the campaign to get Northumberland County Council to install a lamppost on a dangerous bend in the village. One piece in this little booklet had me convulsed with giggles. JS asked me what I found so funny. I tried to read it out, but couldn't for becoming hysterical; it was one of those 'helpless with laughter' moments. He read the article, smiled that wry smile of his and continued downing his pint of Black Sheep.

JS's speech at the wedding was just as I knew it would be, a total triumph, which had the guests both laughing and crying. At the end, he said something I had forgotten until I came across the printed pages on Saturday:

> My daughter asked me to keep this short and not waffle on, so I want to end with this: Helen and I were recently in the north-east of England, and by chance, I came across the following advice to women printed in a small regional journal, and I'd like to share it with you.

It was headed Five Tips for a woman about to be married:

1. It is important that a man helps you around the house and has a job.
2. It is important that a man makes you laugh.
3. It is important to find a man on whom you can depend.
4. It is important that a man loves and spoils you.

And finally...

5. It is important that these four men never meet.

Life is strange isn't it? The words I read in the Packhorse Inn in Northumberland a few years ago were *exactly* the same words I read in Islington a few days ago and yet instead of making me helpless with laughter, I felt shattered with sorrow.

One of the unexpected side-effects of losing your partner is the steady stream of friends who, late at night, steeped in drink and slumped on the sofa, pour out their relationship woes; women bored to tears, literally, by their lives and their husbands, trapped by circumstances, rattled by memories of past loves and missed opportunities, or bitter and scarred from failed relationships. All of them are lovely women, but wine and whisky often lubricates a path to the truth. Henry David Thoreau (1817 – 1862) said: 'The mass of men lead lives of quiet desperation and go to the grave with the song still in them.' Until JS died, I hadn't realised quite how true this is for so many people I know.

When my friends sobbed and poured their hearts out the month before the funeral, I was irritated by what I saw as their self-absorbed behaviour. Now, when I hear these stories, I reflect on what a wonderful life I have had. I know that some people feel sorry for me – it has been said on many occasions – and yet (now) I don't feel sorry for myself at all. Their compassion is welcome, but not their sorrow. I can look back with pain and sadness, but not bitterness or anger or regret. Time and time again, I realise just how lucky I have been to share so much of my life with a man who fulfilled points 1 to 4 of that jokey marriage guidance article.

I would be lying if I told you that two decades of working and living together was all plain sailing, that there were hearts and flowers permanently wound around the door of both the office and our house. There were some very challenging times in our marriage, periods where I stared at the front door and imagined walking through it for the last time, suitcases packed. Once, I stood there in my bright red mac, Rufus on his lead, and dramatically announced that I was going to disappear. I'd seen a programme about people who just vanish to start a new life under a new identity, and bolting appealed to me. JS smiled (which annoyed me) and said he was sure he'd be able to track me down. Indignantly, I told him he wouldn't be able to. *I* had a cunning plan.

'Are you going now?' he asked.

'Maybe,' I pouted, overlooking the fact that the first rule of disappearing is not to announce that you intend to.

'And taking Rufus?'

'Of course!'

He pointed out that a tall, dark-haired girl in black high-heeled boots, a bright red Burberry and a red dachshund (with a red collar) on a lead, was not going to be able to disappear easily. He suggested that I revised my plan, ditched the dog and dyed my hair blonde, which of course had me laughing at the ridiculousness of it all. I'm sure JS also wanted to walk through that door on occasions (probably moments after I took my coat off having decided not to vanish), but unlike so many who have sat on my sofa sobbing, coming through those times strengthened our partnership and underlined what we used to remind each other: that we could get through *anything*, as long as we were together.

I don't feel JS around me as I hoped I would, but remembering that I was truly loved and allowed to be a free spirit whilst still wearing a wedding ring has recently given me a new (if fragile) strength. I am now starting to think about what he would say about how I am trying to live my life, and for brief moments, I feel that he *is* helping me through this maze in some way. Perhaps in some form, if only through memories of our shared past, we *are* still together.

I remember moaning to JS that all I ever wanted after the emotional chaos of my youth was a 'normal' little life without any major dramas. He said that I would be bored to tears. At the time, I felt that he didn't really understand me.

I was wrong. He was right.

I'd like to add another piece of advice to that list of tips to give a woman about to be married.

It is important to find a man who never bores you to tears.

SPIRITS IN THE SKY

I do not have even the slightest wish to receive a sign or message from my wife. Her death came as an inevitable sad blessing – the suffering was over. When she died, I told our three sons that she had gone straight to heaven. I deliberately avoid the 'she will always be looking down on you' since that would be spooky and might make them paranoid. Life is hard enough without the cast of an angelic shadow. ~ **Chris J**

I'd like to share with you one of my recurring fantasies. No, not the one involving Gabriel Byrne and a brown velvet sofa (The Grammar Gestapo has lent me her box set of *In Treatment*), but one that goes something like this: I'm at the cashpoint in Highgate, but as I take my money and walk away, a woman approaches me. She says, 'I don't usually do this, but there's a man here who's desperate to make contact with you.' I swing round hoping to see some shy Stud Muffin who has done the middle-aged equivalent of the teenage, 'my friend fancies you' routine, but the stranger explains that she's a medium and that the man trying to make contact is my husband. She then relays a series of messages that are so stunningly accurate and personal, only he and I could possibly know the significance.

This fantasy is not only played out in Highgate High Street, but also on an aeroplane (like I'm really going to get on one any time soon) where I find myself sat next to international renowned psychic, John Edward. We bond over a packet of airline nuts and a can of G&T (despite being a multimillionaire he obviously travels coach) before he says, 'Look, I don't usually do this, but...' which incidentally is exactly what Gabriel Byrne in his

Dr Paul Weston/*In Treatment* persona says just as we embark on something that could lose him his psychotherapist's licence.

Already I am digressing. Take it as a warning sign of madness ahead.

When Karen died, I was desperate to find out if she was OK, but because I believed that you had to let souls 'rest' for a while, I gave her a year to get used to her new surroundings, after which I promised myself I'd book a session with a medium. JS thought I was nuts – he wasn't a believer – but Karen and I worked together for 14 years on the Snoopy account, often discussed death, and we had a pact that we would use the beagle as a sign if anything happened to either of us. In my head the session would go something like this: the medium would furrow her brow and say, 'There is a woman coming through showing me a black and white dog...' and I would yell, 'KAREN!' and all would be well. The year anniversary arrived, and I didn't go to a medium. I never went to a medium. I didn't need to. There isn't a day that I don't think of Karen. I had a short and very vivid dream about her once, towards the end of the first year. She appeared and I said, 'But you're dead!' She laughed and said, 'Do I look dead?'

I've written elsewhere about the times that I have begged JS for a sign. I'm not looking for his permission to be happy or clues as to how to live my life, I just want to know that he's OK. One moment we were on holiday and he was alive, the next he was dead. I was confused. Was he? I am *still* confused. What about him now? Is there even a 'him' now?

About two months after JS died, our cleaner, a very religious Polish lady, approached me to tell me that JS had come to her in a dream. She felt that this dream was a visitation. She said that he looked fit and strong and well (even pumping her shoulders up to demonstrate) and told me (imagine heavy Polish accent), 'I say to him, Helen, she cry all the time. ALL the time. He say to me, Helen is strong woman. She be OK.' I said, 'Is that it?' If JS had come through from the other side, at the very least he could have told me he was OK, he loved me or what the Virgin Media online password was.

Earlier this week, a friend of a friend had an appointment with a medium. I received word that if I thought of JS at the time she was having her reading, she would let me know if any messages came through for me. I had my instructions: I needed to focus on an object that meant something to JS and to take a flower from the garden. I already wear his watch on a daily basis, but I chose two photos: one of us on our wedding day in Barbados and one of the family; a Terry Pratchett book and a rose from our garden. I put them in the car and drove to St Marylebone Crematorium (Cemetery of the Year 2007, don't you know). JS is still there. According to the lady in the office he's on a shelf in a cupboard. She told me that weeks ago as I sobbed over the counter clutching a letter asking me to confirm when I would be collecting his ashes, something I'm not ready to do.

I arrived at the crem. It was a grey and drizzly early October morning. I took photographs of my mementos so that if the friend once removed said, 'It was so bizarre! The name Terry Pratchett kept coming through,' I could whizz the photo over by email as proof that the message was for me.

In the damp, snivelling and clutching my little pile of keepsakes, I stomped around the vast site. Other than a gardener, I had the place to myself. I've always been fascinated by graveyards and have spent a great deal of time in them over the years, thinking, mooching, reading the inscriptions on the gravestones. I suffer from bouts of melancholia and graveyards bring me face-to-face with mortality, giving me the sort of kick up the arse I sometimes need.

I looked at the stone angels who have toppled off their pedestals, the beautifully tended graves of children long since dead and who would be grown men and women had they survived, graves which are festooned with fresh flowers and toys. I stood wistfully at graves of couples who obviously didn't find new love after death, but have been reunited in the ground decades after life separated them.

And then I came across the grave of the Taubers: Slovakians Emanuel Tauber (90), his wife Blanka (82) and their daughter Lizzy (84), born in Vienna. All three died in London. But there was also their son, Egon Tauber. Egon died on 7th June 1942, but he isn't buried with his parents and his sister, because he died in Auschwitz. He was 26 years old. I don't know why that grave in particular got to me; I've seen such graves before. North London is a very Jewish area, and given that approximately six million Jews were killed in the Holocaust, such memorials are not unusual. But I've never seen one through my 'new' eyes. I spent time crouched by the Taubers' grave, thinking. I left the rose from our garden there.

I got back in the car and drove around the avenues, parked at the front door of the crematorium and went inside. It was empty. I sat in the front pew on the right-hand side, just as I had sat there on 24th March. Clutching my photographs and the book, I cried and cried and cried. I wasn't crying for JS or for his family, or even for me as I am now. On reflection, I *think* I was crying for the woman who sat in that same spot all those months ago, shell-shocked that one moment she could be walking along a beach hand-in-hand with her husband and the next, she was facing hell without the man she loved, a man who made her believe that *whatever* happened, everything would be OK. I was also crying for the Taubers, a family who had lived for decades with the pain of knowing that Egon had been exterminated under terrible conditions. Yes, JS died, but he died quickly and in paradise having had a wonderful life. The hell of Auschwitz is well documented but, still, it can barely be imagined.

Organ music started playing. I'm more of a Scorpions than Bach type of girl, but as I sobbed, alone, it was very moving. I glanced up at the gallery and a man was playing. I assumed that he was practising.

And then I saw a vicar at the door.

I got up and looked at a notice on the wall. There was a funeral due at any moment: a woman called Joan Sandler, the same initials as my husband. I shot out and moved my car, *just* as the funeral procession slowly headed towards me. Quite what they would have thought to see a little white car with red Go-faster stripes and an Arsenal sticker parked where the hearse should be, I daren't think.

I watched from between a row of bushes. There was the hearse and five large funereal limos, only a few guests in each, a very small gathering. Nobody came in their own cars. From the look of the mourners, unlike young Egon Tauber, Joan Sandler had had a good innings. The limos all had personalised number plates, so I knew it was the same funeral directors we used, except we didn't have a hearse: none of the family could bear to sit behind JS's coffin, so it was already in place at the crematorium. We arrived by minicab. It reeked of stale smoke. The driver got the wrong entrance, so I demanded he stopped at the gates and four of us walked up the winding driveway towards the throng of mourners. It was a surreal moment.

Joan Sandler's coffin slid out of the hearse, and they took it inside.

I remember the last time I saw Karen in hospital. She was such a beautiful, lively girl, but in only a few short weeks malignant melanoma had run rampant through her body, robbing her of her looks, her sight, her hearing and a few days later, her life. As I walked out of the door of the hospital that day in late March 2003, despite being devastated by what I knew was an inevitable outcome, I remember feeling a massive surge of energy, a huge shot of strength and almost joy at the understanding that we do only have one life, and it is up to us to make it the best and most fulfilling life we possibly can. I had those same confused feelings watching Joan Sandler's funeral as I sat in my car.

As I drove back through the avenues at a snail's pace, the sun came out and streamed through the glass roof. I wasn't just thinking of JS, I was remembering Egon Tauber who never had a chance to live a full life or even have a dignified death, and I was thinking of a widow who recently left a comment on my *Planet Grief* blog. It was a phrase that has stuck with me. 'Lornz' wrote of her husband's view of life: 'I can hear Davey with his Californian drawl saying, 'It's a joy ride darling, so let's ride it real good."

I banged the steering wheel, let out a double-barrelled expletive about the unfairness of it all and put my foot down.

Did JS come through whilst I was in the graveyard? No, but Joan Sandler was there, as was Egon Tauber, Karen and Californian Davey, all dead, and yet all still teaching the living about life.

CHASING CARS

*James used to prefer driving to having me drive him, but we did take it in turns, and through the last year of his life I drove more and more as his leg got worse and worse. He drove a lot with work, and not long before he died he had to order a new company car, a white Audi A5, automatic, so that if he had to have his leg amputated he would be able to have it adapted. It would have been lovely. He died before it was delivered. I came home from work one day to a message on the answerphone, saying: 'Message for James, your new car is ready to be delivered.' As he had died about a month ago and the car company had already picked up his old car, I was slightly put out that obviously people in these places don't talk to each other. I e-mailed his boss and said that I was off on holiday the next week, but if they could leave the car on the drive and put the keys through the letterbox, that would be great. Unfortunately, it was not waiting for me when I got home! ~ **Linz***

When I was a teenager, I kept a diary. Over the years, I have often been tempted to dump these tomes of angst for fear of dying suddenly and someone finding them. I'm glad I didn't. Not only do they provide a rich source of information for my writing, they are also screamingly funny to get out when school friends visit and we're well down a bottle of wine.

As I teen, I regularly made three vows, all documented in these diaries:

1. I was never going to have children.
2. I was never going to get married.

3. In the horrific event that in a moment of weakness I did agree
    to get married, I would never become the sort of woman who
    let their husband do all the driving.

I loved cars, couldn't wait to drive and with all the passion of a
judgemental teenager, sneered at women who sat meekly in the
passenger seat beside their husbands. Ethel lived next door to Best
Friend Jan (who lived two doors away from me) and epitomised the
sort of woman who I felt let the side down. Driving her little car at
a snail's pace around the roads of the Northumberland village where
we lived, Ethel sat seat forward, clutching the steering wheel at the
top, peering through the window like a startled rabbit. You could
see the change in her expression when she sat beside King of the
Road husband Terry, a man who once cleaned his car on Christmas
Day because the 25th December fell on a Sunday, and he *always*
cleaned the car on a Sunday morning.

Before I was 17, my father would sometimes take me to a disused
airfield, and I'd drive around enjoying all the power that a mustard-
coloured Austin 1800 could provide. If I couldn't get to the airfield,
I would reverse up and down the drive of our house and, no, we
didn't have much of a drive. It was therefore a shock that I failed my
driving test on the first attempt: I shot across an unmarked cross-
roads and the examiner had to do an emergency stop using the dual
controls. Luckily, it was only my pride that was dented.

I passed the second time. I can still remember my BSM instruc-
tor, Keith – a man the spitting image of Steve Coogan's Paul Calf
who chain-smoked throughout every lesson – saying to me as I
drove back from the test centre, 'Aye, go on, open her up!' as we
went past Newcastle Airport. Never has a Mini Metro gone so fast.

My first car was a bright green, multi-owned Toyota Starlet.
I was extraordinarily proud of it, even when my brother ran a

magnet over its chassis and declared that it had more plastic filler than metal.

Fast-forward and a few cars later to 1991. JS and I are living together. He buys me a brand new Lotus Elan SE: Limited Edition, metallic silk red, dark grey leather seats, all the bells and whistles. In retrospect, he probably bought it for himself. Never mind. The test drive that the man from Lotus took me on was exhilarating. To this day, the memory of sitting next to the handsome, blond, professional driver as he flung the open-topped car around corners is still intoxicating. It was a shame he didn't come as an optional extra.

The car was delivered to our flat late one Friday evening. On the Saturday morning, I drove it, alone, from central London to Northumberland. Twenty-seven years old, madly in love and a brand new Lotus. Life didn't get much better than that. Actually, it did, but I didn't know that then.

As you read on, I want you to remember two things I've already told you:

1. My husband bought me a brand new, fully-loaded sports car.
2. I loved driving and had no issue driving anywhere in any conditions.

We are now several years further on. I still had the Lotus, JS had a variety of cars, but at one point, we ended up with two fast cars, both with small boots. I loved the Lotus, but despite umpteen visits to the garage and even a recall to their HQ in Norfolk, the roof always leaked and, in the end, we decided to sell it. The plan was that JS would keep his sporty car that I could drive if I needed a shot of speed and I would change to something sensible, with a bigger boot, which he would drive if he needed more space.

And so began the wilderness years of motoring, the start of my turning into the sort of woman behind the wheel I mocked in my youth and, eventually, a woman who barely got behind the wheel. A woman who wouldn't drive on motorways and felt dizzy with anxiety approaching a busy roundabout, even the Archway gyratory system. A woman whose husband ended up driving everywhere.

I have often given the impression that JS was a man who supported me wholeheartedly in everything I did and who gave me confidence in every area of my life. This is true *if* you discount the sort of person he became in a car. I have always said that although we had disagreements, our styles of arguing were so different (snap v sulk) that we *never* had shouting matches. This is also true – if you discount the sort of people we *both* became in a car. Relatively easy going in real life, I become competitive and confrontational behind the wheel. JS, who at least on the surface was calmness personified, made a jumpy and hypercritical passenger.

If I was driving, any sentence coming from JS's lips would undoubtedly include the following phrases: *Watch out! Have you seen that bike? Whoa! You were very close there. Mind that* [insert object/person]. *It's not a race! Slow down! What are you flashing for? Keep back! I didn't think you were going to stop/see them/make it! Leave the horn alone!*

To name but a few.

At one point, JS developed the irritating habit of leaning over and flicking the indicator for me; he just couldn't help himself. I used to lean over and slam my fist on the horn when he was driving, if I felt he had let someone cut him up without retaliation. We were as bad as each other. Arguments over motoring never spilled over beyond the car. Once outside the motorised tin can, we reverted to our normal, loving, supportive personas.

But over the years, the comments ground me down. In fast sporty cars I felt like myself, and when JS criticised me, I just pressed the accelerator, silently sniggering at his terror. Once I said, 'One more comment like that and you're getting out.' He said, 'I'll save time,' and got out, right in the middle of traffic. But when I changed cars from sporty to sedate, I felt less like the girl with the wind in her hair and more like Taxi Mum (even though I'm not a mum, which is a whole other story). Constant passenger-seat driving comments began to make me doubt my own ability behind the wheel. During one particularly nerve-wracking journey I snapped, 'Do you want to drive?' at which point JS shot back, 'Yes. Pull over.' Instead of pressing the accelerator and feeling wicked, I did what he ordered me to do and stopped the car.

After the Lotus, I had three cars in succession, all of which I hated, because as my confidence waned, the cars I chose gradually got more and nondescript. I blamed the cars, so we changed them, but every time I drove away from the garage in the car that was going to alter things, I knew that I had made a mistake. The problem was I was no longer confident enough to choose a car that turned me on as I put my foot down, and this was at odds with how I wanted to be, how I used to be. I'd kick the wheels of one car I had and growl, 'Hateful car,' as it was parked in the street. JS said there was nothing wrong with it. I used to say that it had it in for me, that it purposefully stalled on hills just to freak me out. I barely drove anywhere. I'd get the bus rather than drive. I took long and complicated bus/train/taxi journeys instead of just getting in the car and heading up the M4 to a see a friend. Sometimes, my car wouldn't move for weeks and when it did move, it was because JS felt he should use it to 'give it a run'. If we were going to a party, I'd dread him suggesting that I drove back so he could have a drink. It would cloud the evening that I was going to have to drive home, in the dark. Just the thought of it made me want to drink.

Eventually, JS suggested that we just kept one car. I was horrified. I'd had my own car since I was 20! I read *What Car?* I watched

Top Gear and knew an M3 from an S5. To lose my car would be the final nail in my motoring coffin. I refused. JS said it made no sense to run a car which never moved; if I wanted/needed to drive, I could drive his. If I wouldn't drive my RAV4 (the last of the Trio of Hate), I knew I wasn't going to use a giant polluting automatic tank with three litres under its German bonnet. I did what I did with the other cars: blamed it on my choice of make and model. If I could just have a sporty little Fiat 500, I would drive again, I knew I would.

JS wasn't having any of it. He told me (nicely) that if I wanted to ditch the Toyota for a new car, I had to buy it myself. He wasn't going to keep buying cars I hated and wouldn't drive.

What a shock! JS was an extraordinarily generous man, but the man who bought me a Lotus (and others) wouldn't even cough up for a little second-hand Fiat.

So I did, but even as I sorted out the money at the garage, I was sure JS would do what he did when he was with me as I bought clothes/shoes/handbags: at the last minute tell me to put away my credit card. But he didn't. He let me buy the ex-demo Fiat myself.

I loved that car. The 1.4 Fiat Sport (pearl with a little spoiler, red wheel inserts and red Go-faster stripes) was *my* car. If it didn't move for weeks, so what? It was mine. I didn't need to feel guilty. Compared to JS's car, it was a low-powered midget so he never wanted to drive it. Gradually, I started zipping around London again.

A few weeks before JS died, we were walking past a Fiat 500 Abarth parked in the street. I'd been lusting after this sporty, turbo-powered version of my car for a while. 'When we get back from holiday, I'll buy you one,' he said. 'I don't need one,' I replied. 'Not with the mileage I do.' 'No, let's go and test-drive one,' he countered. 'If you had an Abarth, I might drive your car more often.'

Warning bells rang. I didn't want him to drive my car. I could see what might happen.

And then before we could have fun test-driving a new car, JS died. Not only had I lost my best friend, my husband and my lover, I'd lost my chauffeur too. Whilst I can drive without fear in London traffic, I still had a phobia of motorways, in particular getting *onto* a motorway, that feeling on a slip road that once you are on it, you can't just change your mind, you're committed to go with the flow.

There are so many people I want to visit, all of whom live a motorway journey away, but none more so than JS's family. They have been very good at coming to me, but that couldn't go on forever, plus, I felt ridiculous having been through so much and yet still feeling unable to tackle a motorway. So, last Friday, with my heart in my mouth, I headed up the M1. At first, I was terrified and probably looked like Ethel behind the wheel. Then I was furious that an old lady in a Toyota Yaris sped past me. I didn't want to pootle along. I wanted to be the man in the Audi R8 that appeared behind me at speed and pulled out, tearing along the outside lane in a flash of low-slung metal and halogen lights. But as I settled down, I began to enjoy the drive.

I felt another demon had been slain. Two, actually: driving and going back to a house that held such happy memories for JS and me. But of course, like all little victories, there is a downside. As I sped back to London relishing being back behind the wheel with rock music blaring, I felt heartbreakingly sad that in order to regain my confidence behind the wheel, I had to lose my husband. I would give up driving for the rest of my life (or be condemned to drive a Nissan Micra 1.0, which perhaps is worse) if I could have just one more journey sat in the passenger seat next to JS, seeing his hands on the steering wheel, his forearms outstretched. So many of my dreams about him have been set in cars. He's driving. I'm the passenger.

Let me tell you about the last 'argument' we had whilst driving.

A few days before we went away, we were powering along the M2. A warning buzzer sounded, and a dashboard light went on. As instructed by the driver, I got the manual from the glove compartment. The advice was to stop at the nearest garage and get the tyres checked. JS didn't wait for the next garage; he pulled over onto the hard shoulder as left-hand drive lorries on their way to the Dover ports thundered by. He got out and started investigating the tyres one by one. I put on the hazard lights and began yelling at him to get back in the car, terrified a Turkish driver in a huge truck would be up our backside before we knew it. He ignored me and carried on looking around the car, crouching beside each tyre. I put the window down and demanded he got back in. Eventually he did – in his own time – and as I banged on about safety on the motorway and why hadn't he used the fluorescent safety jacket a client had given us and which was stored in the boot, he pulled away from the hard shoulder into the traffic at great speed, *not* wearing his seatbelt. The buzzer started going reminding him he wasn't buckled up. He was still trying to do it up as he hit the fast lane. I upped my safety-berating wail. Eventually he snapped, 'Will you give it a rest!' I was tearful. 'I was just scared you were going to die!' I sniffed. 'I don't want to lose you.' 'You're not going to lose me,' he said. 'I knew what I was doing.'

Ten days later, I warned him not to go into the sea. I told him a guest had alerted me to the strong currents near the shore. He dismissed my fears, said he wouldn't go out far, that he would be fine. My last words to him as he walked away from the sun-lounger and into the sea were, 'Be careful! I mean it!'

He thought he knew what he was doing. He didn't. What I feared sitting on the side of the M2 became shocking reality.

WOMEN IN LOVE

It has been my experience at almost seven months that the 'stages' of grief wax and wane for me, rather than come along in the Kübler-Ross set of stages, acceptance being the final one. I can be in and out of denial, anger, sadness, searching for him, yearning, etc. within a few minutes of each other, and that is how it goes every day, lurching from one emotion to another until I eventually exhaust myself and sit down and read a book. I have no sense of moving from 'shock' through set stages. I know that there are days that I still feel shock. Every morning I am shocked at what happened (sudden death). ~ **Lauren***

Let me tell you about my friend, CC, and her husband Rob, a charming, witty, cultured cricket-loving man who adored his spirited wife. Other than the fact Rob was a wonderful cook and JS only ever cooked scrambled eggs and lamb chops, and even that was a performance for which he always wanted at least one Michelin star and a round of applause, JS and Rob had much in common. Over the last twenty years, the four of us had some wonderful dinners at lovely restaurants, but the best times involved me sitting in the kitchen of their home in Camden, gossiping to Rob as he rustled up amazing food whilst CC and JS sat upstairs talking about more cerebral subjects.

On Saturday 13th November 2010, JS and I sat in a pew at St Marylebone Crematorium attending Rob's funeral. It was a beautiful

---

* Postulated in 1969 by the Swiss psychiatrist Elizabeth Kübler-Ross in her book *On Death and Dying*, the stages are denial, anger, bargaining, depression and acceptance.

Humanitarian service, carefully planned by Rob, because for the last year of a torrid four-year battle with bowel and liver cancer, he and CC knew his illness was terminal. It was a second marriage for CC, a third for Rob. At the funeral, one of Rob's sons said that his father loved women, as demonstrated by his three marriages, but that he had saved the best for last. We all laughed and JS squeezed my hand and shot me a smile. I was JS's third wife.

A few weeks before Rob died, he requested that the four of us went for lunch to his favourite restaurant in Islington; we all knew this was to be the final goodbye. The thought of that meal still makes me sad. It took forever to get a pitifully frail Rob into JS's car. The short trip from the kerb into the restaurant was painful on every level. Rob was confused and walked into a glass wall. The restaurant had changed hands; the chef-patron who had been unfailingly kind during Rob's illness had gone. The loos were stinky and blocked. Rob couldn't eat and became anxious. The food was terrible, and I had to run out into the street and physically pull JS away from a traffic warden who was ticketing our car because JS had used Rob's disabled badge incorrectly. We got back to their house to find the front door wide open: in all the confusion of getting Rob into the car, CC had forgotten to close the door.

It was a bleak day.

On 21st February, I went to the West End to get some bits and pieces for my holiday. CC rang and asked if we could meet. She helped me choose some holiday things, and I helped her buy some new bedding and then she asked if I would come back to her house in a taxi. I didn't really have the time, but I went back with her, and whilst there, it was obvious that she wanted company. Some time later, I got on the bus and rang JS to let him know why I was running late. He asked after CC. I didn't want to broadcast my thoughts to the top deck of the 390, so I said I'd tell him when I got home.

JS was in the kitchen when I got back. The moment he saw me, he swung into a well-practised routine of, 'Red or white?'

'So, how is she?' he asked, closing the fridge door and handing me a glass of something white and chilled.

I remember taking a gulp of my wine and saying, 'Lonely. I don't think she wanted me to leave.'

I also distinctly remember feeling incredibly fortunate that whilst I had left CC in her lovely but lonely house, I was at home with my husband in my welcoming kitchen, fairy lights twinkling on a giant ficus tree, chatting about the day over a glass of wine, cooking dinner whilst JS did the crossword, throwing out odd clues for me to solve. I always knew how lucky I was. I can honestly say that I never *ever* took him or our life for granted, not even for a nanosecond.

Six days later, JS drowned.

Just after I got back from Barbados, I went to CC's house. She had invited M, a friend of hers I'd met a few times before, a lovely woman whose husband was murdered after he bumped into a man in a swimming pool in north London. The man followed him in to the changing room and stabbed him. The two widows let me cry and rock in pain and kept the champagne topped up (some standards must be maintained, even in grief).

On 25th March, I sat in the same pew at the crematorium that CC had sat in four months earlier. My life not only felt over, I was convinced it was. Scrub that. I *wanted* it to be over.

I saw CC occasionally after that, but I will admit that her raw grief dragged me even further down. A stylish woman, older than me, fiercely intelligent and witty, CC now looked and acted every inch her age. Her husband's illness and death had diminished her looks *and* her spirit.

After our husbands died, both CC and I felt we faced bleak futures. I felt doubly doomed: if someone as practical and spirited as CC couldn't crack widowhood, what hope was there for me?

Today, we met for lunch. The tapas bar she chose, El Parador, was directly opposite Levertons, the Funeral Directors who handled the arrangements for both Rob and JS's funerals.

I was early and she was late, so I had plenty of time to sip chilled sherry, eat olives and stare out of the window, grimly reflecting on the last time I was in this street.

The funeral director had asked whether I wanted to put anything in JS's coffin, and although initially I said I didn't, as the funeral got closer, I felt I needed to write a letter to him. I kept putting it off; every time I sat at the computer, the pain of writing what I wanted to say was too great.

The funeral was on Thursday morning, and I needed to get something for the coffin by Tuesday evening. On Tuesday afternoon, I wrote a short note at speed in longhand on one side of a card and copied a poem on to the other. Paul, the wonderful Chaplain of Highgate School, let me into their private Chapel and left me alone with my tears as I stood under the stained glass windows and read aloud my letter to JS. Afterwards, waiting for Paul to collect me, I looked around the walls of the Chapel studded with stone memorials to ex-pupils who had been killed in action during the world wars: eighteen, nineteen year-olds, practically children. I cried for so many people, many of them long dead. Later that evening, I wrote instructions to the funeral director as to precisely where I wanted my letter placing in the coffin, got a cab to Levertons and, in the dark, put the envelope through the door and came home.

Sitting in the tapas bar waiting for CC, nursing my drink and thinking back over the last eight months, I mused that I often feel that everything that has happened, has happened to someone else, that it couldn't possibly have happened to someone like me, even though I now know the Grim Reaper is an indiscriminate b*st*rd and there is nothing special about me that means I can protect those

I love from him and his scythe. Sometimes, I feel as if I am dealing with what has happened, with what I saw, as if I am in a movie or a book, that I am playing the character of the woman who wore The Bikini of Death. I am terrified that one day my coping mechanism will fail and I will tumble headfirst back into Hell, whereupon dark shadows will circle around me to the sound of cackling as the voice of The Grief Monster mocks: 'You thought black humour and writing would see you through? You stupid girl! Welcome back to the pit of despair! You won't be getting out this time…'

CC arrived in a flap apologising for London Transport making her late. She looked amazing: there was light in her eyes and a smile on her glossed lips. We chatted for a bit and then she said she had something to tell me. She wasn't sure whether she should, her friend, M, said she shouldn't because I would be upset, that I wouldn't understand. CC felt that we'd been friends for so long she *had* to tell me what had happened, which was this: she had fallen hopelessly and deliriously in love with a man who lost his wife to cancer two years ago. It was unexpected. He had emailed her after a friend of a friend (who had also lost his wife) had suggested it. She knew from his first email there was a connection. They met at 8pm on the eighth day of the eighth month, and from that moment, both of them were smitten kittens. They go to the theatre, to restaurants, to art galleries and, yes, CC giggled, they go to bed.

I burst into tears.

CC was concerned, but as I fished tissues out of my bag, I assured her that I was crying with joy that she was happy again. I want everyone I know to be happy; other people being unhappy makes me unhappy. I wanted to ring JS and tell him that CC was happy again. Not being able to ring him made me unhappy.

It was a glorious girly, emotional, gossipy lunch. There were tears of all varieties from both of us. Just because CC has found love again doesn't mean she is immune from breaking down when she talks about Rob; she did it with me, she does it with New Man, but he has been there too and knows that it doesn't diminish how she feels about him. CC is an independent woman who doesn't need a man to look *after* her financially or emotionally, but she likes one to look *out* for her, and I can understand that. Her new man sounds wonderful. His four children like her too and have welcomed her warmly. Rob's children, her grown-up stepchildren, are divided, but they have lives and families of their own. On the first anniversary of Rob's death, CC will be symbolically removing her diamond wedding band.

We walked up Camden High Street together, laughing.

CC practically skipped home. She was cooking for her new man who was coming round. He would be staying the night. They're going to Malta soon. They're going to drink wine in the sun. She can't wait. She's been buying lots of new clothes for her holiday. There's a trip to New Zealand and Australia planned for next year.

After we parted, I went into M&S Simply Food and bought a microwaveable meal for one.

A few days before we left for Barbados, I was in my kitchen, the heart of my home, with my husband, cooking, drinking wine, new clothes for my holiday still in their bags in the hall, thinking how glad I was that I wasn't CC, alone in her beautiful, soulless house, but instead, looking forward to going away, to sitting in the sun, eating good food and drinking wine with JS. And tonight, eight months later, I was in my kitchen hanging around the microwave for three minutes, waiting for it to ping. The fairy lights haven't been on since JS died, nor have I sat on the sofa or at the kitchen table in the extension, which at night is in darkness. I spend as little time down there as possible; it's a room to feed The Hound, top up the wine glass and get food to take to the TV or my desk. The longest I spend there is the time it takes to unload the dishwasher. I'd like to go away, sit in the sun, drink wine, but given that the Grim Reaper came with me last time, I can't imagine going on holiday ever again and anyway, it would mean I'd have to unpack my suitcase, which remains alongside JS's case, under his desk.

I am genuinely pleased for CC, really I am. I know how much she loved Rob and what a toll his illness and his death took on her. On The Hound's life, I wish her and her new man every happiness, and I never lie when it comes to The Hound.

I just bloody well wish I could stop crying tonight.

WARNING!
SELF PITY AHEAD

*In my darkest moments, when I am most lonely and miserable, thoughts come into my head that I can't get rid of. Thoughts about how frightened James must have been after he called the ambulance and was bleeding uncontrollably on the hall floor. I know that it must have happened quickly – I had spoken to him about half an hour before the ambulance arrived and he was fine, nothing was wrong with him. Thirty minutes later he had called himself an ambulance, and the crew had to break the front door down to find that his heart had stopped. Did he know what was happening? Would it have helped if I had been there? I don't know, and I try to think not. Life is hard and unfair. ~ **Linz***

About a week ago, I went to watch Arsenal play Stoke City. It was a lunchtime kick off and we won. Elsewhere, Manchester United were thrashed 6-1 by Manchester City. Everyone was in high spirits as we left the Emirates, including me. I walked away from the ground, on my own, reflecting on the first game I went to after JS's death. It was 1st May and we'd played Manchester United. I'd missed many games, but I was determined to make that vital showdown. It was emotional to sit in my seat without JS beside me, but our lovely friends, Mr & Mrs Referee, who sit next to us, carried me through, thoughtfully rearranging the seating so that instead of JS and Mr Ref beside each other discussing the game, Mrs Ref and I sat together, nattering about the finer points of Fabregas's – um – legs.

JS and I never left early, but for that match and in an attempt to create a 'new normal', I went ten minutes before the end. As I tottered between the lines of mounted police standing guard outside the ground, I sobbed and sobbed. In fact, I sobbed so much that a policeman let me through a cordon that normally stops fans from using a shortcut onto the Holloway Road. I heard roars from the crowd in the stadium behind me and felt totally and utterly alone. I got on the bus, sat on the top deck and cried all the way back to Highgate. Instead of calling in at the pub for a lager and a packet of cheese and onion crisps with JS, I trudged home, desolate. I thought I would never enjoy another football match ever again. There have been a few games since then with varying degrees of angst, but a week last Sunday was different. I didn't totter out sobbing. I left at the final whistle and sauntered along with the crowd, smiling at the chants, feeling a lightness of heart I hadn't felt since before JS died. I walked down the main ramp and thought to myself: 'I've turned a corner. I can not only see light at the end of the tunnel, I can feel its warmth.'

And then I woke up on Monday morning and what little light and warmth had filtered into my world had vanished.

I'll be honest, it wasn't as bad as those early, terrible months when the pain of my grief was searing and unrelenting, but the image of JS adjusting his swimming trunks, flexing his shoulders and walking away from me into the sapphire-blue sea and the resulting shocking aftermath, footage which constantly runs in my head, somewhere, had shifted back to centre stage.

Everything I did last week seemed to intensify how disorientated I felt, how disconnected from my old life I am now.

My lunch with CC and news of her romance unsettled me.

I met up with friends who were in London on Tuesday evening. We had a lovely time, but after I waved them off, when I went back into the house and cleared away the pizza box and lager bottles, the rooms felt empty of life and energy in a way they hadn't done for some time.

I couldn't sleep. I never get much sleep nowadays. I used to complain I was tired if I didn't get eight hours night after night, but now I get by on two or three hours for days at a time.

I stayed up late sipping whisky and listening to LOUD rock music.

My already erratic appetite nosedived again. Having put some weight on since the scales dipped below seven stone (which frightened me), even with some weight gain, at this point I am still two stone lighter than I was before JS died.

I became a slug: I didn't unload the dishwasher, I left mugs of tea everywhere, I didn't change the sheets when the dog came in from the garden covered in mud and jumped on the bed.

I cried *a lot*.

I was mean to people.

I was selfish.

I rarely answer the house phone, but I let answerphone messages (14) mount up on the mobile and then on Friday night, deleted them without listening to them.

I didn't open the post box, which is on the outside wall.

I ignored paperwork/business issues/emails.

I went to bed one afternoon, something I haven't done for months.

I cancelled an engagement at the last minute.

I dropped a bit of shortbread on the kitchen floor and instead of picking it up, I kicked it to the other end of the kitchen.

I felt out of control in every area of my life.

To be truthful, some of these behaviours have been going on for a while. This makes me feel even more out of control, because those people who knew me before JS died would (kindly) acknowledge that the term 'Control Freak' was invented for me. My wonderful brother flew out to Barbados to help me after the accident and even he had to laugh as we were packing – I had all my vitamins in little envelopes labelled with the days of the week, my outfits for every beach session/sightseeing/dinner date were listed on a sheet of paper, and I took with me medicines and remedies for every possible illness that could be contracted on holiday. (I was the woman who took a packet of Knorr Chicken Stock Cubes to New York because I worried I would get a cold and swore that they cured the sniffles. The sniffer dog at customs sniffed them out.) A seasoned traveller, I was prepared for every disaster.

Except death.

Even typing this, I can feel panic rising again, my heart racing, and my stomach contracting.

Panic.

In the early weeks, I would literally run around the house in panic, as if I was trying to get away from myself. I often had terrible panic attacks on waking, particularly if I'd fallen asleep on the sofa.

I thought that panic had gone away. I was wrong. Panic was just sleeping. But now those terrible, all-engulfing, adrenalin-flooding moments have come back, as the movie of what happened plays out in my brain in high-definition wide-screen Dolby surround sound whilst I silently scream: 'SH*T! MY HUSBAND DROWNED! ON HOLIDAY! ABROAD! IN FRONT OF ME! HOW COULD THIS HAVE HAPPENED TO HIM/US/ME?'

After being out on Friday afternoon, I got in a taxi to go home and I got upset, *very* upset. I cried so loudly, when we got back to Highgate the driver let me off the fare (this is the second time a London Cabbie has done this – I love them). I got in, poured myself a drink before even taking my jacket off, went to the bathroom and caught sight of myself in the mirror: The face looking back at me was the trashed love child of Alice Cooper and Courtney Love. I was shocked by how I looked, how I have been living, by how different my life has become from the cosseted life of (don't hate me) the wife of a charming, successful man. I wondered if JS would recognise the new me. He fell in love with me (he said) because (amongst other things) I was bright, funny, kind and wore a dress and heels with panache. Oh, and I could cook.

What would he say about the wreck in the mirror, still in her jacket, swigging cheap white plonk out of a whisky glass, wondering what the hell she is doing and what she is going to do? I've worked so hard to keep it all together in the last eight months, to make some sort of a life, to honour commitments, to be businesslike and professional, but I'm tired, *so* tired. My brain is dulled from lack of sleep and from grief; I'm sometimes snappy, and I'm clutching on to my sense of humour by the tips of my manky fingernails. I should start a new book – I want to get writing again – but I write books about teenage love and angst, and my current mood feels dangerously dark. I've lost any desire to cook; even when friends come round, I order a takeaway.

After JS died, I repeatedly said that I felt claustrophobic in my own life, that I could feel the walls close in like the trash compactor scene in *Star Wars*. Things have changed. On Saturday night, I was lying in bed, in the dark, in the early hours of the morning and I realised that my feelings of panic are no longer accompanied by the sense that the walls are closing in. Panic now takes a different form: I feel that the universe is unimaginably vast, and I am tiny, insignificant, alone and very *very* scared.

I know now that we only *think* we have control over our lives, that just because something is written in the diary doesn't mean it will happen. After JS died I couldn't bear to look at my diary, at the events we had planned, the trips already booked, the theatre dates and the dinners. I bought a new diary. I know that control is something we manufacture, but be that as it may, I thrived on discipline, structure and routine. *Somehow*, I need to get some order back in my life. I'm just not sure how to do it.

HUNTED

*D's horrible eldest sister who had just separated from her husband of twenty-plus years at the time D was dying (a very unhappy marriage) said to me, 'Well at least you have known true happiness. I have never known what it's like to be really happy with someone.' To this day I will never know how I didn't say, 'Well it's not my fault you married a w****r!' ~ **Amelie***

I'm on the run.

Like a frightened fox, I am being hunted, not across fields and through woods by a pack of hounds, but across Ikat rugs and stripped-wood floors by packs of single women: single by choice ('I never wanted to get married.'); single by chance ('I always thought I would be married.'); or single by divorce ('I married a bastard.').

These women are relentless in their pursuit of new members of The Single Sisterhood, and as a woman without a husband, they have me in their sights.

Unless I'm hiding in the downstairs toilet for so long it appears I might have a bowel disorder, I keep going – a moving target is harder to hit – but at some point I will be cornered, perhaps backed onto the Aga where I have paused to catch my breath and warm my bum, or trapped in the spare bedroom as I try to identify my black coat under a pile of black coats. I'm close to escaping when a woman wobbles towards me with a glass of wine in her hand and says, 'It sucks being single again at our age, doesn't it?'

I feel shock on two levels. The first is that this middle-aged woman with flushed cheeks and crows-feet around her eyes has seen through my hair dye, artfully applied less-is-more make-up and Citizens of Humanity jeans worn with midriff-slimming Spanx, and has recognised me as being the same age as her.

The second shock is that she has classed me as single.

I am *not* single. I am widowed. I don't like being widowed; I like it more than being thought of as single, but a lot less than being called married.

When I completed a form to insure my car, I had to tick a little box as to my marital status. I didn't want to tick 'Widowed'; I wanted to tick 'Married'. I asked a friend who knows about these things whether I could still tick 'Married' because I felt married, but she said no, that insurance companies will do anything to get out of paying up, and that it was an offence to give false information. Not married? Let them try and prove it! If I drove my tiny Fiat into the back of a Yummy Mummy's prestige 4x4, and my insurance company refused to cough up for private counselling for her Post Traumatic Shunt Syndrome, I would take on these jobsworths who wanted to put me in a box labelled 'Widow'. I would fight them, not on the beaches or the landing grounds, but in court, where I would wave my left hand with its wedding and engagement ring on my fourth finger and shout, 'See these rings? *These* are the symbols of a married woman! How dare you brand me a Widow!' But then I could imagine a wig-wearing barrister for the prosecution looking at me over his glasses and saying gravely, 'Madam. Your marriage vows were until death do you part. Your husband *did* die, you *are* parted and you are no longer married. You are legally a widow!' And then I'd end up with a massive legal bill, a criminal record and still a widow with a dead husband.

I ticked the 'Widow' box.

But whereas insurance companies want to compartmentalise their clients depending on their marital status, divorced women want to label *any* woman without a husband as single. The divorced feel an alliance with the widowed, whereas the widowed feel that they have *nothing* in common with the divorced, and why should they? A wife can become an ex-wife for many reasons: cheating, dishonesty, money issues, addiction problems, domestic violence, a change in values and priorities, etc., but there is only one way a wife can become a widow: through the death of their spouse.

I first came across this shortly after JS died. I was outside my house when a neighbour approached me. Until I was widowed, I had never interacted with this woman, partly because she drove her Mercedes up to her house via large electronic gates and there was no chance of human-to-human interaction, but also because JS and I had objected to her plans for an extension on the roof of her house, something which led to her glaring at us if ever our eyes met. But on this post-death day, she pulled her car up beside me and got out.

'I am so sorry to hear about your husband,' she said through a cloud of musky-perfume.

I thanked her for her concern.

'You! Me! We are the same now!' she exclaimed.

Confused, I looked at her, genuinely bewildered as to what she meant. She was exotic, over-familiar with the bleach bottle, heavy-handed with the eyeliner and wore spiky Christian Louboutin shoes *to drive in.*

'I'm single! You're single! We are both single women!' she trilled.

I was flabbergasted. I knew that she was going through a divorce. We'd got some post for her once, in error, and so naturally I'd Google-stalked her and discovered that she was involved in a bitter and expensive divorce battle, the grounds for which seemed to be that she was, according to her estranged husband, a gold-digging bigamist.

'The difference is,' I said through gritted teeth, 'My husband is dead. Yours is still alive.'

'Mine wants me dead!' she cackled. 'He'd like to kill me!'

She got a card out of her designer bag and thrust it towards me. 'Let's meet for coffee.'

Having lived next door this woman for 15 years without exchanging so much as a 'Hello,' she then began to ambush me in the street at every opportunity, regaling me through her car window about her problems with legal bills and solicitors and her dreadful husband, before reminding me of our proposed date. It won't surprise you to know we never bonded over a mug of Nescafé. In hindsight, I realise that she meant well, but at the time it wasn't only her husband who wanted to kill her. It was my first taste of being lumped in the Single Sisterhood, and like the widows on bereavement sites who go into an orbit of snarling fury when they too are considered to be a Single Sister, I didn't like it one little bit. Another example came a few weeks later at a party, where I became cornered by a group of bead-wearing women. I always sound anti-beads, don't I? I'm really not, but there is a particular sort of middle-aged woman for whom no outfit would be complete without a string of ethically sourced and ethnically derived beads. Anyway, apparently people tell you what they want you to know about them within a few minutes of meeting them, so I quickly learned that they were all divorced. They already knew I was widowed as the neighbourhood jungle drums had been beating; either that, or the bereaved give off a strange scent – a mixture of tears, unwashed sheets and alcohol.

'We meet up to go to the cinema,' Bead Woman One said. 'Sometimes, we have a bite to eat too. You'd be welcome to join us.'

I wasn't averse to this. They seemed nice women, if a little beady around the bust area.

But then Bead Woman Two spoke. 'We're all single or divorced too.'

As if I wasn't feeling desolate enough, her words plunged me further into despair.

Not having a husband handy to rescue me, and still being new to the 'Socialising as a Single' scene, I couldn't work out how to extricate from myself from these women, so I hung around. It didn't take long for the conversation to turn to 'useless' ex-husbands, in fact, there seemed to be an undercurrent of competition as to who had married the worst man. Bitterness and resentment flowed out of the mouths of these women at the same rate as the Merlot flowed in. I stood there wondering why these women had married them, let alone merged their respective gene pools to procreate, if these men were such terrible specimens of humanity.

Now, I want to make something clear. I have friends who don't have husbands and I love these women. I'm genuinely interested in their tales of spineless ex-husbands who fail to pick up the children or pay the maintenance. I commiserate with them when yet another internet date turns up six inches shorter and ten years older than their on-line profile claimed. I know women who feel such venom towards their ex they make life impossible for him: cancelling the access visits to their children, poisoning their children against his new partner, bleeding his bank account dry. Whilst I may not agree with their actions, I still love them and value their friendship, because our friendship is based on more than just the fact that we don't have a man to help us put the bins out. But I do know that my friends have been in pain over their failed relationships, that they know what it is like to come home to an empty house, to be ill with no one to bring them chicken soup, to dislike the present and fear for the future, to wonder whether they will grow old alone, to see couples together and think 'Why couldn't that have been us?' Their route to sitting on the sofa alone and in tears night after night may have involved the slutty little poppet with hair-extensions and stick-on nails who works in accounts, rather than the Grim Reaper, but the outcome is the same.

'It sucks being single at our age, doesn't it?' I don't think I could ever have become friends with the woman who said that to me when she caught me rootling through the coats piled on the bed in the spare room. But whatever her marital status, had she said, 'It's hard, isn't it?' with that knowing sad smile of the lonely, I might have said, 'Fancy a coffee sometime?'

And meant it.

COVER GIRL

We don't think about death until it shakes our world, it's just not something we talk about or want to think about, and since this has happened I think, why don't we, before, so we can have some sort of understanding, something for when it does happen, because it's a fact of life. It shouldn't be whispered about or not even talked about. We learn so many things, maths, science, etc. I think something that we should be educated about is death. ~ **Rose**

I was warned about the six-month low, but why did no one alert me to the eight-month pit? I'm a late August baby, the third youngest in my year at school. Research shows that summer babies never catch up with their peers, so perhaps I'm just slow and my six-month slump came at eight months. It's been tough and my coping mechanisms (writing/humour/trashy telly/alcohol) failed me for a while.

Pre-widowhood, one of the routines guaranteed to soothe a low mood was to take a bath with smelly oils, sip a glass of wine and lose myself in a glossy magazine.

I'm a magazine junkie, constantly after my next fix. I blame my mother. There were always magazines in our house and I never lost the thrill of buying a glossy tome, cracking the spine, the smell of perfume samples, print and paper hitting my nostrils.

Whilst my mother was devouring *Good Housekeeping*, *Woman's Own*, *Woman*, *Reader's Digest*, *Here's Health*, *Living* and *Family Circle*, my childhood magazine habits started with *Once Upon A Time*, moved on to *June*, then the iconic *Jackie* and then rather alarmingly (in retrospect), leapfrogged straight to *Cosmopolitan*, a publication which had me wide-eyed, a bit scared and longing to go back to safe *Jackie* with its advice about practising snogging on your arm in the bath. In fact, as I have mentioned before, I realised that it was time to leave a fledgling career in science when it became clear that my colleagues in the post-grad room at St George's Hospital had their heads in scientific journals, highlighting extracts from obscure papers about the mating habits of lampreys to impress their colleagues over pints of real ale in the staff social club, whilst I was flicking through *Cosmo*, using my pen to do racy quizzes and thinking of the cocktails I could enjoy once I dumped my ferret musk-soaked lab coat.

In a life long before me, JS had a job at *Vogue*. I never actually discovered what he did there – he was always vague about his time at *Vogue* – but I suspect he was a 'summer intern'. His links meant that whilst he would body swerve most magazines I bought, he would always pick up *Vogue* and flick through it. I'd often find yellow Post-it Notes marking pages showing fashion shoots: photographs of impossibly long-legged pouting minxes modelling something which JS thought would suit me. In two decades he never stopped doing this, never stopped seeing me as the twenty-something girl he first met in 1987 at the office photocopier wearing a grey jersey dress from BHS (the only dress I owned), but eventually I stopped smiling and giggling and started scorning his choices: *I'm 44 not 24! How can you possibly think that I could wear that? You need to get new glasses! I'd look ridiculous! Yeah, right! Are you ill?* I've never found it easy to accept compliments, but how I wish I had been more gracious when JS put those fashion spreads under my nose. My sneering now makes me sad.

After JS died, I didn't buy any magazines other than the one that every middle-class woman who lives in London succumbs to occasionally: *Country Living*. As someone who believed I would wither and die if my feet didn't spend most of the week on concrete, any form of country living for me always felt doubtful, but during a period when I felt I would be happier anywhere but in this house, I fantasised about living somewhere isolated, wild and tragic, but still on the Ocado delivery route and with reliable broadband and Sky Sports.

But old habits die hard, so during my recent dip and feeling somewhat raddled by grief and age, I happened to come across a magazine trumpeting that it was the ageless issue. There was cover-girl Joanna Lumley looking absolutely fabulous at 65, alongside various quotes suggesting that if I bought this magazine, I would learn the secret to fabulous skin, a flattering wardrobe and other seemingly unobtainable life-scenarios, such as dating, dieting, developing my intuition and boosting my confidence.

So £3.70 felt a small price to pay for something that could change my life, and magazines *can* change your life. It's happened to me before. In a roundabout way I met JS because of *Family Circle*, but that's a digression too far for now.

I went home, flaked out on the sofa with The Hound and, fizzing with hope, turned to the first page.

Dear reader, let me take you through this magazine from the perspective of a recent widow in the pit of despair and you will see why, despite being a relatively mild-mannered girl (parking wars, Virgin call centre operatives and animal cruelty excepted), I wanted to hunt down the editor of that magazine, roll up her 'Ageless Issue', and ram it either up or down her nearest orifice (depending on the position of her body on confrontation) whilst shouting, 'WHAT ABOUT WIDOWS? ARE WE THE FORGOTTEN WOMEN?'

The opening page was crammed with words intended to describe the reader, words such as: Happy; Fabulous; Sexy; Loving; Confident; Witty; Glamorous; In Control. To add insult to severe injury, the words were printed in enormous pink, white and black fonts, mimicking that shouty, excited style that Davina McCall has and which, even when JS was alive, irritated the hell out of me. I could share more of these words with you, but already I can hear you pleading, 'Please don't!' so I won't.

Next to these words, the editor sent me a little message: 'This issue has been inspired by you,' she gushed. 'It's full of women like you and me.'

Clearly, she hasn't met me recently.

Next up came the beautiful Miss Lumley sprawled on a sofa. Now, I love Jo (I'd like to think that as she is a woman like me we'd be on first name terms), but as I started to read that she wouldn't change *anything* at all about her life I thought, 'Clearly she's never found herself wearing The Bikini of Death.' Obviously if she did, she'd look as fabulous as Helen Mirren did when she was photographed in her red bikini, a shot which according to the *Daily Mail* (therefore it must be true) gave hope to mature women everywhere.

I lost interest.

I moved on to the fashion section. Apparently, there are four body shapes that the (ahem) mature woman fits into: Busty; Super Curvy; Apple; Pear.

Au contraire, annoying editor. What about those of us who have been on the Death Diet and are now a string bean? Where is the style advice for those of us whose curves began to disappear the moment the grim-faced doctor walked in to the room and said, 'I'm so sorry…'

Still in the fashion section was an article suggesting a top trick for an ageless look is to wear a fedora. My friend, the aptly named Hat, already knows this and can wear them with panache, but I know (because a photographer once told me) that they make me look 'kooky' (he used that exact word). I was in my twenties at the time. Kooky is not a look I want in my forties. I'm not going for a fedora, but I might wear a burka: it would cover a multitude of sins.

Then, much too early in my opinion, was a large spread entitled: 'The Truth About Dating After Forty!' Four women (one wearing a hat, so it must work), all gave me tips on how to secure a hot or even lukewarm date. None of the women were widowed, two were still single but don't want to be (which makes me wonder whether their dating tips are worth following), and the whole thing sounded so deeply depressing and cattle market-ish, it made me want to stay in with The Hound and watch re-runs of *As Time Goes By*, forever.

Only just getting over the horror of dating as an old crone, I was faced with an article with the title: 'The Secret of a Happy Marriage... My Own Space'. Well, forgive me smug ladies writing about how your marriage is enriched by having a separate basement flat in your house so that you can live together, but apart, but I would like to suggest that the secret of a happy marriage starts with your husband or wife having a pulse...

Then came a gushing article about a couple in their forties who are relishing their life together having had their children young, balanced out by another extolling the unexpected delights of late motherhood at a time when your ovaries should be starting to sleep.

No issue on ageing gracefully would be complete without the Dame in the Red Bikini. Dear, tattooed, often naked, Dame Helen. Like Jo, I do love her, but still I felt cheated. The editor promised me that the magazine would be full of women like me. Just having the same Christian name as Dame H doesn't count.

Sexy in her Sixties Helen was followed by a Christmas gift guide. Do I need to elaborate? I think not.

And now I've lost what little energy or heart I have to describe the rest of the issue with its beauty tips for ageing (but not grief-stricken) skin, health notes where it is clear I face the menopause where one part of me will be gushing with hot sweats at the same time as another part has dried up, recipes for a big family Sunday lunch and perfect homes shown off by perfect couples. Even the hunk of the month on the last page was a bitter disappointment, Kiefer Sutherland, who I am sure is a perfectly nice man, but not in the same league as Hugh Laurie or Alastair Campbell.

A bit of extra research online threw up the same sort of information that this magazine peddled. Apparently, your thirties are the time you are building a secure home and family and forging ahead with your career. Those of you who have lost your partners in your twenties and thirties will have something to say about that.

Your forties are when you have confidence and know exactly what you want in the bedroom, in the boardroom and what suits your face and figure. You are content with your life moving forward. Yeah. Right.

In your fifties you are dealing with ageing parents, children leaving home, but you relish new challenges and having time with your partner, and now you no longer have to worry about contraception, you are able to ignite a love-life which may have dwindled. Any fifty-plus widows and widowers out there will be gnashing their teeth at those words, assuming that they have the energy to do any gnashing.

The article I am quoting from didn't say what happened in your sixties, but I'm guessing they expect everyone to look like Jo Lumley and Dame H.

I am 47. I am winding up the boardroom part of my life. I no longer know what suits me or even what fits me.

I do know what I want in the bedroom. A good night's sleep.

SNOGGING, SLEAZEBAGS AND SAFETY

When I was first widowed, it was the first thing I usually told someone I met, usually as an explanation as to why I walked around looking so haggard or why I suddenly began crying in a crowded place. I no longer divulge this information, I have learned the hard way. A guy at the side of my husband's grave lunged at me. It frightened and angered me beyond all measure, and it left me feeling violated for weeks afterwards. I thought when he stopped to look at the cameo photo that is embedded in my husband's cremation tablet and then asked me why he died so young, that he was genuinely interested. He wasn't. He just wanted the chance to get me talking so he could make his move, and it was horrific.
~ Angela

The subject of finding new love often crops up on bereavement discussion boards, even quite soon after we land blinking and bewildered on Planet Grief. We cannot imagine finding love ever again, in fact, the thought of being with someone other than our loved one is as stomach-churningly horrific as the alternative, a life stretching out in front of us with no one to laugh with, cry with or share sweet-and-sour-prawn balls with on Saturday night whilst watching *Strictly*. We read stories of widows and widowers getting second chances at love and depending on where we are on this journey, we are either heartened or disgusted by such tales, sometimes feeling both emotions within a few minutes of one another.

Shortly after JS's accident, but before the funeral, I began reading Joyce Carol Oates' memoir of being widowed: *A Widow's Story*.

As Janet Maslin, who reviewed the book for *The New York Times* wrote: 'Ms. Oates writes with frantic energy about feeling lost, alone, frightened, disoriented, angry, hurt and "like one who has been slammed over the head with a sledgehammer."' I felt that JCO had not only perfectly captured her own experience of widowhood, but was describing mine too. I felt we had a bond.

Before finishing the book, I Googled Ms Oates and discovered that she had met a new man six months after her husband's death, and had married him before the first anniversary. I was so horrified, I hurled the book across the room as if it was infected with the Ebola virus. I did the same book-chucking routine with Elizabeth Harper Neeld's *Seven Choices*, at the point when she started dating. When my bereavement coach (whose husband died of cancer) told me she had remarried, I was disappointed; I thought I'd found a kindred spirit who understood my grief, but clearly, if she was able to remarry, she couldn't *possibly* have loved her husband as much as I love mine, otherwise how could she let another man into her life?

Some months ago, I remember wading into a discussion online about dating after bereavement. Many of the widows stated that having married 'The One', they wouldn't date again unless they met 'The New One'. With all the naivety of recent grief, finding the idea of dating repellent and with absolutely no experience of any man other than my husband for 22 years, I questioned why we had to wait for The New One? Why, if and when the time was right, couldn't we do what we did before we got married, which is to have a series of lovely boyfriends (or not) and fun casual dates (or not) until such time as The New One came along (or not)? And you know, I really believed *everything* that I wrote. I wasn't considering dating again, I couldn't imagine *ever* dating again, but I assumed that if I did, I would be the girl I was before I met JS.

Dating advice for the newly single is everywhere, but very little specifically for widows. So, I did a bit of online research about dating as a widow, particularly as something happened recently to make me review my previous Girl About Town stance, and made me think about men much sooner than I anticipated.

Amongst the sensible advice about telling a friend if you are meeting a strange man, only meeting him for a coffee or in the afternoon, never giving out your address, paying for yourself, keeping quiet about your financial circumstances and being particularly cautious of anyone you meet online, were the following gems:

Don't talk about how you were bereaved on a first date: Apparently, going into detail puts men off. Does this mean that if they ask I can't tell them? Can I do a silent recap, sort of like grief charades? I'm pretty good at it, right down to the hand signals and everything. I had to do it several times for the authorities in Barbados. It would certainly cause a stir over a pizza in Strada if I did the whole calling for help in the sea through to CPR and falling off the trolley in the ambulance routine. I'd either be asked to leave, or given an extra glass of Merlot.

Don't talk about your late husband or wife: Another turn-off, apparently. As I have been known to accost perfect strangers at the bus stop with tales of JS's life and death, not mentioning him over the carrot cake and coffee (see below) is going to prove difficult if not impossible. I can see me saying, 'The man who shall not be mentioned used to...'

Go somewhere you haven't been with your loved one: This is very limiting and might mean that for the first informal coffee or lunch (as recommended), I'd have to travel from north London to somewhere like Solihull. Such a trek would require me to hire a dog-sitter to look after The Hound for the day, so if the date was a disappointment, I'd feel like handing him the invoice from Animal Aunts and a bill for my travel costs.

Take your time. If you don't want to kiss for six months, don't. He must respect your need to go slowly: Ah, I'm sorry, but I just can't agree with this one. I think you should just go for it, and I'll tell you why…

Like so many others born in the sixties, I spent a good part of my teenage years devouring the pages of *Jackie* magazine. I'd often cut out articles such as how to make a pair of shorts from old jeans, snippets from the Cathy & Claire problem page and of course the photo-love stories. These photographs of a couple *about* to snog were studied in great detail and sometimes stapled to the pages of my diary and annotated, depending on my crush de jour (Chris, Russ, Andrew – it seemed to change all the time). Combined with practising my (untested) snogging technique on my arm in the bath, I felt that not only was I ready for my first smooch, it was bound to be the most wonderfully romantic experience. This little extract is taken from a page of my 1979 diary (written in green ink) where I am anticipating a snog with Chris, a boy who I made no impression on whatsoever and, in retrospect, neither did he on me, as I can't recall his surname, and if he hadn't featured in my teenage diary, I wouldn't have remembered him: 'Can't you see, I dream of your lips pressed softly on mine, in your arms so caring and strong…'

There is more of this nauseating waffle before I end the diary entry with: 'I went for a bike ride with Alex and H & K.'

I got absolutely no chance to put my theory into practice until aged 15, I was invited to my friend A's 16th birthday party. Whereas I lived in the first Barrett house ever built, had parents who hadn't procreated until late in life and exhibited (by my reckoning) old-fashioned attitudes to match, A's parents were young, wealthy, glamorous and lived in the most fabulous modern house surrounded by woodland, a house which her father, an architect of note in the region, had designed and built. Oh, and she had a pony.

But I digress.

The most thrilling part of this birthday party wasn't going to A's house, but that she lived next door to a sixth former who went to an all boys grammar school in town, a sixth former who (gasp of delight) would be bringing other sixth formers to the party. At 15, there was only one thing more glamorous than sixth formers at our large mixed Grange Hill-style comprehensive, and that was sixth formers from a top private school.

At one point in the party, one of the boys, who I will call Johnnie, because that was his name, grabbed my hand and we raced into the wood. When we stopped running, he started snogging me. I was so surprised and shocked I fell over, backwards, into a patch of nettles. The teenage Johnnie obviously took this crumpling to the ground as a sign that my knees had buckled with passion and threw himself on top of me. As I struggled to get him off me and get up, my hands ground into the nettles.

Two things stand out about that night. The first is that my hands were so swollen with nettle stings, I was unable to stir the sugar into my tea when we were all back in the fabulous kitchen of A's fabulous house, and secondly, that instead of my first kiss being a case of lips being pressed softly on mine and melting into someone's strong arms, I was on my back in a wood being *covered* in spit whilst being stung to death.

Yes, Johnnie was a Wet Kisser, and the experience left me so scarred that in one of my books, the teenage heroine, Electra Brown, is given the same treatment, but with a French exchange student at a school disco, rather than a northern posh boy in a private wood. Of the experience Electra said: 'It was like being snogged by one of those machines at the dentist, all noise and suction, making your mouth dry whilst showering the rest of your face with spit and water.'

I did wonder whether because of all the saliva sloshing about, Johnnie was left with the impression that *I* was the Wet Kisser, a horrific slur on my character, which is why Electra spends hours snogging the mirror in her bedroom, checking for moisture levels on the glass. I've never done that, obviously…

I suspect that even a Snog Meister sometimes gets a little moist – dental work, the remains of a cold – and I could forgive a teenage boy for not having the experience to realise that his technique was pants, but you'd think that an older, more experienced man would have noticed if a woman dragged her hand across her face after a kiss. But no. Middle-aged Wet Kissers are out there. Believe me.

I've just met one.

Fast-forward more than three decades, to just before the eight-month low.

I am at a private party with my friend Big Bird. It's a sort of work-related event, which is why I have reluctantly abandoned my slanket and *Corrie* for a bar in the West End of London. There are celebrities milling around and waiters passing by with dainty morsels. All very proper.

Big Bird and I get chatting to a man. Media Man seems fun and bright and interesting, and if I was in a different headspace, he would tick several boxes as potential date material, but I'm not, so he doesn't. We don't know each other, but we know some of the same people and Media Man vaguely knows of my husband. We spend time chatting before he asks whether he can see me the following day. I tell him that I can't because a plumber is coming to help me locate my stopcock; as a widow, I have suddenly become irrationally fearful that I will need to know how to turn the water off in an emergency. Media Man points out that the plumber won't work in the evening. I am polite but firm in my rebuttal. He asks if he can give me his contact details and I say, 'OK,' knowing full well that I won't do anything with them. He scribbles something down. Big Bird says that she has to leave as she has an early start the next day. 'Stay and have another drink with me,' Media Man presses. I decline. I go to leave, and that is when it happens: he lunges at me, sticks his tongue down my throat and snogs my face off, covering me in saliva whilst grabbing my butt in the style of a bowling ball (think, 'finger placement').

I wasn't shocked, but I was so surprised; it was a good job I had a table next to me or it would have been the 'nettles in the wood' incident all over again, but in a carpeted bar with Maureen Lipman nearby. I'd like to take this opportunity to point out that not being of the blonde sex siren type, I am far removed from the sort of woman who men just launch themselves at, and I can prove it. I was once in a room with Charlie Sheen and one other woman, a waitress, and the man who is known for seducing thousands of women not only didn't try it on with me, he looked positively scared as I marched across the room to say 'Hello'. To be rebuffed by Charlie 'Shagger' Sheen says it all.

But back to me and the middle-aged Wet Kisser. Big Bird and I scurried out, me wiping my face with the back of my hand. Big Bird was as incredulous as I was. Despite his persona as Mr Smooth Media Man, he was inappropriate and boorish, not to mention a dreadful kisser. In the taxi going back to my empty house, it made me remember all those times as a youngster when I would spend ages fancying someone, thinking that if we got together it was bound to be wonderful, only to find that the moment we kissed they gasped like a fish out of water and it was at that point I noticed their hands felt like uncooked pork sausages and their breath was rank and why did I never realise that they wore slip on shoes?

Like my first kiss with seventeen-year-old Johnnie, dates often ended in disappointment, but it didn't matter because there would be more dates with other men and life was full of possibilities. And then after years of dating men who weren't quite right, even if they were lovely, when you unexpectedly met The One, it was like coming home; a feeling that this was how it was meant to be. I read an article recently that described a good relationship as being the emotional equivalent of bubble wrap, cushioning you against life's hard knocks. We haven't just been knocked about by life, but as Joyce Carol Oates described, we've been sledgehammered, and the thought of dressing up and going out and spending time with someone, of going slowly, of letting a tiny glimmer of hope come into my head only to find out after one month or six months that he's a Wet Kisser (or worse) is too depressing for words. We've all had so much grief and angst in our lives, we don't need to add 'Date Disappointment' to the list. So, if you find yourself contemplating dipping a toe in the dating pool, I am going to suggest these new dating rules. Yes, some of you may think them radical, others distasteful. I think they are vital:

The moment you meet, before you've even shaken hands, lunge at your date and snog his face off: I know that this seems very forward and might give widows a bad name, but for goodness sake, let's get it over with before we spend time, money and emotional energy on the man. If you feel yourself wanting to wipe your mouth, do a runner. If he does a runner, at least you know he wasn't worth bothering with. Obviously, don't tell the poor man he is a crappy kisser, but if you have friends in common, do warn them should they find him puckering-up in front of them. Forewarned is forearmed and all that jazz.

If the man passes this test and hasn't fainted with shock at your forwardness, tell him in no uncertain terms how your husband died and that you are still a mess: 'My husband drowned in front of me on a beach in Barbados whilst we were on holiday and I was wearing a bikini,' will sort the men from the boys, I think. Do feel free to add any particularly harrowing accounts of illness/death to avoid a scenario later down the line when the man claims that he walked away because he couldn't cope with the fact that your husband died from [insert cause of death], the emotional fall-out from which is still on-going. At least then you can say with all honesty, 'Well, I did warn you!'

Make sure you go somewhere with loads of memories of your time with your husband: If you start sobbing and wailing and he is still around and wants to know you, then he is instantly awarded several million Brownie points. Do make sure that you have enough money for a taxi and a fully juiced mobile phone, so that if he does stalk off a windy beach muttering that he can't stand competing with a ghost any longer and drives away leaving you stranded in the dunes, you can phone a friend or a taxi. Then contact me and I will expose and humiliate him in print and brand him a Wet Kisser, even if it's not true.

Talk incessantly about how wonderful your husband was to be married to: Again, go in at the deep end. Go over the top and claim you were married to a saint. You can always give them the truth later, which is that you actually married a human being who could be annoying, particularly in the car. If they take your claims that your husband could turn Thames tap water into Châteauneuf du Pape and make one M&S seeded batch loaf feed the five thousand of Muswell Hill with grace and good humour, it's a start.

Fish a screwdriver and plug out of your handbag: Based on an Irish electrician I dated when I was 21, I developed a theory which has never let me down, which is that if a man can re-wire a house, he will be exceptional at other things. Even for the new rules of dating, asking a man back to re-wire your house on a first date might be a step too far (particularly if it doesn't need rewiring), but a plug is a start. If like me you have a big handbag, feel free to stick any electrical equipment that has packed up in there too, thereby not only giving him a relationship test, but getting one of those annoying little jobs done at the same time.

Finally, do remember all the sensible rules about telling a friend where you are going and so on. Think lovely Suzy Lamplugh and Mr Kipper... Years ago, JS met Suzy's mother, Diana Lamplugh through The Suzy Lamplugh Trust. She came to our office to talk about personal safety and gave every employee a rape alarm. Every woman should follow personal safety rules,

Clearly, these rules are firmly tongue-in-cheek (which is where that sleaze bag should have kept his), but my unwanted and unexpected experience with Media Man made me realise that where men are concerned, thinking I could be the girl I was before I got married was an unrealistic fantasy. I don't want to be like some of my single friends who go on date after date with men who fall short (sometimes literally) of their not unrealistic expectations. Their dating escapades are hilarious to listen to, but I know they are painful to live with and I've had enough heartache to last me a liftetime. Disappointment follows disappointment; the more they search for The One, the further away he seems. I can't be like them because I'm single through widowhood. It's not that I didn't find Mr Right or that Mr Right turned into Mr Wrong or Mr Unfaithful or Mr Just Want A Womb. I can't be like the woman I was before I got married because I've lived a different sort of life, known true love and witnessed the tragic death of the man I thought I would be married to until it was time for gardening in elasticated slacks. I thought I could, at the right time, be, if not young, certainly feel free and single around town, but I can't. I'm no longer the girl I was and, what's more, I no longer want to be her. I'd rather stay in and snuggle with my favourite bundle of testosterone – The Hound.

In 1979, Johnnie (who went on to be an eminent doctor and married a woman who clearly didn't have the same saliva issues as me) made me realise what I wouldn't put up with, and in 2011, Media Man did the same.

In a funny way, I'm thankful to them both, but particularly Media Man, because he reminded me that however a man might look on the outside, it doesn't mean that they are as respectful as my husband was and that however savvy you think you are, however much you think you are in control, often you're not. Because Media Man stepped over the line in a crowded London bar, his behaviour didn't shock me, it made me laugh with the sheer crassness of it all. But had it happened in a flat or a dark street, I might not be laughing now. I had a lucky escape in my room at college when I was 18. It was the first time I ever met a seriously sleazy man who forced himself on me. Since then, I was not only lucky, but blessed by spending time with wonderful men I trusted; Media Man gave me a sharp wake-up call that sleazebags are out there and that sometimes they are disguised as charming men who look good in a smart jacket.

As we left the bar, Big Bird, a woman I would trust with my life and who has been my Angel in a J Cup for years said to me, 'You're more vulnerable than you think, you know.'

If you only remember one rule about dating or even just living this new life on Planet Grief, it is this: *Stay safe*.

Promise me.

GETTING IN A LATHER

*One of the hardest things I am finding, is wanting to move forward, however small a step, and find happiness in this new life I didn't ask for. The hard part is realising I have to let go of a certain level of my baggage in order to do that. I'm still finding the balance. Some days it feels like Mark is slipping away from me, that no matter how hard I try, I can't keep him at the forefront like I want. And for the record, I am sick of people telling me that I am strong and brave. Feck off! You don't see me broken when I am on my own. ~ **Emma S***

In John Green's young adult novel, *Paper Towns*, troubled teen Margo Roth Spiegelman loves planning adventures for herself in a black notebook. The planning is the fun part, because as Margo reflects, 'Nothing ever happens like you imagine it will.'

Although somewhat unhinged (involvement in suicide, black-mail and spray painting isn't something to be recommended for your average seventeen-year-old, especially as Margo ultimately disappears), she is on the money with her quote. Nothing *ever* happens like you imagine it will, at least, it doesn't for me, and I suspect it doesn't for you either. My career path, my personal life, where I live and so on is far removed from the life I imagined growing up in what was then a small Northumberland village with one bus, but which is now a sprawling town of 'executive' homes owned by footballers. It even has a Waitrose! You'd have to have lived there in the sixties and seventies to appreciate that last sentence.

Like Margo, I have always been a plotter and planner, scribbling down my cunning ideas in the back of my diary, in new notebooks (plans seem more real if you buy a pristine notebook just for the purpose), or sometimes just on scraps of paper.

Doing my hateful tax return recently, I came across a note on which I had made some life plans, imaginatively titled: *Plan A* and *Plan B*. What I hadn't planned on was the Grim Reaper being part of the process and chipping in with his devastating *Plan C*.

Not long after JS died, I had lunch with a widow I'd met through a Facebook grief site. I remember her telling me that she and her husband had always been a 'Go with the flow' type couple, but, unusually and for the first time, they had made plans for the future. A few days later, her husband was killed in an accident. There is a Yiddish proverb: 'Mentsch tracht, Gott lacht', that roughly translates as: 'Man plans, God laughs'. I don't want to offend anyone who has a strong faith, but this is yet another issue I'm going to have to raise with God if it turns out I'm wrong and he does exist. And because I've been wrong about just about everything I thought I was sure about, I expect that there is a God. I'd better start planning what I want to say to him. He doesn't deserve a new notebook though.

Experience has taught me that whilst you think you know how things are going to pan out, how you will react, you absolutely don't. When I was taken back to the hotel room shortly after JS's death was confirmed in hospital, I would have put money on me running around the room like a headless chicken wearing a bikini (now there's a bizarre image), screaming, banging the walls, trying to throw myself off the balcony onto the terrace below. But of course, I didn't. I remember someone telling me how amazingly strong I was, how calm I was being, how other tourists who had lost their partners on holiday had cried hysterically. I remember thinking, 'Am I supposed to cry? How am I supposed to react?' Perhaps in another post I will tell you how I reacted. I still find it difficult to comprehend how in such circumstances the mind does everything it can to grab onto some shred of normality. Certainly, mine behaved in a bizarre and (at the time) inappropriate way, a way that for months made me ashamed. Other widows and widowers I have talked to have similar tales of keeping it all together. The falling apart came later.

But despite all this experience, I still believe that I know what will happen and run through scenarios in my mind, working myself up into a frenzy. One such frenzy was the thought of going back to our cottage in Broadstairs on the east Kent coast. I say cottage, it's a tiny terraced house in the centre of the town with a back yard, not a rose-festooned cottage with hollyhocks in the garden. I didn't mention it before because I could barely think about it without becoming anxious and tearful. I keep a postcard of Broadstairs by my desk; sometimes I'd get it out from behind the envelopes and peer at it as if I was a teenage boy looking at a sleazy image – it would set my heart racing and I'd slip it back, disturbed and yet drawn to it. Several times over the last nine months, I was all set to go there, but pulled out at the last minute, often on the morning of the planned trip. This was because I knew *exactly* how the visit would pan out. Let me take you through it:

The journey down would be an 80-mile sobfest of memories: the stretch of the A2 where a woman slammed into the back of us; the bit of the M2 where we had our last argument on the hard shoulder; the service station where I was terribly car sick and blamed JS's driving ('Who do you think you are, Lewis Hamilton?' I told him); the outside lane where we were forced to stop as around us, cars and lorries bounced off each other and I thought we were both going to die; snapping at JS for going hell-for-leather down the slip road onto the motorway with a coffee in one hand whilst he asked me to lean across him and put his seatbelt on. Happy days. In retrospect.

I was sure the first sighting of water would have me gasping for breath through salty tears as I remembered the dreadful way the sea took my husband from me. I would look at the expanse of coastline and see... Well, you can imagine. I certainly did. Over and over. In this case, familiarity didn't breed contempt, it bred terror.

By this stage my face would be so swollen from sobbing, it would look as if I had been attacked by a swarm of killer bees.

I imagined seeing a neighbour in the street and throwing myself at him, wailing. He'd tell me how scrawny I looked, how my eyes were haunted with grief. Perhaps Janet, the lady at the bakery on the corner, would come out with a cheese scone to soothe and fatten me up. She knows I like them. JS did too.

And then the cottage itself. I had run through the process of going through the front door hundreds of times in my mind. I would walk up the alley with wobbly legs, put my key in the lock with a shaky hand, and on seeing the hallway, my knees would buckle and I'd collapse on to the mountain of post and pizza leaflets. I could imagine my grief and hysteria becoming so intense, to stop me going into orbit, someone would have to slap me like they do in the movies. I was sure that I wouldn't be able to go into any of the rooms and would simply announce, 'Close the door. I'm selling up!' after which I'd be bundled back in the car and driven at high speed either to the nearest hospital or home to Highgate, where I would get smashed on anything I could lay my hands on.

Nine months after JS and I last locked the door and headed back to London, I faced up to the fact that I had to go down and see the place. A neighbour had been keeping an eye on it, but I wanted to check the heating and so on before winter arrived. Even if I sold it, I couldn't bear to think of someone else, even my family, going through the cottage and taking out our personal things. There is nothing of any real value down there: the house was furnished from trips to junk shops and reclamation yards. The thought of those days poking around dusty dumps together seared through my heart like a hot poker. In my mind, I walked through every room, imaging every picture, each piece of furniture and all the knick-knacks and it killed me. The sad thing was that it was only in the last few months before JS died that we spent any money on the cottage. We had decided to spend more time down there and so had ditched the inherited spine-crippling sofas, replaced the fire, sorted out the bum-freezing bathroom, put down carpets and so on. We'd even bought a new television on our last visit there. We had both spent decades working hard and there had been difficult business issues in the last few years. JS was exhausted and stressed. It felt time to slow down and start enjoying life. In 2008 when we became embroiled in a legal issue that kept JS awake at night and anxious during the day, I wrote in a notebook a quote from Elizabeth Gilbert's, *Eat, Pray, Love*, a book I was obsessed with at the time: 'I wanted to live a smaller, bigger life.' I urged JS to slow down, to simplify our life. I really did want to live a smaller life in material terms, but a richer life as a couple. I didn't need money in the bank. I only needed him. He said, 'Let's give it two more years.'

Two years later, in 2010, he was still stressed. I begged him to stop, to let me help him, but he wouldn't, or couldn't, step back, and he wouldn't talk about it. I couldn't reach him or share his worries and he was too preoccupied for mine. It made the last year of our relationship the most challenging period in two decades. I look back at photos and am saddened at how tired he looked. He always wanted to take on all the problems, to keep me free from worry, to treat me like a princess. The sad irony is now I have to deal with far more problems than he did, but without the support of a loving spouse. Another sadness (or happiness, depending on how I am feeling) is that the moment we got to Barbados, JS relaxed and was the man I fell in love with all those years ago. At the point he died, he was happy. I know that because, sitting on a sun lounger, he told me.

The visit.

My friend, Mac, drove me down. On the morning of the trip, I nearly rang him and cancelled, but I didn't. And this is how the visit went:

We were so busy chatting and laughing on the journey, I barely noticed that we had arrived.

As Mac parked the car, I saw the sea, but instead of hyperventilating with shock, I remembered why I loved Broadstairs and this stretch of coast. It may seem odd to say this given what has happened, but JS and I found the coast a very healing place and looking at it, the outline of France just visible 32 miles across the English Channel, for me now widowed by water, it still was.

Janet wasn't there to give me a cheese scone because the shop had been sold and was empty.

As we walked towards the cottage, I saw Trevor, one of my favourite neighbours. Instead of collapsing in a heap at his feet, I was thrilled to see him. He was another link with JS and happy times. It felt good to hug him.

Yes, going into the cottage was difficult, yes, my heart was in my mouth, but when I stood in the entrance, it reminded me of the first time I walked through the front door.

I love negotiating, it was part of my job for two decades, but as I stood in the hall on that first viewing in 2001, any thought of haggling over the asking price vanished. I hissed at JS, 'I want this place.' I hadn't even put my head in one of the rooms, but it felt a happy house. JS, ever the canny businessman, hissed back at me to keep quiet. 'I don't care,' I whispered. 'I want it.' We bought it and had some glorious times there.

So even though I was back again without JS, it was the happy times I remembered as I walked through the house with my friend. I was surprised at how glad I was to be there, how at home I felt. We opened the place up, put the heating and hot water on (which turned out not to be working) and went out to lunch on the sea front.

I had spent months in terror at the thought of walking through the door, but it was a lovely trip made so much easier by Mac being there for me both on an emotional and physical level (lots of plumbing and electrical stuff had gone wrong/seized up). That night, I had drinks with my neighbours, and we reminisced about the times we all spent together. We had brunch overlooking Ramsgate Harbour. We walked The Hound who loved being back at the coast and dived for stones we threw in the sea. I was amazed at how easy it all seemed to be there, how natural. The weather was spectacularly good; the skies were clear and blue.

It's going to take another visit and a heating engineer to sort out the boiler, but in the meantime, I found the switch to put the immersion heater on so there was hot water. I went into the tiny shower room that we had renovated late last year, the bathroom that JS used (I used the one on the top floor, both of us believing that one of the secrets of a happy marriage is separate basins).

And that is when I saw it.

A bar of white soap in a soap dish, by the side of the sink.

And I just crumpled. The tears came and they wouldn't stop. The house, the pictures, the decorating that we had done together, none of those 'big' things had stabbed me in the heart in the way that I thought they would. But that little bar of soap on the side, just as JS had left it, crucified me. And suddenly it seemed so unfair that here I was in the cottage we had bought ten years ago, but only recently made changes to and JS wasn't there to enjoy it. I sat at the kitchen table and wept. I kept saying how ridiculous it was that a bar of soap should get to me. It felt absurd that an entire furnished house hadn't moved me to tears, but a bar of cheap, white soap had pressed all the grief buttons. Through my tears, I started pointing out the things that we had recently bought: sofas barely sat on; a television hardly watched; a fire which cost more than we intended, but which JS said we should go for because we were going to spend more time in the cottage; carpet barely walked on; a bathroom hardly used when he had spent years freezing to death in the little outside extension. It wasn't the physical things; they were just a symbol of the promise of further good times that never happened. Mac was wonderful. He knows the pain of suddenly losing your spouse, of waking up married and going to bed widowed; he knows that no one can make it better, there is no fast forward button through grief. He sat with me and listened as I wailed and then sometime later when the tears subsided, he poured me a glass of red wine and went out to get fish and chips.

There was another sticky moment as I locked up the cottage to head back to London.

I've thought a lot about those few days in Broadstairs. Perhaps in London, I subconsciously felt that JS was in Broadstairs. When I got to Broadstairs it all felt so normal, it was as if JS was at golf or back in London whilst I was there writing, a not unusual scenario. But then I saw the soap and I knew once and for all he wasn't coming back. He's *never* coming back. Just typing those words has me in tears again. When the front door was locked as we left, I realised that for the first time I had gone there without him *and* left without him and that was how it was always going to be. There could be no more fantasises about waking up from the dream like Bobby Ewing and the shower scene in *Dallas*. This is my life now.

Just before we left for that final, fateful holiday, JS visited one of his businesses in the north of England. When he got back, he looked drained. I remember him sitting on the stairs, still in his coat, playing with The Hound who was doing back-flips with joy at his master coming home. JS said he didn't know whether all the hassle with the company was worth it. Over the years, we had always said that if everything went wrong we could sell the London house and live in the cottage. We used to say that if we had each other and The Hound, we could live anywhere, even in one room as long as it had Sky Sports. I sat beside him, clutched his arm and reminded him of what we had talked about. 'Just give it all up,' I urged. 'Let's sell up and move to the coast, take a breather whilst we decide what to do next.'

'Just two more years,' he said. 'I'm planning on two more years and then we'll be fine.'

We never even got one more week, let alone two more years.

Mentsch tracht, Gott lacht.

You'd think I'd stop making plans, wouldn't you?

Let me take you back to John Green's *Paper Towns*. Seventeen-year-old, straight-laced Quentin is in love with wild-child Margo. This is one of the exchanges between them.

Margo: 'Nothing ever happens like you imagine it will.'

Quentin: 'But then again, if you don't imagine, nothing ever happens at all.'

I'll keep planning, I know I will.

Still, cheap, white soap.

Who would have guessed?

A PIG OF A SEASON

Although I desperately wanted to delay giving them this information until after Christmas, due to circumstances beyond our control I had to tell our three sons that the Christmas coming up in the next two weeks would be the last with their mother. I managed decorations and the usual trimmings apart from presents to each other: mutual presents were considered rather pointless since the one thing we wished for, i.e. her recovery, was not, ever, going to fit into Santa's sack. The one thing that she wanted, a quiet 'normal' Christmas at home, was slightly tarnished and denied because of what we had to tell the children. Sadly, the decorations stayed in the loft last year. I just did not have the motivation. ~ **Chris J**

Almost ten months since JS died, and I'm still constantly wrong-footed by this grief business.

Take Christmas.

Actually, please, someone, *anyone*, take Christmas, I beg you.

I wasn't always like this about the festive season: grouchy, tearful, wanting to strangle every adult in the Morrison's Christmas advert with a string of tinsel, especially the flirty butcher in the boater who says suggestively to Freddie Flintoff, '*And* the British beef.'

Pre you-know-what-you-know-when, I loved Christmas, becoming ridiculously excited when Selfridges opened their Christmas grotto in August. Being somewhat of a control freak (oh, the irony now), by October I had my presents bought and wrapped, menus planned and a list of ingredients to procure.

In mid-December, our house would be decorated. Lots of holly, flowers and foliage; two trees: one enormous real one that had to be sawn up in the front room on Twelfth Night, as, once unfurled from its mesh condom, we could never manoeuvre it out of the front door; and a small artificial one in the kitchen. We put a garland with lights winding up the stairs, lights in the garden, lights on the garage, lights strung around the mirrors, lights on the pot plants. Not quite *Home Alone*, but enough to push EDF Energy's profits up.

Sadly, last Christmas was the worst Christmas and New Year JS and I spent together, because in December I got every bug imaginable, peaking with the winter vomiting bug making a spectacular appearance on Christmas Day. Then, because what was mine was his and vice versa, I generously passed it on to JS. When we took the decorations down in early January, I started sobbing, 'What if this is our last Christmas together, *ever*?' I told JS of my feeling of impending doom. He put my fears down to post-viral slump and told me not to be so silly...

If I was a betting woman instead of someone who once a year gets anxious that I'm wasting a fiver on a £2.50 each way bet on the Grand National, I would have put good money on my going into hysterical orbit at writing Christmas cards without JS's name on them, guaranteeing I would need sedation if I so much as thought of putting up a tree without him. Which is why I had no intention of doing either of those things.

Christmas was cancelled.

But life drags you along in its wake, and I ended up writing cards and putting up a tree. And did either of those things reduce me to floods of tears and a lake of snot?

No, they did not.

What did was the following:

1. Smug round-robin Christmas letters.

2. The stack of cards written and ready to post.
3. Shrink-wrapped cured pig.

Let's start with the Christmas letters and go downhill from there.

I thought that this year I might be spared these self-satisfied, smug missives trumpeting fantastic lives and amazing holidays with perfect, gifted children, who not only got 15 A*s in their GCSEs, but who, if only they didn't have to train for the Olympics/sing in a professional choir/compete in *Junior Masterchef*, would have developed a cure for the common cold in their bedroom.

Oh my god, we've had some corkers in the past. One year, when it was well known that we (along with many of our friends) were having serious financial business issues relating to the recession, a letter dived straight in with: '2008 saw us start the year as we went on – in a fabulous hotel in the Seychelles!'

Another highlight which had JS and me sniggering every time we remembered it, was the letter which discussed in detail a newly purchased washing machine and separate tumble dryer: 'Because with a new kitchen and a large family doing sport at the highest level [see how they smoothly incorporated two subjects], it is important that we have household equipment that is both reliable *and* stylish.'

With the advent of digital cameras and sophisticated computer programmes, these letters have become increasingly elaborate. Now they feature coloured fonts, each photo in a frame, ivy around the border, and even angels in the corner, presumably trumpeting the arrival of the letter rather than the baby Jesus. In the next few years I'm fully expecting a DVD to be included in the card, a mini-movie of the year in review starring Mr & Mrs Smug and the gifted Smuglettes, possibly directed by Martin Scorsese.

When I was a child in the sixties and seventies, my father and mother sat at the table and laboriously wrote the Christmas cards and letters, an event that took days to complete. I know it took days because so as not to disturb the piles of cards in their varying states of signing (thereby incurring the wrath of our mother), we had to eat our meals around them. But nowadays communication is so easy, you would think that Mr Smug or Mrs Smug might be able to add a personal paragraph to a letter to someone who, for argument's sake, lost her husband to drowning whilst on holiday earlier in the year, perhaps cutting out some of the more 'Aren't we a fabulous family!' sections. Even if the fabulously exciting couple can't locate the 'Select' and 'Delete' sequence on their state-of-the art computer, or are too busy being absolutely fabulous to get around to doing it, surely one of their amazingly gifted children could stop swotting up for Cambridge at the age of 13 and help them out by pressing a couple of buttons? But no, those letters have been slipped in the 2011 cards, many of which wish me a 'Magical Christmas!' or even, 'Have A Wonderful Year!'

Now, let me put my non-festive cards on the table and say that I am not the sort of widow who on seeing elderly couples holding hands wants to stick a magnet near their pacemakers because they have each other and I have The Hound and my V+ Box for company. Wistful, yes. Angry, no. I do want people to be happy and I am genuinely interested in the lives of my friends and family; I relish their successes. Some letters are a joy to receive, such as the witty self-depreciating ones my friend Gill P always sends or the chatty round-up from our friends, Bonnie and Eric, whom JS and I met in Bermuda years ago. This year, when the first letter came through oozing with self-congratulatory smugness, I felt sad that I couldn't mock it with JS. Standing alone in my kitchen, there was no one to share my evil fantasy that one day Perfect Child A would run off to the circus with a lad working on the Wall of Death and forget all about 'A' Levels and a Nobel Prize, whilst Perfect Child B was on remand for growing skunk in the school greenhouse. Reading about these oh-so-fabulous families felt isolating, and then I became mad that these people hadn't had an ounce of thought or humility to realise how they must sound to someone in my situation.

So, I did what I always do when I am mad.

Firstly, I cried.

Then I poured a glass of wine.

Finally, I started bashing away on the computer, in this case, composing my own 2011 Christmas letter.

It started pretty well. I wanted to keep it light and upbeat with a touch of self-depreciating humour:

2011 has been a year of change for me, and I don't just mean the menopause...

But fuelled by Merlot and misery, it soon degenerated into sarcasm and bitterness.

Whilst I have had a difficult year, I want to acknowledge that many of you had problems in 2011 too. I remember the email I received from an old friend after JS's funeral, apologising for not being in touch because as she said, her life was currently a nightmare. There was me grieving, and until I got that message, I hadn't grasped just how life-changing it must be to have to deal with a leaking washing machine in one of the properties she and her husband rent out.

Or:

I was touched to receive hundreds of cards after JS died and really appreciated all the kind offers of help and support. Since the funeral (JS would be proud of the enormous bar bill we ran up!) I've only heard from a handful of you, but the thought was there, even if you weren't.

See what I mean?

So, I opted not to send a letter, but I did decide to send cards.

Originally, I was only going to send cards to those people that have been there for me this year.

So, I bought ten.

Then I started going through our address books and in a spirit of two-fingered (victory or otherwise) defiance, I decided to send cards to pretty much everybody, which meant I had to rush out and buy more. I ended up with 79 UK cards, six overseas and eight neighbours. I know these figures, because I had to go back out and buy stamps. Anyway, I signed away, sometimes from me, sometimes from me and The Hound, often putting a few comments in too. I wanted people to know that with or without them and JS, life goes on. And it was OK, it really was. I found I didn't mind signing the cards. I finished them, stamped them and flicked through them.

And that is when I realised something.

Not one of my circle of (pre-accident) friends had lost a spouse suddenly. Not one. Now, of course, I know that the world is full of those who have lost a loved one in tragic circumstances, but sitting on the stairs flicking through those white rectangles, I felt horribly picked on by life. The early emotions of 'Why me?' surfaced for the first time in months. Even during the recent low period I never thought 'Why me?' because I know it's not just me; there are many other widows and widowers out there in considerably more difficult circumstances. But with my previous social circle stamped and in my hands, I felt victimised. How could this have happened to me? To him? To us? That old, stuck record started playing, and I started crying. And then I gave myself a mental slapping, dragged The Hound from his bed and went out and posted them.

The next day I went food shopping.

I was back in defiant two-fingered mood, though this time the fingers weren't aimed at anyone in my address book, they were aimed at the Grim Reaper.

I powered my trolley up the first aisle. At the top, I spotted packets of smoked salmon and blinis. JS and I had a tradition on

Christmas Eve night: smoked salmon on blinis with mock caviar, sour cream and champagne. It was 'our' time, the calm before the storm of Christmas Day. There was a lump in my throat when I saw them, but, still defiant, I decided: Sod it! I'm going to buy them for myself'. I tossed them into the trolley with a flourish.

'This is going to be OK!' I thought. 'I can do this!'

I swung round the next corner to come trolley-to-shelf with a massive display of hams of different sizes: breaded, smoked, honey cured, glazed, studded, browny pink, luminous pink, pale pink; a piece of cured pig for everyone.

Except me.

We always got a big ham at Christmas: we had it in sandwiches, with salad, baked potatoes, chips; fried up with leftover veg or with eggs for breakfast. Those ruddy hams represented relaxed Christmas meals when we had come in from visiting friends, walking The Hound or hitting the sales.

The floodgates opened.

I am very lucky in my life in so many ways, but standing by those hunks of shrink-wrapped pink meat, I didn't feel defiant, I felt desolate.

On a shelf by the Hams of Despair were some Heston Blumenthal pies for one. I bought two. Instead of powering along the aisles with my trolley, I trudged around, using it like a walking frame with wheels. I felt low and slow and defeated. When I got to the checkout and put my things on the conveyor belt, I noticed the woman behind me. She was elderly and hump-backed. In her basket were a couple of meals for one and a small tin of macaroni cheese. When she put them behind my shopping, I noticed her hands were mottled, the skin papery thin, a narrow gold band on her wedding finger. I had more items (and much more booze) than she did, but both of us were clearly shopping for one. Now, in my usual Pollyanna-ish state of mind I could re-frame this situation by thinking, 'At least she is shopping in Waitrose! Things can't be all bad!' But with Ham Head, I just cried. I cried for her, for me, for everyone who had been affected by JS's death, for everyone facing Christmas without someone we love and miss. I also cried for my lost youth. I cried so much I forgot to put my green token in the charity collection: I found it in my coat pocket when I was sitting in my car in the car park sobbing and I fished out a tissue. When I got home and unpacked the shopping, I realised I had bought two packets of blinis, even though this year, there's just me. Old habits are hard to break.

I talked to my bereavement coach, Shelley, about what had happened with the hams and the cards, about how these events had not only ripped the fragile scab off my grief, but also made me feel different to those around me. She reminded me of what I already know, but what I need to hear from time to time: that whatever good things are going on in my life, mourning is part of healing and is healthy. Sobbing over cured pork is part of my healing process, although quite frankly, I'd prefer to sob over something more glamorous, like champagne and diamonds.

Shelley and I talked about making new traditions whilst honouring old ones, or keeping up old traditions but with a new twist.

I drove home and on the spur of the moment and against everything I said, got back in the car, went to the garden centre and bought a small Christmas tree in a pot; I liked the fact that it was living. I bought some new baubles and then at home, opened the trunk where two decades of Christmas decorations are kept, decorations that I had put away whilst sobbing, gripped with fear that JS and I wouldn't have another Christmas together.

I was right.

We didn't.

It was strange to see everything there, but not bad strange, comforting strange. JS and I had so many fun-filled Christmases together, but not putting up a tree, sitting in a bare room, refusing to send cards, mired in denial and becoming bitter over others and their lives isn't going to bring him back. Nothing is *ever* going to bring my husband back, not even a letter to Santa telling him I've been a good girl this year. As lovely Denise, a Geordie Angel I met whilst walking The Hound on Hampstead Heath on a particularly low day wrote on my Facebook page: 'If you're going to be sad, be sad in fairy lit magic.' She's a canny lass that woman, a pragmatic Geordie.

On Thursday night, waiting for my friend, Big Bird, to arrive for the evening, I sat sipping red wine looking at my new tree whilst The Hound lay in front of the fire. Yes, I felt sad and wistful for the days when I sat there next to a towering brightly lit monster, the rest of the house buzzing with life and light and love, but I didn't feel painfully desolate in the way that I thought I would.

The next day, I went back to the garden centre. Amongst all the Peace, Love, and Merry Christmas signs, I chose a new decoration. I hung it near the top of the tree, under the po-faced angel we've had for years, the one that we always made jokes about as we stuck the top of the tree under her skirt.

Holocaust survivor, Viktor E Frankl, wrote in his amazing book, *Man's Search for Meaning*: 'Everything can be taken from a man or a woman but one thing: the last of human freedoms to choose one's attitude in any given set of circumstances.'

The decoration I chose says: *Hope*.

The future terrifies me, the past still haunts me, the thought of the year ending and a new one starting and the countdown to the first-year anniversary and the inquest fills me with anxiety. I am dreading Christmas Day: it will be the first time in 47 years that I will wake up on the 25th December alone in an empty house.

To drag me through, I'll be thinking of my fellow Planet Grief inhabitants. I've had generous invitations from friends to stay with them, but this year, I need to do it alone. There will be a visit to the Crematorium in the morning and then a relaxed lunch with my brother, his partner and their friend, Rob, before I head home for the soaps and *Absolutely Fabulous*.

It won't be a Merry Christmas, but perhaps it can be a hopeful one.

DRAWING THE
SHORT STRAW

I was thirty-one when the accident happened, thirty-three now. Being told by his family a month after the accident that I was still young and had time to move on, meet someone else, fall in love again, have a child was just about more than I could bear and possibly the worst thing that anyone at any point has ever said to me. They were stricken by their own grief of course, but made me feel that my loss should be replaceable whilst theirs wasn't. ~ **Sophie Day**

It's everywhere at this time of year, isn't it? No, not Slade's *Merry Christmas Everybody*, but the phrase: 'Christmas is for the children.'

I have wonderful stepchildren and a huge tribe of much-loved godchildren, but I don't have biological children of my own. At 47, that ship has if not sailed into the sunset, certainly turned its engines on, pulled its anchor up and is heading out of the port leaving me slightly wistful on the quayside, wondering what the daughter I never had might have looked like and what she would be doing. Possibly she'd have dreadlocks, a ring in her nose and be shacked up in a squat writing experimental poetry with a guitar-playing dropout, just to freak me out. Still, I can't help but wonder.

Such an early digression signals trouble ahead, but PLEASE don't stop reading because you have children and I don't and you feel that there is a wall between us.

I've had that before.

Many times.

I'd meet a woman, we'd start chatting, get on well and then she'd ask me how old my children were. The moment I said I didn't have any, The Breeder v The Barren barrier would come down, often initiated by The Breeder. I am perfectly capable of being friends with someone who has sprogged, indeed some of my closest friends have shelled babies like peas from a pod.

Sometimes there would be a look of pity, sometimes curiosity. Once, whilst bobbing about in a warm, turquoise-blue sea, there was downright hostility from a woman with four children, culminating in a remark made with withering judgement, 'I find it sad when women choose a selfish lifestyle over having a family.' To avoid sitting on her head until the bubbles stopped rising, I abandoned my neon noodle and breast-stroked at Ian 'Thorpedo' Thorpe speed back to the beach, where, alone (JS was playing golf or he'd have got my hurt anger with both barrels), I sat tearfully on my sun-lounger having evil thoughts about trying to seduce her husband as revenge.

I've never claimed to be an angel...

So, I'm childless or childfree or however you want to put it. I mentioned in an earlier post that as I teenager, I vowed never to have children, but of course it's not that simple. It's one of life's great ironies that you spend your late teenage years and beyond trying not to get pregnant, at times panicking that you are (oh the agony of peeing on a stick and waiting to see if you got two blue lines), only to find out much later that there's no point in buying anything designed to change colour.

So, it was hardly surprising that the very first post I started on a bereavement site was about children and a rather a self-pitying one at that. So many of the comments were along the lines of: 'I am only keeping going for the children,' or, 'Without the children, I'd end it all,' so the gist of my initial post was: 'What about those of us without children? Without even nieces or nephews? Those of us for whom our family DNA has been discontinued? Who do *we* go on for?'

All my life when things have gone Pete Tong I have tried to think of those in worse situations than me. This is probably because my mother was one of those mothers who would trot out the, 'Finish your food there are starving children in Africa,' routine, or remind me of hundreds of scenarios where I was lucky and others weren't. And for the most part this has been a good way of living; you can't feel aggrieved that you can't afford a conservatory when you remember that there are children in India living on the tops of trains and searching rubbish dumps for bottle tops to sell.

So when I began to hear of widows and widowers battling with their grief alongside their children's pain, the old 'It could be worse' instinct kicked in. On nights when I felt low, I'd read about single parents going to school concerts alone and reflect that at least I could stay in on the sofa with Charlie Sheen on the box and wallow. On mornings when I couldn't face getting up (though I always did or The Hound would complain), I'd remind myself that I didn't have to tackle the school gate swarming with smug, married mums. Posts about coping with ill children in the night had me thankful (whilst I was awake in the small hours) that at least I didn't have to strip off another urine-soaked/vomit-covered sheet. And what of those bereaved whilst pregnant or because their wife had died in childbirth or soon after? I couldn't imagine it. I felt fortunate in so many ways.

But somewhere along the line, counting my blessings was replaced by guilt about grieving and more recently, that compared to so many, I had no right still to be grieving.

On days when I felt I couldn't go on, I'd feel guilty I felt so low when it wasn't as if I had to make the sandwiches and get a child off to school who was asking, when Daddy, or Mummy, was coming home.

When I was so exhausted through lack of sleep the doctor told me I *had* to rest for a couple of hours in the afternoon, I'd feel guilty that I was snoozing on the sofa instead of dragging myself out to pick up children, organise play dates, make meals and so on.

How was it that I, childfree, couldn't cope, when others with far more on their plate than me were battling on? What was wrong with me? I felt I had no right to grieve because whilst I am still relatively young, the facts are that my husband was much older than me, had enjoyed a wonderful life, had two beautiful children, three (newly born) grandchildren, been successful in business and died quickly in a place that can only be described as paradise (though it turned into Hell for me). He was happy and still in love with his wife right up to the moment it all ended. He'd travelled the world, was hugely respected in his career and had a long list of friends and a loving and supportive family. What a life! I wasn't left in penury with young children. JS *did* see his family grow up, he saw them married to partners he was very fond of and he knew his branch of the family tree had extended. His DNA continued. In so many ways, his life could be thought of as shorter than we imagined but complete, even if our marriage, our life together and his influence on his children and their offspring wasn't.

But pushing grief away never works; like trying to control belly flab with power pants, it simply pops up again in another place and is just as uncomfortable. I feel that part of my slump at eight months was to do with all of the above, that I didn't deserve to grieve compared to others whose young families had been ripped apart by death. I was zooming around, powering through grief because I had no right to wallow, no right to feel sorry for myself even for a nanosecond. I had so many great things going for me despite losing JS.

After sleep, food and reflection, I thought I'd put that particular train of thought to bed, stopped judging myself against others, but then a couple of weeks ago I had a dream.

This time, I dreamt that my husband had come back to life, but instead of rushing into my arms crying, 'Darling! I've missed you! Where is Arsenal in the league table?' JS behaved as if I had something nasty on the bottom of my shoe, i.e. he kept his distance, had an odd look on his face and seemed uncomfortable in my presence.

I was confused. This was far from the big reunion I used to fantasise about, said reunion either taking place as he walked through the front door as if nothing had happened, or in some amorphous, cloud-filled area loosely called Heaven, where a man with a flowing white beard and clipboard ushered me through enormous wrought-iron gates and into the greatest party imaginable with an out-of-this-world (literally) guest list.

As I became distressed, JS explained the situation. Far from being dead or dead-then-alive and missing me, he was (gasp!) living with another woman. Not only another woman, but (brace yourself) a widow. He told me her name. I could instantly picture her face and that of her family, because although back in the real world we have never met, she participates in two 'closed' Facebook bereavement groups I contribute to. Despite the fact that she nabbed my husband (in the dream world), seeing how she interacts online with other widows and widowers, I know I would like her. If my dead husband was going to run off with a cyber-woman he couldn't have made a better choice, though I suspect if he was here and I asked him, he'd have chosen a young blonde Page Three model sporting a pair of pneumatic puppies.

'Why her?' I cried. 'Why not me?'

'She needs me,' he said.

'I need you!' I countered.

'You'll be fine,' he retorted. 'She needs me more than you. *She* has children.'

Ah. Children. Clearly, my subconscious mind is still working on that subject.

The other night I was walking The Hound around the streets of Highgate. I could take my time looking through the windows of the posh houses as The Hound cocks his leg at every gatepost he comes across. I saw children in kitchens and living rooms, sparkling Christmas trees, family life, fridge magnets clasping childish pictures to fridge doors, framed family photographs. Sometimes, like that night, it rips me apart, especially when I let myself back in to my empty house. But what if I was widowed with children? I suspect that I would look in on those family scenes and see couples in those brightly lit rooms, a traditional family unit, knowing that when I went home, there would be children, but no spouse, no one to share the trials and tribulations of having children.

On Christmas Day, I will wake up alone in an empty house (except for The Hound). Some widows and widowers will wake up on Christmas Day to a house filled with children, but no partner. In our own ways, we will all feel searingly disconnected from the life we once knew.

Widowed but childless, widowed with children at home, widowed with your children grown up: we've all drawn the short straw.

DONE AND DUSTED

*Last Christmas day was the three-month anniversary. With a four-year-old who had already lost a lot, I ploughed on regardless. I put the tree up, I wrote the cards (not sure I remembered to post them or not!), I cooked Christmas dinner for all the family (well not ALL the family), negotiated the empty seat at the dinner table dilemma, had my first glass of champagne at 10, then didn't trust myself to hold it together until everyone had gone, so stopped then. When everyone finally left, I wailed, but I did survive it all. One of my very dear friends, who has been amazing since 'the day', bought me a present even though we don't usually as she wanted me to 'have something nice to open,' so in the bag there were a few small girly things and a small pebble with the word 'Hope' written on it. It made me well up. The pebble is still on the shrine/hall table. I think of it often. ~ **Tracey***

So, after dreading Christmas for months, it was nothing like I predicted, i.e. constant wailing, a desire to hurl sprouts at anyone who wished me 'Merry Christmas' and having to be physically restrained from trashing the nativity scene outside the local church. No, on balance and given the circumstances, I actually had quite a reasonable Christmas, and I feel slightly guilty admitting it, although I should point out that this Christmas wasn't like getting three purple Quality Street in a row when you dip your hand into the tin, i.e. too good to be true. Admittedly, I didn't gnaw my own hands off with grief, or get smashed on Widows Cocktails (a mix of everything in the drinks cupboard, including liqueurs that should have stayed in the Duty Free shop on that Greek Island 15 years ago, all watered down with salty tears), but I was *very* glad when it was all over.

Post-lunch (two slices of toast and peanut butter) on Christmas Eve saw me sobbing for England, St George and any other European country David Cameron hasn't alienated yet. Tears and tantrums were pretty much the form for the rest of Christmas Eve. Tears wrapping up presents, tears listening to the carols from Kings College, Cambridge, tears on the phone to friends and family. The entire world seemed to be preparing for a fun, loved-up family Christmas.

Except me.

Yeah, yeah, I know that all over the country there were couples in kitchens hissing at each other over in-laws who were *already* doing their head in, even though said relations had only just arrived, but still, it hurt. *They* were couples in kitchens. Me and The Hound standing waiting for the toaster to pop up, doesn't count as a couple.

Instead of my usual Christmas Eve spread of champagne and smoked salmon blinis whilst wearing something nice, I ordered a takeaway from the local curry house. Already in my nightclothes, I rang them at 6:25pm as they quote at least an hour for delivery.

A man on a moped turned up at 6:45pm.

Clearly, I was the only saddo in my area of north London who was ordering a curry for one on Christmas Eve, something which added to my sense of isolation as I watched a programme I'd recorded about a man in Surrey who was an obsessive-compulsive hoarder. He slept, worked and ate in the same chair surrounded by newspapers and said he went downhill after his mother died six years ago. Ramming poppadums and garlic naan in my mouth, sluttishly ignoring the crumbs and curry dropping on my nightwear and reflecting that most days I eat all my meals (such as they are) sitting at my desk in the study, I knew the feeling of going downhill, even if I stick my newspapers in the recycling bin rather than up against a window.

I expected to wake up on Christmas morning wanting to tie a string of tinsel around my neck and sky-dive over the banisters, but I didn't because, firstly, I couldn't leave The Hound to fend for himself, not on Christmas Day and, secondly, our banisters are not very high. Knowing my luck, instead of sudden death resulting in me hammering on the gates of Heaven demanding to see JS to wish him 'Happy Christmas,' I'd probably end up in a hospital bed with a broken neck and unable to wipe my own butt.

I woke up early and dry-eyed and thought, 'How weird that this is Christmas Day.' I felt *totally* disconnected from *everyone* and *everything*; it could have been any day.

I got up and (more slutty confessions) threw yesterday's clothes on and, without even washing or flashing a toothbrush over my gnashers (I have no proof, but I believe the dead don't care about parrot-cage breath), chucked The Hound in the little Fiat and drove to the crematorium. JS's ashes are still there. I know where I want to scatter his ashes, but there are logistical problems as important family members live on the other side of the world, so, at the moment, my husband is still on a shelf.

As I drove through Finchley, an ambulance came up behind me at speed, sirens wailing, lights flashing. I pulled over. It brought back memories and brought on tears as I thought of the terrifying high-speed, blue-light dash we had in Barbados, a journey where we were all thrown around so badly, I ended up terribly bruised. With my back to the driver and in The Bikini of Death, I hauled my husband back on to the trolley whilst the paramedic carried on the CPR. To think, I'm such a poor traveller I used to have to take travel sickness tablets when we drove to Kent. I *was* sick after that ambulance journey, but it wasn't the drive that had me retching on the grass verge in the blazing sunshine. That happened after I walked out of the hospital and every morning for months afterwards.

As I sat on the side of the road, I wondered who was waiting for that ambulance to arrive, whose Christmas morning was ruined, whether it would be more than just one day that was in tatters.

At the crem, I found I wasn't alone. Dotted around the vast site, visitors were tying wreaths to a fence, laying flowers and cards, sitting on benches, reflecting. I got out of the car and with The Hound, began to walk around, crying, whilst trying to stop him cocking his leg against gravestones (no respect these young dogs). No one wished each other 'Merry Christmas', but we nodded, a nod of grief and understanding. A man who looked in his late sixties had set up a table groaning with flowers. He had a vase with foam in it and was cutting the stems off flowers, making an elaborate arrangement. A taxi driver arrived in a smart suit and took a bouquet of flowers to a grave. Families arrived en masse; toddlers holding balloons tottered between gravestones, laughing. Balloons were tied to rose trees, to benches, to tiny memorial plaques.

I had taken a pink flower with me intending to put it on the memorial to the Tauber family. Obviously, being Jewish and not celebrating Christmas, the Taubers hid from my festive flower, as despite walking and driving around for ages, I couldn't find their stone. I put the flower I'd brought at the door of the Chapel, as near to the office where JS sits on a shelf with other departed souls as I could find.

Back in the car, I wailed, I upset The Hound, I read a touching and timely message on my phone from Lynsey, a widow in Kent who had been thinking of me, and then I drove home, had breakfast, took The Hound on the Heath for a long walk and drove a few miles to my family for lunch. There were four of us. I had a good time, a really good time with people I love. There was great food, lively conversation and lots of silliness.

I was home by five. To avoid the delivery charge (never an issue when I was married and ordering for two), I over-ordered the Christmas Eve takeaway and ate the leftovers (curried chickpeas) in my dressing gown on Christmas night. I didn't laugh at *Ab Fab*. I wondered if my sense of humour had deserted me once and for all, but Big Bird (a woman with a first-class sense of humour) told me she didn't laugh once either, so it was the show, not my grief, that had me granite-faced on the sofa. Late in the evening, I sorted out the charger drawer, working out which bundle of wires went with which electronic device, labelling them all with my labelling machine.

Like I say, I had a good first Christmas Day without JS, but I was relieved it was over.

On Boxing Day, a last-minute decision to visit a widower and his family in Hertfordshire turned into a lovely day with dog-walking, lunch and lots of laughter. But back in London that night I was restless again, desperate to escape the black cloud chasing me. I've spent the days since searching the internet, looking at places I could move to as far apart as Northumberland and Kent. I learnt that Karen's husband has had a baby with his new partner. Karen would have loved a child: she had two miscarriages before she died. She would have been thrilled for her husband. So was I, but I still wept buckets for what might have been.

So Christmas 2011 was not as I expected – either a year ago or a week ago. Life continues to surprise me and drag me along at a rate I sometimes feel unprepared for.

On the 27th of December it was ten months on from the day that I hauled my husband's body back on to the trolley in that ambulance, sometimes screaming at the driver, begging him to get us to the hospital, sometimes chanting, 'What will be will be.' Christmas will never be the same again, I know that, and yes, it makes me sad, but perhaps different can be good after all.

DIARYMANIA

I can't help but feel that I should have known what was happening, that our love was so strong that I would have had some sort of feeling that he was in danger. ~ **Emma A**

For me, a new year doesn't mean getting squiffy, singing Auld Lang Syne and kissing a policeman in Trafalgar Square, although in my youth, I've done all those things. No, for a long time now, New Year has always been about the thrill of a new diary.

Since I was a little girl, I've loved diaries: keeping one, buying one, filling in the details at the start of a year. They've been incredibly useful items in my life and not just for making sure that I got to the dentist at two-thirty on a Thursday afternoon, kept a track of my periods or marked significant 'romantic days' denoted by a blizzard of asterisks and exclamation marks, something which years later left me wondering who and what it was that deserved such a row of *****!!!! Diaries have helped me get things into perspective by writing reams of angst, let my mother know I knew all about where babies came from and made me realise that she snooped on my diary because she *knew* I knew where babies came from. Decades later, my teenage diaries provided rich material for my books and my adult ones proved useful in a court case.

Despite this diary love-in, I have only ever exhibited 'vanilla' monogamous behaviour when it comes to dated pages, i.e. committing myself to one at the start of the year and sticking faithfully to it until the year did us part. But when JS died, I was afflicted by a dreadful bout of Diarymania: in 2011 I used FIVE diaries.

This diary-addiction wasn't because grief had mucked up my brain to the point where I had some sort of weird calendar fetish that saw me rolling around on John Lewis non-iron polycotton bedding in my Snoopy nightshirt whilst fingering Lett's mock leather covers. It came about because I couldn't bear to look at the diary I started at the beginning of 2011. My world was shattered, but there, marked in the pages, was the life I intended to lead, *expected* to lead: holidays planned, weekends away, social engagements, work commitments, not to mention birthdays, anniversaries and football fixtures.

I found the burgundy-covered diary so painful, I dumped it in the back of the basket I stick all my paperwork in, but with so many businesses to sort out, meetings to attend and people to see, I still needed a diary.

I bought a Moleskin one. I hated that diary, hated the blank pages devoid of life or fun, but punctuated with trips to the undertakers, the lawyers and so on. Moleskin lasted about two weeks before I turned it into a Gratitude Diary, another phase which didn't last long as I had very little to feel grateful for. To cheer myself up, I bought a tiny pink Filofax, but it felt cramped. I know it sounds bizarre to say a diary felt claustrophobic, but it did. My diary had shrunk along with my life.

I dug out my old 1980s Filofax and bought new inserts. How I loved that Filofax in the eighties; I felt like a character who worked for Gordon Gekko in the film *Wall Street*, though in reality I was more Del Boy. But in grief-stricken 2011, that once-flash diary didn't seem right. I dumped diary number four.

I was now becoming diary-desperate. I bought yet *more* Filofax inserts, this time for my ancient, A5, mock-croc, work Filofax, a weighty tome to lug around. It was the fifth diary of the year, and, thankfully, I stopped there.

As 2012 loomed, yet again I treated myself to a new diary. I bought the type of diary I have used for years: slim, pleather cover, page to a week. Back at home, I despised the fact that it was the same as all the other years, just a different colour. I chucked the latest Letts and treated myself to a slimline Filofax in soft brown leather. It's lovely, but of course the pages are blank.

Traditionally, I used to fill in my diary on New Year's Eve with two sorts of information: firstly, the usual anniversaries and, secondly, my New Year's resolutions.

Even though I can be shockingly melancholic at times, all my life I have started a new year with great gusto and optimism, looking forward to a fresh start, wiping the slate of the previous year clean and throwing myself at life. Crucial to this process was making a list of New Year's Resolutions. They never lasted. Usually by 14th January I was fed up of the dark nights and the bad weather, but mostly disappointed with myself that after only two weeks I'd broken all my resolutions and turned back into the creature riddled with faults I was the year before.

Let me give you an example: these are the resolutions I wrote in the front of my diary when I was 14:

New Year Resolutions (no order)
1. I must work hard at school.
2. I must not think about health.
3. I must not be so quick. (My mother was forever telling me I did everything too quickly: ate, spoke, walked.)
4. I must smile more often.
5. I must stick to the same style of handwriting.
6. I must be more glamerous [sic] *and take more care over my appearance (to attract boys!!).*
7. Have more self confidence and not let other people run me down, but where boys are concerned play hard to get!!

8. Save money, earn money and spend it wisely.
9. Be tidier and more organised.

Clearly, most of these resolutions didn't work, as at 17 I was still writing the same old tosh:

1. I must work hard and get my head down and swot.
2. I must be more glamourus [sic, but getting closer].
3. I must have more self confidence.
4. I must be more sophisticated.

Under number four I have helpfully written the following tips:

Sophistication – how to get it
Walk slowly everywhere
Don't fidget
Smoke
Carry a small dog
If bored yawn slightly and look into the distance
Don't blow your nose in public

For anyone reading my tips for instant sophistication, please note that they didn't work at 17 and wouldn't work at 47. However, there is some progress on the glamour front: I am still not glamorous, but at least I now know how to spell it.

My resolutions were always a case of optimism over experience, but just the thought that in 12 months I might turn from an ungainly caterpillar into a beautiful butterfly with poise, tidy cupboards and qualifications was very uplifting.

But I digress (perhaps that should be a resolution – no digressing – I'd fail at just past midnight).

I didn't get to fill in my spiffy new Filofax on New Year's Eve, because I spent a lovely evening in Hertfordshire with a widower and his family, but on New Year's Day, I flipped open the pages which is when I realised something: in order to fill in important and recurring dates, I was going to have to look back at the diary I started at the beginning of 2011. During the terrible days of last year, I was excused not remembering the wedding anniversary of school friends or the date of birth of yet another child and didn't need to look at the old diary, but we are now in 2012. I do want life to go on, and I do want to mark the dates I used to.

I opened the original and first diary of 2011 and felt incredibly sad. The run up to JS's death was filled with the minutiae of my old life: *1:30pm Jade Nails*; *JS to Crewe office*; *7:30 Dinner Mick & Kath*; *2pm Hair, Roger*; *4pm Jennie's tea*.

Then there were the diary entries for our holiday. We knew the restaurants we liked to go to in Barbados, so I'd booked some of them before we left: *25th 8pm The Fish Pot*; *8pm 26th The Lone Star*; *27th Midday Atlantis for Brunch*.

We never got to the Atlantis Hotel for our Sunday brunch. My husband was dead by midday.

The day before JS drowned I was in a gift shop fretting over what colour flip-flops to buy. JS wanted to go and look at the books, but I wanted his opinion on whether to buy gold or silver flip-flops. I stood next to the rack of rubber footwear and took him through my wardrobe: 'The silver would go with the white beach dress, but so would the gold. I've already got some gold ones, but they give me blisters.' How ridiculously trivial this seems now, what a waste of time in our precious last 24 hours together. Megan, whose partner drowned, wrote on my blog that none of us had any idea of what was barrelling towards us. That image has always stuck with me; it makes me weep – the thought that I was doing ordinary things whilst this terrible life-ending and life-changing event was hurtling towards me, to us, to our marriage, to our family. Looking back at that 2011 diary, I was gripped by a feeling of panic that JS's death was heading my way, but there was nothing I could do about it. We had booked a waterside table at The Cliff on the 1st of March. It was there in the diary, so how could it not have happened? We were due to go to Northumberland the weekend after we got back from holiday. Surely, it was set in stone because it was in the diary, in ink, not even in pencil? Pencil meant the entry was only tentative, subject to change.

This year is the first year I can ever remember that I haven't made any New Year Resolutions. Instead, I am going to set goals. I don't need the start of a year to set myself goals; I can and I will set goals throughout the year, but there is one goal that I set myself on the 1st of January and which I am determined to face soon.

It's now ten months since the accident. Both our suitcases are still packed, still standing with their luggage labels intact. I'm not going to unpack JS's suitcase – what would I do with his clothes? – but I'm starting to feel that I need to unpack mine, the green one. I don't have a big enough house to hide the cases away, and we have no loft, so I see them daily. They are constant reminders of not just of a holiday interrupted by death, but a life forever altered by it too.

FACEBOOK, FRIEND OR FOE

*Within a few days of being widowed, whilst at the Church Office booking Malc's funeral, a woman I know, widowed some time ago, came into the office. After a brief discussion with her, she informed me that, 'It never gets any better'. Her words filled me with utter despair and panic. I was already half-mad with grief and drugged up because I wasn't coping, so the thought that this was how it was going to be for me for the rest of my days was more than I could bear. Twelve months later, I realised that this foolish woman and her words were wrong. Yes, it was still awful, but there were now better days, sometimes, and even laughs and things to 'look forward' to, things that would bring me quiet pleasures. I was getting stronger, and some days were definitely getting better. ~ **Angela***

I've been in hiding from my fellow widows on the internet and Facebook, not because I'm tired (which I am), or ill (which I have been), or lazy (OK, maybe a bit), but because (imagine Carrie Bradshaw at the beginning of *Sex and the City* at her laptop, but minus the blonde locks and little strappy top) I can't help but wonder:

Is Facebook Hampering My Healing?

At 11 months, sometimes I wake up without the crushing blow of grief pressing on my skinny frame. Since the dark days of Christmas, I've felt reasonably OK and (gasp!) hopeful about the future. This is an amazing statement for me to make, because even before JS died I was allergic to mornings. Coming round from my nightly coma, I'd fester between the sheets groaning that I felt too [insert pathetically weedy excuse such as tired/ill/spotty] to go to the meeting, give the presentation or throw the party. My long-suffering husband bearing a cup of tea would remind me that once I had taken a dose of PG Tips, stuck my bod under the shower and put some slap on, I'd be ready to take on the world, or, at least, a class of teenage girls keen to become writers.

But back then, before the Grim Reaper gatecrashed our holiday, I didn't look at Facebook almost as soon as I regained consciousness. Now I do, and sometimes I'll read a post along the lines of: 'My life is sh*t.'

I'm a bit slow in the morning and need to be reminded of things, but I'd like to be reminded of nice things such as puppies and how lovely roses smell, or the fact that I have a lunch date with a friend, not how terrible life can be. And feeling sorry for myself (not just because my husband has died, but because these days I have to make my own cuppa) I'd think, 'Life *can* be sh*t, can't it?' before my neurones sparked all over the place sending my thoughts to dark places: 'My husband drowned! On holiday! In front of me! That's sh*ttier than just mere sh*t. That's traveller's sh*t, and everyone knows getting the raging squits away from home is the worst sort of sh*t EVER!' So sh*t would be my mood for the rest of the day.

And even if my brain didn't go into 'Oh woe is me, for I am widow,' meltdown, I'd read the posts of others and feel pain at *their* pain and it would drag me down, pouring cold water on what tiny flames of hopeful energy I possessed.

Recently, there was a long and active thread of pictures on a Facebook bereavement site: wedding shots full of hope, couples in love, families intact. I stared at those photos with deep sadness. When husbands and wives and children and lovers smiled for the camera, they had no idea what was about to happen, that their lives together would be blown to smithereens. In photos of young children, it's often the innocence in the child's face that touches the viewer. Even though these photos were of adults, it was their innocence of what lay ahead that ripped me apart.

I wept buckets over my keyboard. Eventually, I had to stop looking.

When new people join these bereavement groups and I read about their struggles, their tears, their bleakness and their fears, I can hardly bear it. Perhaps it's just a stage I'm at. Perhaps it's the run up to the first anniversary of JS's death at the end of the month. There are widows and widowers further down the line than me who post encouraging words and have given me hope for the future and support for the present. I'd like to do the same for those coming up behind me, but, strangely, I felt more able to offer support in the early days of grief than I do now. I also have Facebook Fear, fear that during one of my fragile moods I will read a post by someone who is, say, two years down the line, reporting that they have found the second year harder (how *can* it be harder? If it is, I will surely break), or have become depressed (I had a bout of severe depression 11 years ago – what if it comes back?) or ill (who would look after The Hound if I was whisked into hospital in the night?).

In the past, I'd see posts from widows who would dramatically (so I thought) announce that they were leaving a grief group to 'move forward'. I'd turn my nose up at these statements and wonder why they had to leave the group, why they couldn't just ignore the posts and dip in and out when they wanted. Attention seekers! Now, I understand. The temptation to just pop in to see what is happening is overwhelming and then: BANG! You're immersed in the lives and grief of others when you're still processing your own.

Although I'm currently feeling somewhat ambivalent towards Facebook, I acknowledge that the internet has been a lifeline to me, there for me during bleak days and sleepless nights.

For months after JS died, much of my life obsessively revolved around message boards: reading, posting and contacting other widows. Not all these widows were purely cyber friends: I met and spoke to some of them in real life. They are fabulous and resilient human specimens, determined despite tragic circumstances not to become a Professional Widow.

I live near a PW. I knew her before JS died. Bereaved with two young children, she blames everything that goes wrong on her spouse's death, telling anyone and everyone at every opportunity how hard her life has been, wearing her loss like a badge of honour. After JS died, she told me horror stories of how my life would be as a widow (damaged, bleak, merely existing). She scared the sh*t out of me. Before you want to slap me around the chops with a wet kipper for mocking a widow, I should point out that this particular woman lost her husband more than 30 years ago, but if you were to bump into her in a shop or on the street, you'd think she had recently been bereaved, such is the torrent of widow's woe which pours from her.

In the last 11 months, I've done a lifetime's worth of weeping and wailing and stomping my feet and shouting, 'Why me?' I'm still doing it, though not every waking hour of every day as I did for most of last year. Only the other morning, I was walking The Hound round the park, mulling stuff over and out of nowhere I slapped a wooden bench in anger, which was daft because I hurt my hand. But I don't want to be forever telling someone I meet for the first time and in graphic detail how my husband died. OK, I've done it to excess this past year or so, but I'll be damned if I'm going to be doing it years from now.

In the early days after JS died, another widow of some years sent me some very kind, supportive and viciously funny emails. In one of those early emails she wrote that whilst loss is forever, grief is finite, that if grief is dealt with it doesn't *have* to last, it *can* be expunged and life can be good again.

I didn't believe her.

At the point she wrote those words I was still playing Kamikaze Pedestrian, walking out into the traffic without looking, hoping for a direct hit from one of the enormous gas guzzlers that populate north London, in the hopes that this was a one-way ticket to see JS. As I've mentioned before, I only managed to annoy cyclists, which is ironic because usually I'm a model member of The Tufty Club, waiting patiently at the zebra crossing at the top of the road, often ending up remonstrating with some idiot on a mobile phone driving a tank who fails to see me and takes the corner too fast.

But I digress.

Back then, a life without JS seemed impossible: a grey stretch of existence without any respite from pain. But whilst I am still a long way from totally expunging my grief, as I anxiously approach the year mark, I believe that life *can* be good again, if only at first in short bursts. I also believe that at some point you can make a decision to live again, to say: I can't have my old life back; there is no point in longing for something I will never have, my husband is *never* coming back to life. My marriage vows were until death us do part and I honoured them, but JS is dead and I'm alive, and I have to keep living and make it the most fulfilling life I can.

It's a simple strategy.

Simple doesn't mean easy.

I desperately want to move forward and leave grief (not JS) behind. Sometimes I long to be normal and to me, normal isn't writing or reading about grief. The problem is that even if I did leave Facebook, close the blog, refuse to see anyone who reminds me of what has happened and start running around London in a short skirt with a smile plastered across my face, I suspect this ruddy widowhood business would follow me around like a flatulent Labrador.

Recently I went to a smart party.

There were well over a hundred guests there and I knew only two people, but that was fine because there was champagne, and I don't mind mingling with people I don't know. Also, as I was anonymous, I could be me, not a widow. The idea of normality if only for a few hours was exciting.

At the party, I pushed my way through the crowd, saw one of the people I knew and went over. After double air-kissing, the opening conversation went something like this:

Friend: 'You made it! How wonderful! I wasn't sure if you would be up to it.'

Me: 'I'm fine.'

Friend: 'You look fabulous. Still thin, but fabulous. Are you sure you're OK? I'm sure parties must be an ordeal for you.'

Me: 'I'm OK, honestly. I can just slip out if it gets too much.'

Random Guest to me: 'Have you been ill?'

Me: 'Er… no.' Takes huge gulp of champagne.

Friend: 'Helen's husband died a few months ago.' (Said in grave, explaining tone.)

Random Guest: 'Oh! God! How dreadful! I'm *so* sorry. You're amazingly strong to come to something like this. Isn't she?'

Murmurs and nods from the assembled group.

Me, hoping that the ground will swallow me up before I burp from gulping bubbly too quickly: 'Um…'

Random Guest 2: 'Was it cancer? I know *so* many people who've had cancer.'

More nods, mutterings and glances.

Me: 'Er… no.'

By now, there's a group of people standing around waiting for more details. I wanted to laugh and drink champagne, not be reminded of my new marital status. I'm fed up and irritated. I tell them what happened in short sharp bursts.

'He drowned. On holiday. In front of me.'

And then I see their horrified embarrassed faces and wish I hadn't been quite so brutal.

I gulp more champagne, the group disperses and then a little while later someone comes up to me, touches me on the arm and says, 'I've just been told about what happened. I'm so sorry for your loss.'

And it happens again, and again. They mean well, but I don't want to be the guest whose husband drowned. I want to be the slightly silly, occasionally shallow woman I was before. The weight of widowhood makes me feel weary.

I'm the first to extract my coat and leave. In the back of the cab I feel angry and tearful that for a few hours I can't just be 'normal'.

I guess the moral of the story is, when it comes to grief and widowhood, you can run, but you can't hide.

HE'S ELECTRIC

*When I was at that awful paperwork stage, phoning call centres and transferring names from two names to one, I had to sometimes guess a password and usually got it right – the name of our previous Labrador. I like to think G and our dog met again at Rainbow Bridge. Childish, I know, but it gave me comfort. ~ **Denise***

I'm pretty good at celebrity spotting. Almost every day when I'm grubbing about in the street picking up steaming dog poo (The Hound's poo obviously; I'm not so public spirited as to scoop-the-poop of random mutts) I'll see someone famous – Kate Moss, Geri Halliwell, Alastair Campbell. I love Alastair when he's powering towards me in his running gear, breathing like Darth Vader with a fifty-a-day fag habit. I always hope he'll stop, wipe the sweat out of his eyes and pant, 'Ever since I saw you that day in Carphone Warehouse I've found you *fascinating*,' and then we'll start a conversation where I'll ask him how he managed to cope with depression and anxiety spin-doctoring for a Government during turbulent times, whereas I can't even cope with standing in a queue at Waitrose. To be fair, I doubt he even sees me as I'm bent double scooping the poop. If he notices me at all, he probably thinks I'm bowing as he thunders past.

My celebrity-spotting talents are good, but mainly because I live in a part of London stuffed with them. Finding a celebrity on my doorstep is like shooting fish in a barrel, not that I ever want to dump a whole load of fish in my water butt, borrow an air rifle and see whether it's quicker to kill a brown trout or find Geri Halliwell jogging along Hampstead Lane.

The real pro when it comes to celebrity spotting is my friend Big Bird, a woman whose two regrets in life are that she didn't make the most of her natural assets and talents when she was young, namely becoming a Page Three model and getting a job with *heat* magazine.

Big Bird would have been brilliant at both, but now, at fifty, she's modelling bras for the 'fuller bust' and her celeb spotting is confined to whispering to me, 'See that man in the corner? It's Sean Penn!' It wouldn't be that I hadn't noticed the man in the corner, but rather that I'd marked down the small man slouched on a seat in the restaurant as a regular London tourist, rather than an international film star once married to Madonna.

So, whilst I'm not at the professional level of Big Bird in spotting a celebrity, I am considerably better than my late husband who, quite frankly, was rubbish. This isn't speaking ill of the dead, it's a fact, but one that he would vehemently deny.

JS suffered from Celebrity Spotting Dysmorphia; in other words, his view of his ability to spot a star was completely at odds with the reality. Unless it was totally obvious he was in the presence of someone famous (standing next to Sean Connery in the toilets for instance, in which case JS said it was the voice that gave it away) he either got celebs mixed up or didn't recognise them at all. I gave up whispering to him, 'Don't look now, that's Annie Lennox,' because JS would say in a loud voice, 'Where? Annie Lennox? No, it can't be. That woman's *much* too old.'

The problem with living in London and in an area full of A-listers, was that if I wasn't there to verify a star spot, it was sometimes difficult to know whether someone JS had labelled as a 'celebrity' was indeed a star of stage and screen, or just an ordinary Joe buying some Hovis and a lottery ticket.

JS reporting back that, 'I've just seen Gwyneth Paltrow in M&S in Muswell Hill,' could indeed mean Gwynnie was out and about in

N10, or it could mean that JS had seen a glossy willowy blonde and *thought* it was Gwyneth. Had I been there, I would have not only have been able to verify whether it was Miss Paltrow by her face, but by the contents of her trolley: organic, wheat-free and fat-free – possibly. Packets of Percy Pigs – unlikely.

Not long after we got The Hound, I fell ill. I don't think it was anything serious or I would have remembered, but there was a period of a few of weeks when I didn't feel up to getting out of bed at the crack of dawn to traipse across Hampstead Heath with The Hound, so JS did.

Every day he'd come back, and I would cross-examine him from my sick bed: Had The Hound run off? Had JS met anyone he knew? Had The Hound played with any cute dogs? How many poos had The Hound done and what was their consistency?

One day amongst this question-and-answer session, JS mentioned that he'd met a nice couple with their dachshund.

Any mention of a dachshund merited further interrogation, but disappointingly, 'a nice couple with a dachshund' was the extent of the information I could extract.

A few days later, JS reported that he had again met the 'nice couple with the dachshund', and I gleaned a few more details. Their dachshund was female, but the man really wanted another dachshund, this time a male. He'd played with The Hound and, according to JS, had been quite taken with him.

I can't remember how many of these meetings with the 'nice couple with the dachshund' JS had, other than I would ask him on his return whether he had seen them, and sometimes he would say, 'Yes,' and sometimes he would say, 'No,' but that was about the extent of it.

And then I got better and I started to walk The Hound again, sometimes with JS and sometimes alone.

One day, as we were crossing a field near Kenwood House, a woman waved at us. JS waved back. The Hound galloped towards them.

'Do you know them?' I asked, as we wandered in their direction.

'It's that nice couple with the dachshund I told you about,' JS explained.

I stood there as JS chatted to his new friends. JS stroked their dachshund. The man stroked ours. Everyone said how much they liked each other's dogs.

JS said he hadn't seen them about recently.

They'd been in Ireland, they said. JS enquired as to whether they had taken their dachsie. They had.

'Did you take the car ferry?' JS asked.

'We flew,' came the reply.

'They allow dogs on the plane?' JS was surprised. 'What airline did you fly with?'

'We made special arrangements,' explained the man.

Discussing pet transportation methods over, we said goodbye, retrieved our dogs and went our separate ways.

'Do you know who they are?' I hissed when we were out of earshot. 'Have you any idea who you were talking to?'

'Yes,' JS said. 'That was the couple I told you about. The nice couple with the dachshund. He really loves Boris, doesn't he?'

My husband had been completely unaware that he had been discussing sausage dogs with rock wild man and Oasis front man, Liam Gallagher, and his then wife, Nicole 'All Saints' Appleton.

And yes, they really were a nice couple, and they had a dachshund.

THE RING THING

I have taken my wedding ring off – one day a few weeks ago it felt like the right thing to do. I am no longer married, and I felt that I wasn't, and I'm not. I wear my engagement ring on and off, sometimes on my left hand, sometimes on my right, but while I automatically used to put it on every morning, without fail, it is surprising how quickly the habit has been lost. The days I put it on I do so because I want people to know that I was loved, I had found a wonderful man who loved me, and chose me, and would have done anything for me; I used to be someone's special person. I will probably get it re-sized and wear it on my right hand, as it is a beautiful ring. What happens if I meet someone else? Do I get a new one? This weekend I went and bought a new carpet. I took my mum, and the carpet man assumed that I was a 'Miss'. I didn't correct him, but it made me sad. ~ **Linz**

Twenty-five years ago, I chaperoned an American woman around an international trade show. She worked for one of our biggest New York-based clients and my role was to show her what a fantastic job we had done licensing bubble bath in the shape of a black and white beagle.

Bored of pressing the flesh of manufacturers, she asked to visit one of the jewellery halls. Our business involved fake fur and plastic rather than diamonds, but who was I to argue with a client?

As I trailed after her, this woman drooled over the brightly lit displays of sparkling engagement rings, pointing out what sort of finger-bling she was going to choose when she got engaged. I can't remember her precise requirements, but it was a bit like being in a restaurant when someone orders Off Menu. You know the sort of thing: 'I'll have the bacon and blue cheese burger with fries, but with Monterey Jack cheese instead of blue cheese, and no fries, just salad, but if the bun has sesame seeds on it, I won't have the bun, but then I *will* have the fries as long as they're cooked in vegetable oil. Oh, and no bacon. I'm Jewish.'

That happened to me once in a restaurant in Frankfurt with (again) an American client. I thought that the stern, German waiter was going to boot us out. I expect that the chef gobbed on our food as revenge.

But I digress.

At some point in this 'I want an emerald-cut, one-carat diamond with yellow baguette diamond shoulders in a platinum rub over setting' speech, I asked the woman what her boyfriend did for a living.

She confessed she didn't yet have a boyfriend.

She knew what engagement ring she wanted, even what style of dress would suit her (and probably whether to have chicken or fish at the reception). The only uncertainty in all these plans was who was going to be her husband. Eventually she walked up the aisle in her dream dress wearing her dream ring. Unfortunately, it wasn't with her dream guy. A few years later, they divorced.

This bride-in-waiting attitude was totally alien to me. I was never going to get married or wear a wedding ring. To me, a wedding and engagement ring was a sign of being owned, an old-fashioned symbol of an outdated institution tantamount to having 'Taken' tattooed across my forehead.

Back in the days when I had a waist and no wrinkles, I was young, foolish and stroppy, but when I changed my mind about marriage and found myself outside a jewellers in London's Hatton Garden with JS, I knew exactly what sort of ring what I wanted: a modern design which looked nothing like a traditional engagement ring.

I walked out with the same style of ring as my grandmother and mother wore, a diamond solitaire, possibly the most traditional and engagement-like ring you could choose.

I've never pretended that my mind works in a rational way.

So there I was, married with rings. I know women who say that their ring has never been off their finger since their wedding day, but because of bouts of contact dermatitis, my nuptial bling has been on and off like a new bride's nightie. At the first itch I'd remove all my rings (I wear two on my right hand as well) and holding them with the bacon tongs, JS would clean them by blasting them under the steam nozzle of the cappuccino machine and scrub them with an old toothbrush. I'd leave my hands naked for a week or so until everything calmed down and when it did, I'd pop them back on.

Sometimes I enjoyed the feeling of a naked ring finger. Sometimes I would look at my hand and waggle my fingers and feel a heady sense of freedom. However much I loved JS, that old fear of entrapment was never far away. I kept my maiden name, we didn't have a joint bank account and even at the funeral some mourners didn't realise JS and I were married until I was referred to as his wife. With one dead wife and one divorced wife, I used to joke that becoming Mrs John Sinfield was unlucky.

Now there is a widowed wife.

Me.

Hat trick.

When JS died, my relaxed attitude to my wedding rings was turned on its head and I began to exhibit some bizarre ring-related behaviour.

At some point in the first few months on Planet Grief, standing at a bus stop or in a shop queue, I became obsessed with looking at the wedding ring finger of other women. If the woman was pretty and not wearing a wedding ring, I'd wonder what was wrong with her to still be single. If she was overweight and unkempt and ring-less I'd think, 'No wonder she isn't married!' If she was overweight and unkempt and had a wedding ring, I'd feel annoyed that she hadn't kept herself nice for her husband. If she was gorgeous and had a ring I'd think, 'Lucky cow.'

Like I say, I have never pretended that my mind works in a rational way at the best of times, but in grief I was completely bonkers.

In one trauma counselling session, I rounded angrily on Doktor R when she pointed out that I was no longer married. I would *always* be married to JS, whatever the legalities of the situation were. I would wear my rings and even if hell froze over and I met someone else, I would *never ever* take my rings off.

Doktor R suggested that some widows hold on to the idea of being married to their late husbands (even though the stark fact is that they are no longer married as marriage vows are a contract between two people 'until death do us part') because it gives them status in society, their rings a symbol that they had been desired enough to be someone's wife and a safety net against being single in a challenging, couples-dominated world. I was incensed. Marriage to me meant more than a ring on my finger or the prefix Mrs. It wasn't just about romantic love. It meant looking out for each other, looking after each other, supporting each other. Teamwork.

And yet now, ten months after that session, I wonder if Doktor R had a point about safety and status.

A little while ago, I was in a hair salon in north London. I'd nipped in to buy some shampoo. I'd been walking The Hound and was out sans slap, hair piled up and in my old Puffa coat; in other words, I looked pants. I found myself waiting at the till behind a couple of over-groomed, snotty Yummy Mummies with big rocks. There was an argument between the sales assistant and the women and everyone became restless. I sighed, 'Oh come on!' under my breath. The Gruesome Twosome glared at me.

And then I found myself doing the once unthinkable.

Because of the Death Diet, my rings are looser than they were, so my solitaire often faces my palm. I swivelled my diamond to the front and put my hand so they could see I was wearing a wedding and engagement ring. Never in a million years would I have done that before. Why was it so important to me that those stuck-up women thought I was married, that I was one of them, that I had a husband at home rather than just some saddo singleton off the street with a dog and nothing better to do than wait to buy a bottle of colour-protecting shampoo before going home to a glass of sherry and a chilled meal for one? You'd have to ask my subconscious mind, because my conscious mind was freaked (and intrigued) by my behaviour.

Shortly after this 'Look At My Ring! I'm Wearing One So I Must Be Married!' peacock strut, I had a problem with a creepy tree surgeon doing work at my house. He must have noticed that I was wearing a wedding ring because he asked me what my husband did and whether he was around. At that point, I was glad that he thought I was married, though it didn't stop him being difficult over something else, an argument which ended up with me phoning the gorgeous grey-haired widower I know in Hertfordshire and pretending to the tree guy that I was on the phone to my husband who was working away. (He was a lawyer working on a libel case in New York, in case you're wondering what other tale I spun.)

Showing those women in the shop I was married; giving tree surgeons, men in bars and mini cab drivers the impression there is a husband on the scene; pretending I still *have* a husband: perhaps Doktor R was right about status and safety. A woman I know still wears her rings many years after a very bitter divorce because she says it makes her feel safer. Pre-JS's death I couldn't understand her stance, now I do, although my experience of meeting men in my married days is that if they are going to hit on you, they'll hit on you, even if you're displaying a symbol of betrothal.

So, I'm still wearing my rings and yet as I approach the first anniversary of JS's death, I no longer feel married, or at least as married as I felt this time last year or even just before Christmas. Christmas without JS was a turning point for me. Before Christmas, I went on a date and ended up bursting into tears and sobbing, 'I still feel married!' in front of the poor man. I still spontaneously burst into tears, but with every hurdle I either jump or crash through, I can feel the bonds of my marriage vows loosening.

To confuse matters, I don't feel *unmarried*, single in the way I did before I met JS, and I still feel very cherished and loved by my late husband and vice versa. But married in the true sense and present tense?

No.

JS and I were a team both at home and at work, with each other 24/7/365 for more than two decades, and now there is just me. You can't be a team of one. For me (and I know many widows will disagree vehemently with me), to be married, *truly* married, means you need a spouse who is still alive.

In some ways this feeling is a relief; I know it is a marker of moving forward and yet in others, a great sadness as it means acknowledging that a phase of my life is over. Now, when I look at my rings they still remind me of being loved, but they also remind me of loss, of a marriage that ended in tragedy. JS put them on my finger in Barbados overlooking the same stretch of sea that destroyed his life and our marriage. That circle of fate still takes my breath away.

Talking of things circular, since my 40th birthday, when JS gave me diamond earrings, it was a standing joke between us that he'd have to come up with something even more spectacular if I was to get out of bed on my much-dreaded 50th. JS promised to buy me a yellow-diamond ring. He'd tell our friends that he had diamond mines all over the world looking for just the right gems, because if they were the wrong ones, his life wouldn't be worth living. He was teasing of course, but I knew he'd do it. It makes me tearful to think of it, not because of the lack of birthday bling, but because JS won't be here for my half-century to tell me all those things he used to say to me when I moaned about ageing: that he loved me more the older I got; that to him I would always be the girl of 23 he saw standing by the photocopier in a grey jersey BHS dress, sent from the temp agency in place of the more experienced fifty-year-old secretary they had been promised.

In the privacy of my own home I've moved my rings and other dress rings about, but nothing feels right, particularly a naked finger, although oddly taking *all* my rings off, left *and* right hand, feels fine. Once, I removed them prior to a lunch date with friends and family, only to sit in the car at traffic lights and frantically put them back. That time, it wasn't because it didn't feel right, but because I worried what others would think if they noticed. I still worry what others might think.

One night, I Googled grief boards to see what other widows had done. Some had diamonds made from their husband's ashes and incorporated into a new ring to wear on their left hand, but that's not for me. I don't want to wear my rings around my neck, which was another popular option. Some had bought a 'Widow's Ring', a dark-stoned ring for their left hand and moved their wedding rings to their right hand, but I'm not a fan of black stones, nor do I want to be reminded that I am a widow. Others had opted to have their gems re-set into a different ring incorporating the gold from their husband's ring. JS hated jewellery and didn't wear a ring, so although this would be my favoured choice, it's not an option, but I did start looking at designs these widows had posted. I found myself becoming that American woman I knew 25 years ago, looking at rings and thinking, 'I could do that, but without this and maybe in platinum instead of gold…' and then I thought, 'WTF am I doing slobbering over ring designs as if I'm newly engaged?'

A week or so ago I made a decision that on 27th February 2012 I was going to remove my wedding rings. I was firm in my intentions.

A few days later, I went to a party. I had a fantastic time. Again I found myself checking out which women were wearing wedding rings, and I felt thankful to be wearing mine.

I may no longer feel married, but the madness of grief isn't over yet, far from it. I'm still living in some sort of marital limbo land.

For now, the rings are staying put.

OSCAR NIGHT

*The day J died, I left the hospital at 6am and arrived home in time to wake each of my three children one by one, to say the same thing to each of them, to hear their squeal of pain and watch their face crumple. I then dressed them, fed them and walked them to school. I was so wired and edgy, I persuaded my eldest age nine it was a good idea for her to appear in her school play!!! I turned up at school at 2pm; someone had saved me a seat on the front row. There was a moment when one of the characters had been shopping and arrived on stage clutching shopping bags. I laughed to myself because the bags were Prada, Mulberry and Jo Malone. I thought, 'Wait until I tell J!' Then it hit me. I dug my fingernails into my hands, trying not to let my beautiful nine-year-old see my tears. The first day of the new life. I started to run and still haven't stopped. ~ **Bonnie***

In the latter part of the first year after JS's death, I had a little fantasy.

No, not the one involving me, Alastair Campbell in his Lycra cycling shorts and a mobile phone charger, but that the day after the first-year anniversary, I would burst forth from this debilitating darkness like a stripper out of a giant birthday cake, a smile on my face whilst yelling, 'Watch out world! I'm back!' though wearing clothes, *obviously*.

Now the anniversary is upon me, I realise that I was as unrealistic about my entrance back into the 'normal' world as I was about me and sex-on-a stool Alastair C, when we met by chance in Carphone Warehouse.

Whilst I am smiling (sometimes through tears), my appearance at the first-year finishing line is less dramatic, more akin to a butterfly slowly emerging from a rather ugly chrysalis: there's been quite a lot of thrashing around, tentative antenna waving and cracking of my protective carapace, but parts of my wings are yet to totally unfurl. There is still a chance that just as I take flight, some passing toad sticks its tongue out and has me as a tasty little snack.

Quite why I thought I'd be different from everyone else, that I could approach the anniversary of JS's death with a spirit of feisty 'F**k you, Grief Monster!' defiance, I really don't know. I should have remembered that acts of great defiance in the face of adversity often end up with me in tears, something which JS (were he still alive) would attest to, having witnessed me haranguing a bus driver, numerous stuck-up mothers parked outside my garage and a particularly nasty member of staff who tried to run me over with her moped in the underground car park at work. In all cases (and there are plenty more to which I plead guilty), I boasted that I was going to show that driver/mother/colleague what for. And I did, with bells on, only to collapse in a snivelling wailing heap later.

But still, I was totally prepared for 27th February 2012. There was absolutely no point (I told myself) to rehash the run-up to that terrible day. I've done it all year, hundreds of times a day and it does me no good at all. It doesn't bring JS back, it's simply a total waste of time and energy. These few days prior to the anniversary are just ordinary days.

Except, they're not.

Perhaps they will never be. I've written before that years after JS's first wife died, the days in the run up to the anniversary of her death were always a tense and fraught time in our household. I'm not saying that I was unsympathetic, but I will admit to occasionally thinking, 'Oh for goodness sake! Get over it!'

But it's not that easy.

In the run up to the 27th, I've had bizarre dreams. There was one where JS was alive and sitting at a bar in the Caribbean with friends of ours. I've only seen his face once in a dream and he was dead. In this dream, JS was very much alive and wearing a white short-sleeved shirt. I saw his face. He was chatting, making plans for the future. I told him not to. He asked why. I told him that he was going to drown. He didn't believe me. I handed him a thin sheet of paper on which his autopsy results were printed in old-fashioned typewriter type. It was definitely a dream and not a 'visitation', as in the dream I was on holiday with Rio Ferdinand. As an Arsenal season ticket holder, going away with a Manchester United player counts as a nightmare.

No matter how hard I tried not to do the whole, 'This time last year' thing, I have done, every day this week. No wonder there have been tears and the occasional tantrum.

Tonight, the Oscars are taking place in Los Angeles. I have Sky News on in the background, and they're covering them.

There is one aspect of JS's death that I have hardly thought about. I don't know whether this is because I couldn't bear to, or because I have been focused on the actual events surrounding JS's death. And yet, as I approach the first year, it has become massively traumatic for me to remember.

The first night after the day of JS's death.

It was terrible to witness my husband's drowning and the appalling circus on the beach. For such a private, dignified man, he had a very public and undignified death, though now I feel sure that he would not have known anything about it, that my screaming the names of his children and tickling his feet to bring him round, the yells of the crowd, my pleading for a jet ski to rescue him, for an ambulance to save him, for someone to help him, all fell on ears wired into an oxygen-starved brain. The rest of the day was a blur: of a terrifying blue-light ambulance ride; of the hospital; of doctors; of police; the Foreign Office; the British Consulate; of tour reps; of hotel staff; of hotel guests; of heartbreaking phone calls with screams on the other end of the line.

And then everyone left and there was just me, thousands of miles away in paradise in a hotel room overlooking the sea that killed JS and the beach on which I learned life would never be the same again.

That first night alone, was, in some ways, worse than the day when the momentum of death kept me going, kept me hauled up by the armpits even though my feet were barely touching the ground.

Friends in the UK knew friends in Barbados and arranged for them to ring me. They suggested that they came to pick me up and take me to their house. It was a Sunday night and they were staying in to watch the Oscars. I would be very welcome to join them. I declined. I didn't know them. I didn't know anything except that my husband was dead, and I was alone and far from home.

The sun went down.

The restaurant below my hotel room began to prepare for dinner.

I paced the room that was the same as we'd left it in the morning: JS's clothes over the back of the chair, his toiletries in the bathroom, the bed unmade. It was the Marie Celeste of rooms. Nothing had changed, and yet everything had changed.

I could hear guests going into dinner, leaving their rooms, chatting as they walked along the corridor outside.

The band struck up.

I couldn't bear it.

I rang the friends of friends and asked if I could change my mind and watch the Oscars with them. They said they were on their way.

I went down to reception, an area that overlooked the restaurant. As I waited, all eyes turned to me. For a moment, the band slowed down. It was surreal, almost comedic. I remember giving a slight wave and saying (to no one in particular) with an ironic laugh (not the right word, but if you were next to me, I could do an impression and you'd see what I mean), 'Yes, I'm the woman on the beach whose husband drowned today.' I'll never forget it. I want to forget it, but I can't.

The friends of friends arrived. They were lovely. Warm northerners working in Barbados. They drove me to their house, which was on the edge of a golf course. It was absolutely fabulous. As I walked in I thought, 'I must tell JS about this place!'

They made me tea and cheese and biscuits. They were terribly kind. They wanted me to stay with them.

I couldn't settle. I couldn't sit still. I needed to pace. Pace and pace and pace. I paced in their bathroom to try and get some pacing out of my system.

Warm Northerners had the Oscars on the television. I tried to watch them, the pretty dresses and the handsome film stars, but I couldn't. I just couldn't sit still. My body was jumping inside.

I'd only been there (I think) half-an-hour or so when I asked them to run me back to the hotel. They wrapped up the cheese and crackers, and we drove back.

The moment their car lights left the property, I desperately wanted to run out of the gate and up the road and beg them to take me back with them.

Armed with my snacks, I went back to the hotel room. I remember the band was playing Chris de Burgh's *Lady in Red*. I hate the sentimental pap of *Lady in Red* at the best of times.

I put the television on. Coverage of the Oscars was still in full flow.

I kept pacing.

I could hear footsteps outside and doors close around me, couples going back to their room after dinner. Together.

The band stopped playing.

I looked over the balcony. The restaurant was almost empty.

I couldn't stay in the room.

I went down to the bar. It was outside. I could hear the sea lap on the beach.

I drank whisky with the hotel manager and two of his friends who were in Barbados on a golfing holiday.

They were kind men, but they couldn't sit up drinking spirits forever.

We all went back to our rooms.

There was still Oscar stuff on the TV.

I got undressed, put the white hotel dressing gown on and paced the room.

Everything was deathly quiet except for the noise of the whistling tree frogs. The first time we went to Barbados, JS made up a song for me. It won't mean anything unless you know the tune, but the words go like this:

The whistling tree frog went over the hill
Down to the valley so shady
He whistled and he sang 'til the greenwood rang
And he won the heart of his lay-ay-dy frog

This trip, JS promised that he would finally get round to composing a second verse by the end of the holiday.

I turned the TV off, lay on the top of the bed and turned the light out.

Seconds later I turned it on, terrified, images of what I had witnessed flooding my brain.

I put the TV back on.

I started pacing again.

Pacing. Pacing. Pacing.

In the early hours of the morning, I had to get out of the room. Still in my dressing gown, I started pacing around the property, *desperate* for human company. There was a man sitting underneath the pergoda where earlier the band had been playing. He was on a chair, asleep. I wanted to talk to him. To someone. To anyone. I paced round and round that bl**dy pergoda in my white dressing gown, but the man didn't wake up. I went over to the bar and started poking around, not for a drink, just because I didn't know what else to do. A big, black man appeared. I explained who I was and what had happened. He had heard all about it. He was sorry. I asked who the man under the pergoda was, the man who I couldn't wake up despite circling him in a snowy white dressing gown. The man said he was the hotel's security guard.

I went back to our (my?) room.

The TV was still burbling away: news. Oscars.

The time difference between Barbados and the UK meant people were getting up at home. I rang them or they rang me. They kept me talking. I can't remember what I said or in what order I spoke to people, I just know that those people I spoke to prevented me from doing something stupid thousands of miles away in paradise until my wonderful brother could arrive from the UK, which he did about five o'clock later that day.

The sun came up.

There was the sound of the clattering of dishes from the restaurant below as the breakfast buffet got underway.

I ran a bath, but felt too weak to get in it.

I lay on the bed.

The phone rang.

I can't remember who it was, I just know that I was asked to go to reception as a car was being sent for me to take me to the hospital.

I put on a dress, shoes, make up and all my jewellery and went downstairs.

Couples were going to the beach.

I was going to the mortuary.

TRUST ME, I'M A WIDOW

On the first year anniversary, I threw a 'Flotilla Party' to thank the people who had kept me afloat. It had a nautical theme and I got noisily drunk. It's not what everyone would want to do, but anniversaries don't have to be about quiet reflection. ~ **Sue Ab**

On the morning of the first anniversary of JS's death, I woke up feeling anxious, tired, desolate, terrified and physically sick.

Retching into the bathroom sink, the toilet, the kitchen sink and the flowerbed, when I let The Hound out, was a constant feature of mornings for months after JS died, so much so, I worried that my gnashers would turn in to little acid-worn pegs. That might still happen, but once I stopped worrying about being sick every morning, the heaving decreased and then vanished.

But on 27th February 2012, like the alien bursting forth from Ripley's gut, my vomiting made a spectacular reappearance.

As the kettle boiled whilst I did an impression of a cat chucking up a hairball, I wondered what on earth had possessed to me to make anniversary plans beyond lying in bed, listening to James Taylor and sobbing into The Hound's fur.

I tell you what had possessed me – advice from other widows.

So many had assured me that the actual day wasn't as bad as they had feared, that the anticipation was worse than the event. With this knowledge, I had taken the bold step of planning a lunch for a select group of industry colleagues. Some of this inner circle had known JS for decades, and all of them had stuck by me for the year, even if at times I'd refused to take their calls, answer their emails or let them into the house. I'd booked a table for ten at L'Escargot, one of JS's once-favourite restaurants, not only the venue of many lunches and dinners, but of our first proper date where we sat at the table in the window and I was filled with love and awe, not just for JS, but for the gold foil-wrapped chocolate snails they gave you at the end of the meal.

'These widows with their advice were wrong!' I told myself. 'The day is going to be a disaster.'

In tears, I thought about cancelling lunch, the pre-lunch hair appointment and the dog-sitter. Why put myself through all this? Couldn't I have found a quiet mountain to sit on, rather than a bustling Soho restaurant?

Some hours and copious cuppas later, my hair coiffed and my eyelashes groaning with waterproof mascara, I arrived at the restaurant. The round table for ten was set up in the window, the very spot where more than two decades before, I had first sat with my future husband. For a moment, the ground shifted beneath my heels and then friends began to arrive, and all my anxieties melted away. I'd brought with me photos of JS and we laughed and reminisced and drank champagne; it was all great fun and, at times, rather raucous. The only thing wrong was that JS wasn't there and having changed ownership many times over the years, the chocolate snails were no longer on the menu.

We also remembered Karen, who died in March 2003.

At one point, one of the guests remarked that this was the second first-year memorial lunch she had been to recently, the first being held by the widow of a man I vaguely knew. 'E is dealing with widowhood very differently to you,' my friend remarked. 'She's very elegant and calm and quiet.' Everyone laughed as I cried with mock indignity, 'Are you saying I'm not elegant?' It was a funny, poignant moment, a reminder that just like our marriages, our way of dealing with grief is unique.

After lunch, my wonderful friend Big Bird and I mooched around the shops. I had promised to buy myself some memorial bling. Any excuse! I ended up buying a jacket from Selfridges. A memorial jacket isn't what I had in mind, but I know JS would have approved. He loved good clothes and buying them for me, and Selfridges was his favourite shop.

In the evening it was Dim Sum with Big Bird and then home, alone.

With The Hound on my lap, I sat on the sofa in my dressing gown and watched *The Only Way is Essex* on catch-up. I suspect that my choice of TV programme would be the one part of the day JS would *not* have approved of.

Those widows who told me that the actual day would be OK, that the run-up would be the difficult part, were right, just as they have been right about so many things on this journey. It was a great day: a day with friends in the West End of London with good food, champagne, a touch of glamour and shopping. Very much a JS type of day.

And now I am officially in year two.

Gulp.

TIME HOP:
COMING CLEAN

Do I want a 'grown up' relationship again? Yes, I think so – don't hold me to it, but I am a realist. I'm virtually fifty, a short, fat grey-haired bloke with two children. I'm not going to meet someone and sweep them off their feet. This is it for me. The ship has passed over the horizon. If you're young enough and disposed to try again, then damn it, go do it!
~ David

Almost four years after I wrote the chapter 'Getting in a Lather' at the end of November 2011, I can now reveal something that my friends and family knew, and some readers of my blog guessed at the time, which is that 'Mac' who came to Broadstairs with me, was Ian, aka Gorgeous Grey-Haired Widower (GGHW), a man I met online through a Facebook bereavement group, and whose entirely innocent support and friendship turned into romance. It took until the end of March 2012 to reveal this new relationship in print, though I had left clues in the blog about a widower in Hertfordshire along the way. Why didn't I come clean about GGHW sooner? Why didn't I rush to my keyboard and announce to the readers of my blog that there had been a snog on the sofa in the same way that I had poured my heart out about anxiety vomiting in the morning, or getting drunk in the evening? Partly, I didn't want to tempt fate so that the moment I put my head above the parapet of grief to admit that I was dating again, everything fell apart, but mostly, my silence was a desire to protect the innocent: GGHW and his family, especially his two sons whose mother died suddenly in the garden of their home when they had just turned 15 and 18. I didn't want to become *Planet Grief*'s version of Liz Jones, the *Mail on Sunday* columnist who chronicles her life in *You* magazine, a writer whose entertaining prose, has, she admits, hurt, angered and alienated scores of people, some of whom she cared deeply about. It was *my* decision to start the blog and chronicle my grief, not theirs, and any reference to them was always treated with the utmost caution, though I did used to joke that if GGHW dumped me or treated me badly, I would get my revenge in print and fatally wound him through the power of words.

One of the other reasons for my desire to keep things under wraps was that, for months, I had no idea whether GGHW was going to simply have a walk-on part in my life, or become a permanent cast member. Some years ago, a friend of mine lost his wife to cancer and, by his own admission, badly misjudged how to announce the news of his first relationship. Soon after his wife's death, he embarked on an affair with a woman he'd met in a hotel whilst working away from home during the week. It was through a desire to be completely open and honest about this relationship – rather than because he felt swept off his feet – that he told everyone about it. I was surprised, but pleased for him. His late wife's family were devastated. Most people thought the relationship was too soon for his own emotional wellbeing. To him, his wife could never be replaced. To them, she had been superseded with indecent haste. The affair (which was more about comfort than love) fell apart, and my friend was left picking up the pieces in the full 'I told you so' public glare. He told me at the time that he wished he hadn't said anything until he knew that there was something long-lasting to tell, that it would have been kinder to keep quiet, and that sometimes it's better to grasp the nettle slowly. However happy people are that you are dating again, many – especially children and close relatives

– find a big announcement difficult to take, embarrassing even. Drip-feeding details into a conversation ('I'm going to the theatre with a friend, Ian, who was widowed too,') gently paves the way and gives both of you time to assess whether the new romance is the real deal or just 'any port in a storm'. I have often read (sometimes with the disgust of the newly widowed) excited announcements on internet bereavement sites along the lines of: 'I can't put this on my main page yet for obvious reasons, but I've met this man, we've had a couple of dates and it's fantastic! I never thought that I would feel this way ever again!' only for them report back a few days later that it was all off as this new Stud Muffin hadn't called or he had shouted at the widow's children or that it turned out he was still married. Facebook relationship updates could go from 'Widowed' to 'In a relationship' to 'Engaged' and back to 'Widowed' within weeks, cue a torrent of tears and an online postmortem of where it all went wrong.

When GGHW and I met, we were both vulnerable, emotional wrecks; our relationship could easily have collapsed as we worked through our grief and became stronger. JS – who was widowed in his twenties and married his second wife less than 15 months after his first wife's death – told me that the sort of person you need when you are broken through bereavement is not necessarily the person you want to spend the rest of your life with, that the very qualities in a partner you need when you are widowed can become unbearably suffocating as you grow stronger. So, I didn't write about GGHW until everyone in my 'real' life knew about him, but I thought that the clues in my blog had gently revealed that he was part of my life without the need for a fanfare announcement. I was wrong. When I finally made it clear I was in a relationship, as you will read in the next chapter, it was like stepping on the internet equivalent of a landmine...

BRIGHTON BELLE

*I've had a lot of judgment from fellow widows, who I would have thought would have understood more than most people. However much we loved our husbands – and don't get me, wrong, I loved him with all of my being – sometimes it feels right to move forward relatively quickly. Maybe our loved one suffered from a terminal illness for a long time so we had more time to come to terms with their death, maybe we want more children, maybe we can't just do it all on our own and we need a little support and love, maybe there is the need for physical comfort and it hasn't been possible owing to terminal illness. Having spoken to a few widows my own age (I'm thirty-eight) there seems to be a band of us who are young enough to want to have more children, who are therefore willing enough to put ourselves 'out there' and to risk a new life. ~ **Holly***

Once upon a time, I firmly believed that one of the very few positives to come out of JS's death was that having witnessed and lived through unimaginable horror, I would no longer sweat the small stuff. In other words, grieving aside, I would reserve my tears and tantrums for issues such as child poverty and animal cruelty, serenely brushing aside minor domestic incidents and people who annoyed me, unless they were parking-related, in which case I gave myself permission to go nuclear.

Having also experienced the worst sort of post-holiday blues possible, I felt sure that just getting everyone through the front door with a pulse would be such a relief, never again would I suffer from a post-trip slump.

Fast forward to last weekend which found me in a room cleared of furniture, sitting on the carpet in damp jeans, wishing I was back on Brighton Pier and sobbing as if The Hound had just choked to death on a squeaky ball.

Have you seen those adverts for VAX carpet cleaners? The one with the perfect house filled with pale furnishings, cute children and a mucky dog called Beckham? A woman glides this contraption over her slightly grubby floor and – Ta-da! –the once-tainted carpet regains its virginal status.

My carpets have not only lost their virginity, they look as if they've been working the streets for the last 15 years, so I decided to invest in a carpet washer. I had visions of whizzing around the house, transforming the flooring, perhaps even putting a sparklingly positive review on Argos along with all the other reviews which waxed lyrical about this wonder-machine, a mechanical marvel which had saved having to re-mortgage the house in order to afford a new Axminster from John Lewis.

Unfortunately, whilst Advert Woman didn't even glow whilst using her VAX, after wrestling with the box, the packaging, assembling the thing and moving all the furniture, I was sweating like a pig on a spit before I'd even flicked the switch.

And when I did, it didn't work.

After much fiddling and swearing, I rang VAX who agreed it needed to be returned. Before ramming it back in to its wardrobe-sized box, I looked on the internet. I no longer saw glowing reviews but a sorry tale of dirty water, foamy streaks and non-rotating brushes (although to be fair, these were the search words I put into Google). Some bright spark suggested tipping the machine at 45 degrees and switching it on. I tried it and – hey presto! – it sprung into life.

Then it stopped and made the sort of rumbling noises my insides make after a prawn bhuna.

Then it worked again.

Ooh! A patch of clean carpet! And look at the filthy water! How grimly fascinating!

Then it stopped.

Finally, like an incontinent drunk standing in the street outside a pub at closing time, the damn machine expelled the contents of its tank in a mucky puddle on my carpet, whilst I looked down at my sodden feet, bewildered at its lack of control.

It was all too much. Recently, there has been one (mostly expensive) domestic disaster after another, a state of affairs that has led me to having a little fantasy that the house will burn down, whereupon I can start again courtesy of Sainsbury's Home Insurance. And then I remember the saying: 'Be careful what you wish for' and totally freak, because of course I don't really want the house to go up in flames, it's just that sometimes I feel so tired of it all, I want to close the door and run away, not just from incontinent vacuums and intermittent electrics, but accountants and lawyers and financial advisers and endless paperwork relating to the last three professions, but mostly from being a widow.

Which is why having two nights and three days in Brighton with Gorgeous Grey-Haired Widower was so lovely. It was (in memory terms) neutral ground, the weather was great, the hotel lovely. We had breakfast in greasy spoons and dinner in smart restaurants; we went wild, spending 50p each on the push 2p machines and won a pencil; we ate fresh doughnuts and drank champagne; we lay fully clothed on the nudist beach and felt the early spring sunshine warm our faces. But most of all, we laughed and laughed.

At one point, sitting on Brighton Pier, GGHW announced that he was going to 'Check In' on Facebook on his phone. 'Shall I put who I'm with?' he teased.

It's well known that women can go mad when they're on holiday, particularly middle-aged ones, witness *Shirley Valentine*. They sleep with waiters or have a scorpion tattooed on their butt or get their nipple pierced, and there are usually consequences to such things, such as a nasty infection requiring a dose of antibiotics and/or something to rub on twice a day.

My *Shirley Valentine* moment was a little less dramatic, but still had a consequence. Throwing caution to the wind and in holiday mood, I urged GGHW to go ahead and tag me on Facebook.

The button got pressed.

We giggled like teenagers at our recklessness.

I then posted a picture on my Facebook page.

I have written of my disgust that when reading *A Widow's Story* by Joyce Carol Oates, I discovered Ms Oates had remarried. The same was true of Elizabeth Harper Neeld's account of dating after death in her book, *Seven Choices*. In both cases, my reaction to their new lives was extreme: I *threw* the book down. These women with whom I had identified had betrayed me; we had nothing in common any more. At the point where they accepted new men into their lives, the bond between us was broken. As a new widow, as far as I was concerned the moment a man came on the scene, the pain of widowhood was over; these women had no right to continue to chronicle their struggles.

A few hours after the Facebook post, the first of a succession of disapproving (and angry) messages started coming through on my phone. My Facebook friend count dwindled. This was the social media equivalent of my throwing those books down in disgust. Widows who had identified with me through my blog, who had charted their pain and grief alongside mine, felt betrayed, accused me of being a fraud, of letting them down. To be honest, the reaction of this small group didn't surprise me and not just because I had experienced similar feelings in the past, but because I had been on the receiving end of such behaviour before, at a time when only a few widows knew about GGHW. Most (all widowed around the same time) were fine, one even confessed that she had been secretly seeing someone too. But from other quarters there were barbed comments about dishonour and disrespect – and one particularly vicious (and unfounded) side-swipe implying that whether in a bar or online (both were mentioned), I have always been on the look-out for a man.

I've spoken to other widows (who have dated) about this reaction. Their feeling was that this behaviour was driven by jealousy.

Perhaps I need more time and experience to reflect on their diagnosis, but I'm not sure that I agree with them.

Thinking back to my own extreme reaction to discovering that others (both in print and on screen) were dating, I wonder if our reaction is driven by fear? Fear of being alone; fear of being with someone and all that a new relationship entails; fear of new loss; fear of new feelings; perhaps fear that our old partners will somehow be eclipsed by the new. I won't deny that in amongst the laughter there can be sadness about the strangest things. For instance, I like my tea made a certain way. It was a constant joke between JS and me that no one would ever make a cup of tea as good he did. I really believed him. I remember standing by the kettle after he died and feeling bereft at the thought.

GGHW makes a lovely cuppa. When it first happened I felt incredibly sad that JS wasn't right, that there was someone else who could take over his tea duties.

Daft, isn't it? Do I want to drink rank tea for the rest of my life just to prove JS right?

So, despite upsetting a small band of widows, I had a wonderful time in Brighton. But coming home was unsettling. I love my home now, I really do, but having been away where everything was fresh and clean (and I mean clean of memories), the weight of widowhood quickly settled back on my bony shoulders. GGHW said he felt the same when he walked into his house. I felt low and down and had there been a paint pot and roller handy, I might have gone mad and painted all the walls white in an attempt to make the place feel different, fresher.

Which could have been why, 24 hours later, I bought the carpet cleaner.

So there I was, sobbing on the carpet, when I see where I've parked my butt: next to my husband's desk. I knew what was in there, a concertina file of personal (not financial) documents, but I've never looked through it. It's always scared me a little, though quite what I thought I would find I have no idea, but in the last year, I've avoided that file like the plague. But sitting on the carpet with wet ankles and post-Brighton blues, I suddenly wanted to see what was slipped between those dividers.

JS wasn't a hoarder and the documents were hand-picked items, kept because they meant something to him: things his children had made him; cuttings from newspapers; his first pay slip; a letter from the BBC telling him he'd got the job; and so on.

And then there was a collection of certificates, including the birth certificate of his first wife Kay, their marriage certificate and her death certificate that gave details of the findings of the inquest. She was 28.

Birth. Marriage. Death.

The perfect circle.

Except JS's life didn't run in parallel to Kay's, though I suspect when they married at Kensington Registry Office, he assumed it would.

Then there was JS's marriage certificate to his second wife and their subsequent divorce papers.

JS's birth certificate and our marriage certificate were missing, presumably with the lawyers, but I had his death certificate. Seeing his often-complicated life from start to finish in a handful of paperwork was incredibly moving.

I sat mesmerised by these documents, flicking through them, taking in every full stop as I reflected on the man and his life. There were things he did and decisions he made and behaviours he exhibited which previously I couldn't understand, but having experienced sudden and traumatic bereavement and the process of trying to rebuild my life, I do now. I longed to talk to him about what I'd found, to talk to him in a way that he would never have been comfortable with had he still been alive. JS was a man who cried buckets when he watched *ET*, but otherwise found showing his emotions difficult.

Looking through the file, it occurred to me that despite – or possibly because of – such a terrible loss (including that of his mother), my husband went on to carve out a full and rich life. He was a man who wasn't afraid to take risks (and yes, I get the irony) or change direction if something wasn't working for him, a man who focused on what he wanted and strived for it both personally and professionally, a man who refused to let fear rule him. After all that had happened, JS could have given up on love and become bitter about loss, retreated to live a quiet life free of drama and angst, but he didn't. He embraced life and seized opportunities.

If I can be slightly less stubborn and more emotionally open than JS, the way my husband lived his life is a role model for how to live *my* life after *his* death.

I'm sorry those widows are angry and disappointed in me, I really am, but they are not living my life, nor I theirs. Whilst I will always cherish the memories of JS and our time together, I believe there is a difference between honouring the past and clinging to it.

David, a widower with two teenage children, recently wrote something that resonates with me: '...*move on we must, or stagnate in our own misery. What speed we move is of course very personal and no one should judge another because they are apparently different.*'

PAINFUL PLEASURE

*I don't believe that for every person on earth, there is only one person that can ever make them happy. I mean, it would be quite a coincidence that out of six billion people, our one soulmate tends to live in the same town or work in the same office. I have already met one of my soulmates. Why would I deny myself finding one of the other ones? Why would anyone? ~ **Marieke***

WARNING!

Tales of underwear and men ahead!

You!

Yes, you! I'm talking directly to you, the woman whose life is so shattered she begs to die rather than go on living without her husband.

Or you, who stood in the shower this morning so shell-shocked, you walked out and got dressed in dirty clothes that hang off you, a cloud of shampoo still in your hair.

And to the lady who stands in the park screaming at the sky, 'Where are you? Give me a sign to say you're OK! Anything! *Please*!' before crumpling in a heap on a memorial bench and sobbing until you vomit, turn the page now, I beg you.

Because all of those women above were me and during those terrible raw times, I didn't want to read about relationships and nor do some widows, if the vicious war of words that broke out last Friday night on one of the Facebook forums I belong to is anything to go by.

A widow, a regular contributor whose deep grief I have witnessed through her anguished posts, began a thread about internet dating. It was light-hearted, poking fun at the plonkers she was encountering, and there was plenty of good-natured banter, something I badly needed. A miserable Friday afternoon had turned into a very miserable sofa-slumped Merlot-sloshed Friday evening, the sort where I not only looked around my living room and thought, 'JS, where are you?' but noticed the cobwebs and the peeling paintwork and felt overwhelmed.

But then, in amongst the light-hearted and supportive comments came darker posts dripping with distaste, the general gist of which was that a grief forum was *not* the place to mention new relationships. Like porn on the top shelf in a newsagent's, such discussions should be taken out of the gaze of those who wear the veil of widowhood and have no intention of ever lifting it, not even for a peck on the cheek, let alone a snog. Those who had joined in the fun were admonished for encouraging such posts, slapped down for 'revelling' in the details of dating.

The atmosphere on the board changed as the charges were set out against those who had the temerity to think about forming a new relationship: We were hiding from our grief; settling for second best; 'crowing' about finding a new partner ('Look at me! I'm so in love!'), ramming new relationships down others' throats. It transpired that some widows had pulled out of attending a recent meet-up when they discovered they would see something undignified and distasteful: widowed couples newly in love.

The blue touch paper was lit and everything exploded with a bang, the aftershocks of which were still rumbling on the board days later. Words can wound and people cornered (or perhaps plastered) lashed out. I was watching the fight unfold on my iPad and might have joined in if I could have sat up to type, but it meant moving The Hound who was lying across me, legs akimbo, snoring contentedly. Also, I was a bit squiffy and in danger of lobbing a nuclear bomb into an already flaming forum.

Wise and experienced widows tried to calm the situation, but the newbies, still raw and with the self-righteousness of the recently bereaved, carried on scorning the life-choices of long-standing members.

Self-righteous? I know that in the early days I had a very 'holier than thou' attitude. *Clearly*, my grief was greater than anyone else's: *I* had no time to say goodbye to my husband or ask him what the password for the Virgin Media account was; *I'd* seen him drown in front of me, on a beach, on holiday, thousands of miles away whilst I was wearing a bikini. *I* had no children to get up for and pull me through. *I'd* worked for JS so I lost my job *and* my husband. *I* couldn't just go to work and sit and do my job and be surrounded by others who would make me tea and jolly me along. *I* had a financial and business minefield to unravel. *I* couldn't join a counselling group because JS didn't die in a local hospice or hospital, yada yada yada.

It was a load of bollocks, but at the time I believed those things just as I believed that I would never again be happy, be able to put the bins out without sobbing or read the Sunday newspapers. If we can't imagine ever doing something as simple as laughing again, how could we possibly imagine a new relationship? And if one comes along when we are least expecting it, when not only are we not looking for one, but we don't want one, when we are still banging the drum of life-long marriage even if our partner is now in a box on a shelf rather than on the sofa beside us, what then?

Through an online grief forum, I had been corresponding with widows and widowers since before JS's (much delayed) funeral. These people were supportive and warm and often bleakly funny. Some fell by the wayside as their lives moved forward and they distanced themselves from shared grief, but there remained a core group who dragged each other through significant dates: anniversaries and birthdays, social events attempted alone and so on.

Towards the end of last year, I was walking through the women's underwear department of M&S when out of the blue, I had a seriously X-rated thought about one of the widowers I corresponded with. I stood amongst the lace-trimmed push-up bras and matching G-strings *horrified,* shaking my head as if a wasp had flown into my ear, trying to rid my brain of such a disgustingly inappropriate thought.

I walked on.

It happened again.

I was rocked to my core. There had been absolutely no hint of anything remotely racy in our emails. Unlike other widows who found themselves at the end of saucy messages asking what colour underwear they were wearing and graphical anatomical pictures of male genitalia, our conversations on Facebook Messenger went like this:

Me: Got to go as going to have a bacon sarnie for lunch.

Him: Red or brown sauce?

Me: Mustard!

I rushed out of M&S into Oxford Street, got on a bus and wept. I felt sleazy, guilty and ashamed. My heart said I had been unfaithful, that I had broken my marriage vows. My head told my heart to bog off and get real, that my vows were until death us do part. I was frightened and bewildered that the part of being a woman I thought had died along with my husband had returned whilst surrounded by mass-market underwear. I was disgusted at Media Man when he pounced on me, but this was far worse: I was disgusted with myself.

Only being an hour up the motorway, The Widower and I had talked about meeting up to walk The Hound, but after the M&S incident, I stalled. We'd meet up before the end of the year. Or not. Maybe never. I encouraged The Widower to start dating whilst hating myself for hoping he wouldn't. Our correspondence continued, witty messages that I looked forward to receiving. When one morning my first thought was to reach for my phone and smile at a 'Good Morning' text The Widower had sent me, rather than look at the empty pillow beside me and howl for my husband, I plunged into a spiral of despair, confusion and, later that day, whisky drinking and loud rock music.

I told my bereavement coach, Shelley, about what had happened in M&S. She was delighted and felt it was a shift in my grief, a new stage in the process. I was freaked and scared and confused. How could I be sobbing over my husband one moment, yet having lustful thoughts over a stranger the next? I looked at photos of JS around the house, and my face burned wondering if he knew what my brain was up to.

As it turned out and due to a genuine misunderstanding between us, I met The Widower when I was least expecting to, as demonstrated by my outfit. Instead of the carefully thrown together, glossy-haired, understated, tons-of-make-up/no-make-up look, we first came eye-to-eye when I was wearing shrunken tracksuit bottoms, bare feet, a stripy dressing gown, wet hair and no make-up.

After months of messages, it was good to meet him. *Very* good.

That first meeting and sitting outside a pub, I laid the law down in no uncertain terms. I did *not* want a relationship. I was *not* going to be anyone's girlfriend; the odd date with a lawyer or a rich banker, maybe, but *never* again would I have a long-term partnership. My advice to The Widower was that he should sow some wild oats and then settle down with a lovely woman. He deserved a lovely woman, but that woman wouldn't be me because, as I had clearly stated, I would be racing around with lawyers and bankers.

It was quite a speech, worthy of Churchill or Martin Luther King.

It was also totally inappropriate, as the poor man had only come to walk The Hound with me.

It's a mark of the man that he didn't tell me to pull my head out of my own butt and stop being such a stroppy, self-centred princess, but instead, he listened with calm, good humour.

And then he told me he was not the slightest bit interested in a relationship either.

But, just to ram my point home, after he left, I emailed him a copy of my speech.

Was I telling The Widower that I didn't want a relationship or telling myself? I know that at the time I meant everything I said. I talked again to Shelley. She asked what I liked about The Widower. I reeled off a long list of his qualities. She asked me what I didn't like. There was nothing about him I didn't like. What I didn't like was that he had come into my life now. It was too soon, not part of my plan. She said, 'OK, don't see him for another 18 months or two years or whatever time scale you think is appropriate. Then look him up and when you find he is happy with someone else, we'll deal with your tears of regret then.'

'If he finds someone else before I'm ready, then that's fate', I told myself, trying to ignore the fact that I would be devastated if in one of my 'You should date lots of women!' conversations The Widower had confessed, 'Actually, I've found someone I really like…'

There was more dog-walking and friendship and deeper talking and, at some point, we agreed to go out on a date. Traipsing across Hampstead Heath in wellies was one thing, but a proper grown-up date in good clothes was quite another. It ended in tearful, angst-ridden disaster, and an acknowledgement that it was all too soon*.

---

* Our first date was lunch at the National Portrait Gallery and an afternoon screening of *Tinker Tailor Soldier Spy* in Leicester Square, an outing which ended up with me becoming hysterical and getting a taxi home as detailed in 'Warning! Self Pity Ahead'. (see page 154)

There were no more funny emails, no witty texts. Life felt even darker than it was already.

I missed him.

After a gap, we went back to uncomplicated dog-walking.

One day, it was muddy on the Heath and The Widower got stuck in the mud. I was laughing so much I doubled-up and could hardly breathe. When I straightened up he was still trying to pull his wellies out of the mud and laughing and I thought, 'I don't want to lose that man from my life.' Which is the moment The Widower became Gorgeous Grey-Haired Widower.

I suspect that those who have been widowed and look on as others make new relationships feel (as I would have done) that a new partner erases grief, but the reality is much more complicated. I don't want to speak for GGHW, but what I will say is that I doubt there is any widow or widower out there who hasn't struggled with the idea of a new relationship and the problems and unexpected feelings it brings.

The first weekend GGHW stayed with me we had a lovely time, walking The Hound, going to the local farmers' market, reading the Sunday papers. When GGHW drove away that evening I was happy. I was happy as I made something to eat. Then, suddenly, I became convulsed with hysterical sobs. I stood in the kitchen shouting into space, 'JS, I'm sorry! I'm sorry, but you're not here! You're not bloody here!' whilst waving a wooden spoon aggressively in the air. It frightened me and it frightened The Hound.

And then there is the fear of the future. Whichever way you look at things, there will be upheaval and angst. If things don't work out then it will be heartbreaking. If they do work out and we live happily ever after, the cruel reality is that one of us will be widowed again. When I first thought of this, I burst into tears and wept that I couldn't do it all over again. Always calm and optimistic, GGHW pointed out the fun we would have in the meantime. But still…

I had also firmly believed that if I did ever date again, I would be forever comparing JS to other men and that other men would always fall short and be second best. It has been a shock to find out and painful to admit that in some areas, the tables are turned.

And then there is the most distressing part of the entire dating-a-widower process, and something I still find incredibly difficult and painful to cope with.

GGHW has two gorgeous sons who have been nothing less than welcoming to me. They are tremendous and I adore them, but in amongst the laughter we have when we are together comes terrible flashes of why I am there: I am there because their mother isn't. It should be Gorgeous Son No 2's mum sitting at the kitchen table as he recounts his day. It should be Gorgeous Son No 1's mum visiting him at university. Sometimes it all becomes so overwhelming, I feel as I did in the early days of grief when I used to sink to my knees and cover my head, waiting for the tidal wave of despair to wash over me.

I remember one night at GGHW's house sobbing and saying that if I had my car with me I would leave, even though it was the early hours of the morning, such was the overwhelming grief I felt for everyone. GGHW put his arms around me and said that if I really wanted to go home he would drive me. I stayed. The terrible truth is that me not being there won't bring the boys' mother back, however much I long it would, but sometimes the practical side of me becomes swamped with emotion and I weep for what should have been for those young lads and their lovely mum.

All these emotions; is it any wonder that some of us simply decide we can't face any further upheaval and pull up the drawbridge?

To those who think that finding new love means we no longer have a place on widow forums, the truth is that, whilst it is undeniably lovely to have someone who cares whether you've got home safely, new love doesn't erase old loss and neutralise grief. It brings with it new issues and painful reminders. It holds up a magnifying glass to past relationships. It makes you examine how you behaved and uncovers deep hurts and unresolved regrets. After the lows of bereavement, the highs of a new relationship are undeniably heady, but when you come home to an empty house and legal wrangles and a cold side of the bed and a wardrobe still full of your husband's clothes and wake alone and anxious after yet another terrible dream and you *still* can't get the little movie of your husband walking into the sea and all that happened in the moments afterwards out of your head, I promise you, life can feel just as bleak and despairing as ever.

SHUT AND OPEN CASE

Not one of us can predict how we are going to react to something. If we could plan our emotions in that way, then hey, I would get all the sad stuff out of the way at the beginning of the week and have a lovely six-day weekend. ~ **Emma S**

JS and I were *very* different. I used to joke that were we to appear on the TV game show *Mr & Mrs*, not only would no one believe we *were* Mr and Mrs, we would lose because my husband seemed to know so little about me. Examples of this included his comment that my favourite shop was Harvey Nicks (it's Selfridges), I like oxtail soup (I don't) and that I'm afraid of flying (I'm not, but I suffer from travel sickness).

One of the areas in which we differed was our behaviour when we came home from holiday.

JS's routine after a long-haul flight (him watching movies, me snoring with an eye mask) was to sort through the post, fret over the garden and unpack his suitcase, a process which involved flinging dirty washing down the stairs towards the general direction of the utility room. I took a more relaxed approach to coming home, preferring to dump my case in the hall, interrogate the dog-sitter over the state of The Hound's bowels and then take a cup of tea to bed and, against all the advice as to how to avoid jet-lag, sleep for a few hours. Invariably, I'd wake up to the sound of the washing machine (we did our washing separately after one too many incidents of dying all my white shirts a dirty grey because JS couldn't be bothered to sort the washing and bunged it all in together) and the rasp of the lawnmower. Sometimes, I'd start unpacking, but only if I wanted something; if there was no need for white jeans in London in November, why rush?

I'm giving you this background info to show that I have form when it comes to leaving a suitcase packed, but even by my sluttish standards, never did I envisage leaving a suitcase packed for one year, two months and 25 days.

But yesterday, I decided to open the battered, green Antler my husband bought me in 1990, a case last packed amongst terror and tears in Barbados as I prepared to make the return journey home without my husband, a man who instead of sitting next to me watching the movies as I snored, was still in the Caribbean, lying in a mortuary.

I know my case was purchased in 1990, because JS bought me the suitcase just after he jetted off across America whilst British Airways left me stranded at JFK Airport in New York, mistook me for another passenger's wife (really!) and so flew me home on Concorde (seat 2A!) as compensation. At Heathrow, it was easy to spot my borrowed suitcase plastered with 'Save Madagascar' stickers amongst the Louis Vuitton on the luggage carousel. I thought it was funny, but JS decided if we were to travel together, I needed something smarter.

The case I chose ended up going around the world with me for more than two decades. Its frame became bent which made it a devil to close, I used an elastic hair-band to keep one of the straps in place and there were several attempts to repair rips with layers of superglue, but I loved that case. When I saw it coming round the carousel at the airport with its red and white (Arsenal!) ribbons as extra identification, I would become ridiculously excited that we were being reunited, something that didn't always go down well on the numerous occasions when JS's case decided to take itself on holiday, often to Miami, even if we were nowhere near Florida.

For me, my suitcase wasn't *just* a suitcase. When I chose it and JS bought it, the case promised a lifetime of adventures, *together*. It was a symbol of excitement, of romance, of high-powered business trips, of balmy nights on foreign shores, of giggles trying to get it closed by sitting on it after buying one too many holiday souvenirs.

And now, of death.

I don't have a house big enough to 'lose' the case and nor do I have a loft, so I've seen this symbol of tragedy most days. Like a thirty-year-old who has yet to lose their virginity, it was becoming a millstone around my neck. People were asking about the suitcase in hushed, concerned tones; girlfriends were telling me that I HAD to open the case in order to move forward with my life. Once, I had to body-block the wretched thing to stop a well-meaning but slightly squiffy friend from opening it for me.

But on a sunny Sunday at the end of May, it felt time.

It felt right.

Ever practical, I also wanted some summer clothes.

I dragged the suitcase from under JS's desk, took it into the living room and opened it on the cleared coffee table.

I thought that I knew what was in there, such as the numbered packages of vitamin tablets, which after a few days were never used, because when you've watched your husband die you don't really care about balancing your perimenopausal hormones, and of course there was the symbolic Bikini of Death, but it was strange to see a couple of items I hadn't realised were packed: the shoulder bag JS used to travel with and the black polo shirt he was wearing on the beach just before he went for his last swim. And then there was the fine sprinkling of Barbados sand at the bottom of the case…

Until now, I thought that I would wail over the open case, sob into the pile of used underwear and dresses never worn.

I didn't.

As I took the clothes out and threw them into piles (dry cleaning; white load; coloured load; and several 'What the hell do I do with this?' piles) it felt like someone else's case and another woman's laundry, so much has happened since I packed to go on holiday in February 2011. I've put back on most of the two stones I lost after JS's death so I mostly *look* the same, but for the eyes that stare back at me in the mirror; eyes that have seen too much and cried too often. I *feel* like a different person in good, bad and sad ways.

JS's case is still packed, but, just as other widows promised me about my case, there will come the right time to open his.

So there we are, another hurdle jumped. At first, straight after I opened the suitcase, I was fine. Relieved.

But old habits die hard: I didn't put the piles of washing in the machine or store away the case or put away the sun lotion and the beach bag. I left the empty case in the hall and the piles of laundry dotted around the living room.

Last night, just before I went to bed, I went around the house switching the lights off.

I saw the contents of my suitcase scattered around in the darkened room and the empty suitcase in the hall illuminated by the streetlights and thought, 'Why the fuck did this have to happen to me?'

THE SAMARITANS

My youngest son told me last night before he went to sleep about how he'd managed to put a deflated rubber pig on his head, and how it had become stuck in his hair. I burst into laughter for the first time in I don't know how long, and then the hurt came. The one person who would be laughing harder than me wasn't here. I went to his photo and told him that I hoped he'd been listening. – **Rose**

Last week, I watched a programme that looked back on Queen Elizabeth II's 60 years on the throne. During it, I found myself reflecting on one of the darkest days of my life – no, not June 1977, the Queen's Silver Jubilee, when I ran on to the school playground and danced like a scalded cat for three minutes with lumpen scowly lads as part of a bizarre musical tableau – but the wedding of Kate Middleton and Prince William.

I'd planned to go to a friend's house and drink champagne whilst watching the nuptials, possibly even adding a waspish running commentary on the outfits (think Joan Rivers at The Oscars for *E!*), but I woke up on Friday 29th April 2011 (one month after the funeral, two months after JS's accident) so low, I was seriously scared that I could do something that others might regret.

The morning began with the same routine that had plagued me for weeks, a routine which would continue for months afterwards: I'd wake up, momentarily think that I'd had a bad dream and then seeing the empty side of the bed, JS's death would flood my brain in high-definition Technicolor, whereupon I'd rush to the bathroom to vomit. Some days I didn't make it and threw up en-route into my hand, or, depending on what I'd gone to bed wearing the night before (which depended on how drunk I was), I used my nightie as a make-shift cotton barf-bag, yanking it up from the hem to cover my mouth. After I'd thrown up, I'd go downstairs to let The Hound out and make a cup of tea and, multi-tasking woman that I am, throw up again in the sink and in the flowerbed whilst the kettle boiled and The Hound peed.

Every morning was shocking, but the morning of the Royal Wedding was so grim, it was one of the handful of times I rang The Samaritans*, sobbing and pacing the bedroom as the man on the end of the phone patiently listened to my panic and despair.

I can't remember how long I was on the phone for – I know that some of the phone calls went on for hours – but eventually I calmed down, hung up and got dressed.

I took The Hound to the Heath for a walk. There was hardly anyone around. All of London seemed to be partying whilst I was grief-stricken. A woman walked past me and said cheerfully, 'Another Republican boycotting the wedding! Good for you!'

In my head I raged at her in the same vicious tones I'd used to my mother the day before, spitting down the phone, 'You haven't got a clue, have you, sitting there with your husband of 49 years!'

Having had a sob and a walk, I felt better, so at home I put the telly on. With seriously bad timing I just caught the 'Until death do us part' bit and wailed and screamed and rocked in pain and then cried not just for JS and me, but because I'd frightened The Hound with my vocal hysterics.

I can't remember what I did for the rest of the day. After all that emotion I suspect I just drank, ate Mr Kipling Almond Slices and

---

* The Samaritans are not just for those who feel suicidal. They can be telephoned at any time, day or night, to talk things through. www.samaritans.org

flaked out on the sofa watching *Two and a Half Men*, which is pretty much what I did every evening during those dark months.

If, back then, anyone had told me that 14 months later I would be marking the Queen's Diamond Jubilee, firstly I wouldn't have believed them (finding it hard to imagine getting through another day let alone a slew of months) and, secondly, I would have been outraged at their suggestion that life and love could ever rise again from the ashes of my shattered life.

But I did celebrate the Queen's Diamond Jubilee, and I had a fabulous time.

The long weekend was split between my area of London where it was a case of 'Spot the Bunting' (and when you did, it was so tastefully understated you almost missed it) and the pretty village where Gorgeous Grey-Haired Widower lives, a village festooned with so much bunting, even the bus couldn't make it along the High Street without becoming gift-wrapped in flags.

We decorated the outside of GGHW's house with streamers, flags and balloons (it looked like a used car lot) and GGHW, me, The Hound and GGHW's two sons sat in his bright-red vintage MG and took part in the village parade.

The Hound, resplendent in a Union Jack collar and lead, waved a regal paw to the crowds. Son No 2 took him round a canine agility course (no mean feat for a dachshund), all the humans ate ice cream and drank beer, and the rain stayed off until it was time to go home. It was great fun and *almost* converted a die-hard townie like me to country living. We even got our picture in the local paper.

But as with so much in this new life, there were flashes of pain and sadness amongst the red, white and blue jollity, the feeling that my new life hasn't quite caught up with my old brain. Many bereaved will identify with feeling sad that you *can* be happy again, deep pain that your loved one isn't here to see how bravely you are trying to make a new life, tearful when you know how proud they would be of you for coming so far since the days when The Samaritans had to talk you down from the cliff of despair, if only temporarily.

And make no mistake, there is still panic, sometimes during the day, sometimes waking me at night. Perhaps this anxiety isn't grief, perhaps it's the menopause which is knocking on my door. But do shrivelling ovaries cause vivid dreams, dreams of speeding cars where I am the passenger, but I look over to see there is no driver, or of JS finding a new partner and running away from me, in one, even climbing over a wall at the back of a shop to escape?

All the positive thinking in the world can't trick your subconscious mind and mine comes out to play at night.

I hear from widows who are roughly at the same stage as me who say: 'I feel just as bad as when it first happened. It's like I'm back at the beginning again.'

For me, nothing could be as bad as those early days when I would literally run around the house, panic-stricken, trying to escape from the inescapable. Back then the grief was relentless, unmanageable and uncontrollable. Now, it isn't relentless, but it is still uncontrollable, catching me out in the strangest of places. The difference is, now I can manage it. I know that the kick to the gut or the wrench to the heart will ebb away, that tears can be healing, that when the stiff upper lip crumbles it doesn't mean that you aren't coping, but that breaking down once in a while is actually a way of coping.

To see how far you've come, sometimes you have to look back, and sometimes you just have to watch a TV programme.

ANGRY BIRD

When I started out grieving in those very first days, all I could say to my husband was 'I'm so sorry...' because I myself had a lot of guilt. Later it became, 'How could you? Do you even see? Do you even see all of this?' when I'd have a moment alone in the car screaming, shaking. At this point when I see him – I'm not sure whether I'll hug him or punch him.
*~ **Julia Cho***

I've been feeling angry lately, the sort of angry that makes me glad I don't live in a country that makes it legal to carry a Smith & Wesson in my glove-box, otherwise I would be writing this blog from a prison cell, having leant out of my Fiat 500 on the Holloway Road and blasted the person in front for chucking the remains of their McDonald's meal through their car window.

As an example of my anger, in the space of a couple of hours I ranted at two Smug Breeders, a disabled person and a seventeen-year-old schoolboy. The Smug Breeders deserved getting it with both barrels, the disabled person was in the wrong too, as was the schoolboy in his mother's car, but perhaps shouting at the boy to, 'Go home and come back out when you've learnt how to drive, how to shave and your balls have dropped!' was a little over the top. On the other hand, perhaps the lad is used to middle-aged women going mental, as he stared at me and said with gum-chewing nonchalance, 'Oh, I get it. It's your age.'

I've screamed at cold callers, fired off angry letters to financial institutions and accountants and been uncharacteristically abusive to a man who keeps asking me to help him with a business issue which is no longer anything to do with me, something I have pointed out (nicely) for months. I've written a stinging email to a company telling them they will never get my business ever again, even though they didn't want it in the first place, and threatened to report the block of flats next door to the council if they didn't sort out their monster light-sapping hedge (which they did).

I've even been angry that I started blogging, furious that I should find myself in a position to write about grief, when I'd much rather be writing about travelling around the UK with The Hound in search of the best plate of ham, egg and chips (top spot so far: the Swan in the Rushes pub in Loughborough).

I'm not going to pretend that before JS died I was St Helen of Highgate, floating through life in a wrap dress and heels proclaiming in honeyed tones, 'Forgive them for they know not what they do.' I'm not perfect; even Jesus threw a hissy fit and started flipping over tables in the temple. Tolerance has never been my middle name (it's Elizabeth), and my friends know that if I ever become ruler of this great land, as a born-and-bred Geordie, I intend to pass a law whereby anyone who lets their dog foul the pavement is forced to live in Sunderland. But whereas usually I'm a blow-up-for-30-seconds-and-get-over-it girl, I've been simmering with rage for weeks.

What started this current bout of anger was reading an interview in *The Times* with the Olympic rower, James Cracknell. In it, he said: 'If you are cycling without a helmet, you are being selfish. If I don't wear a helmet and I get knocked off and devastatingly hurt, how can I look my wife, kids or parents in the eye and say I did everything possible to make it home safely to them?'

I read the article and felt *furious* with JS.

JS loved cycling, proper London-Brighton type cycling, but he refused point-blank to wear a helmet, claiming that as he had been both a driver *and* a cyclist in London all his life, he was able to think ahead and avoid an accident. After seeing one too many bunches of flowers tied to railings and white 'Ghost bikes' on our way to work, I begged him to wear a helmet. He said I could buy him one. We went to a shop, I bought a red one, we took it home and then he refused to use it, pointing out that he had said I could *buy* him one, *not* that he would wear it. At the time, I was exasperated, but shrugged it off as being just JS and his personality. But reading the James Cracknell interview, I was incensed at JS for being so selfish, for putting himself first, just because he always rebelled against being told what to do. I was mad, but I couldn't confront him with the article, tell him that I was mad not just for the sake of being mad, but because I was scared of losing him. My anger built. I knew I was being ridiculous: I was angry at a dead man over his refusal to wear a helmet I had bought years ago, in the hope of avoiding an accident which never happened and could no longer happen.

Fuelled by fury, I remembered his tantrum over the seat belt alarm in his new car. He hated the fact that it buzzed with increasing intensity if he didn't put his seat belt on, which, often, he didn't. One day, the buzzing went on and on. It was driving me crazy. I urged him to put his seat belt on. 'I will not have this car tell me what to do!' he snapped. 'I'm going to get it disconnected.' And so we drove with the thing going mental, me upset and him determined to prove a point that some German engineer with safety in mind at BMW wasn't going to dictate to a man in north London that he should buckle up.

Before this recent bout of anger, I would remember incidents like these (and there are many) and fondly roll my teary eyes, shaking my head with a wry smile as if I was talking about an exasperating child who is naughty one moment, but melts your heart with a beaming smile the next.

I'm in a new phase of grieving, and JS wasn't a child. He was an educated grown man, interested in the arts, obsessed by books, intelligent and cultured with a wide vocabulary, a man who could write the most beautiful letters and give breathtakingly eloquent speeches.

But despite his first-class command of the English language, there was one word he never used.

Sorry.

JS never said 'Sorry' because he could never admit that he was wrong, even when the evidence was overwhelming that he was. He was *never* to blame; it was always someone else or something else: the thief's fault for stealing things from my car, even though I had reminded him to lock it and not leave the boot wide open as he trotted between street and house with luggage; the bank's fault for not having a more efficient clearing system, thereby bouncing a large cheque (incurring costs) I had given him along with strict instructions not to bank it for five days to allow money to move between accounts, but which he had deposited straightaway; Rufus's fault for running out into the road because JS had opened the garage door and then gone wandering down the street to talk to a neighbour (which incidentally happened another time, which meant a bike got stolen; again, not his fault). He never said, 'Yes, sorry, it was a bad call. I shouldn't have done it.' *Never*.

At times, I did get very upset, but though stubborn, JS was also a man who could charm the birds from the trees. I would be angry with him, but I could direct that anger *at* him, get some response which might be him sulking for a week or a meal out/dog walk/trip to the coast where we would end up laughing and all would be well.

But lately, more and more I have been feeling anger towards JS over incidents long ago forgotten and forgiven when he was alive. The problem is, now he isn't here to explain himself or to charm me out of my fury. The dead can't defend themselves. My anger has nowhere to go, which is why, perhaps, I've been lashing out at strangers. As well as anger, I feel overwhelmed, restless and directionless; annoyed that many of the issues I foresaw when JS was alive and which he wouldn't talk about because he refused to have his judgement questioned are now problems *I* have to deal with, alone, problems which have sapped my resources, both emotionally and financially. I have had to 'man up' very fast and confront issues that my husband either couldn't or wouldn't. No wonder I'm angry.

After JS died, I used to sit on the sofa in my living room and look at the front door and imagine him coming through it. In the first six months or so, I used to think that I wouldn't be the slightest bit surprised if he walked back in. It would seem such a normal thing to do, as if all the horror was just a bad dream. Later, I imagined him coming in and me flying to the door and flinging my arms around him, sobbing, The Hound hysterical with delight.

The other night I was sitting on the sofa, alone and fed up, eating a cold sausage. I imagined JS coming through the front door, 18 months after he walked into the sea despite my warnings.

I was shocked that my first reaction was, 'Don't you dare you just waltz back in here as if nothing has happened.'

Like I said, I'm angry.

Sad and angry.

COMPETITIVE GRIEVING

A corker said to me by a social worker who was based in my school was, 'Oh you're lucky your husband's dead. I still have to see my bastard ex-husband regularly'. She then went on to moan about how hard it was to get on with her life after her husband had left her for another woman.
~ Amelie

'I feel like slapping Meryl Streep with a wet fish,' isn't a phrase you come across every day, nor one I ever thought I'd utter, but I do, and if you're widowed you might want to join me in my piscatorial slap-fest. We could take it in turns or perform synchronised slapping, me with a piece of cod, you with some haddock, all sustainably sourced and responsibly caught of course.

Why, might you ask, am I encouraging other widows to partake in a spot of fishy thuggery towards one of Hollywood's finest and most revered actresses?

Read on.

Have you seen the film *It's Complicated*?

It's a rom-com starring the aforementioned Ms Streep as Jane, and Alec Baldwin as Jake, a once-married, now-divorced, LA-based couple who start an affair, ten years after Jake cheats on Jane with the woman he's now married to. Confused? Like the film's title says, it's complicated.

I saw the DVD languishing in a bargain bucket at a local shop, and tossed it in my trolley because it also stars Steve Martin. I *love* Steve Martin. I once sat next to him in a restaurant and was focusing so hard on pretending not to look at him or listen to what he was saying, that I dropped a great big blob of satay sauce on my top, something I didn't realise until I sauntered through the restaurant on the way to the theatre, feeling fabulous, only to get to the coat check and see a nasty brown stain across my boobs, as if I'd been cradling a breast-fed baby with an overflowing nappy. I asked JS why he didn't notice the offending stain. He loved Steve Martin too, and had been too busy looking at him out of the corner of his eye to notice my sullied top.

Anyway, it took me a while to get round to watching *It's Complicated* as my DVD player didn't work, and all the jiggling and fiddling of leads and banging of the top and sides didn't make any difference, so in the end, I propped my laptop on a pile of books on the coffee table and watched it from there.

So, there I was with snacks and vino, wondering where Meryl's cute earrings were from (Ted Muehling – I Googled them) when about half-a-glass of Merlot and several handfuls of Twiglets later, the action cut to a scene featuring Jane/Meryl and three of her friends (one divorced, one never married, one widowed) sitting around Jane's fabulous kitchen table with a bottle of wine, picking apart what went wrong with Jane's marriage, and reflecting on an awkward meeting Jane had had with Jake in an elevator earlier that day, something which involved plastic surgery and sperm samples.

It was light-hearted and gossipy, and the dialogue went like this:

Diane (divorced, lustrous hair): 'Janey, come on, he cheats on you with her, your 20-year marriage ends then six months later she leaves Jake for some random guy, has a baby, leaves that guy, marries Jake and she's not nuts!'

Jane (divorced, lovely hair, fabulous earrings): 'Jo, you're so lucky Jerry's dead.'

Joanne (widowed, short hair, rather dowdy): 'Oh, thanks.'

Jane: 'No, I mean, you never have to bump into him.'

What! Did I hear right? Did Jane really tell her widowed friend that she was luckier to have a dead husband than an alive ex-husband? That it would be preferable for the ex to be dead to avoid any awkward embarrassment in an elevator?

I re-wound the DVD for confirmation. There it was again: 'Jo, you're so lucky Jerry's dead.'

I began to fantasise about meeting Miss Streep in a lift. In my fantasy, I'd stop the lift between floors and start waving a wet fish in her beautiful face, berating her for her crassness whilst rejecting her pleas that she was 'in character'. This little fantasy ended with her apologising profusely, and handing over the earrings she was wearing. I never did work out why I was in a lift with an unwrapped piece of haddock.

Sucking thoughtfully on a Twiglet, I realised that it wasn't Meryl or her character I wanted to confront, it was the countless divorced women I've come across since JS died, who seem to feel that widows have it easy compared to divorcees.

A day or two after JS drowned and still in Barbados waiting for the formalities to be completed, I walked past the pool area where a 40-something woman in a bikini was sitting on the edge, dangling her legs in the water. She looked up at me with puffy tearful eyes and said, 'I'm so sorry about what happened to your husband.' Even in my shocked state, I was aware that watching a man drowning and the attempts to resuscitate him on the beach must have been very distressing for other holidaymakers, and I knew that some of the guests were in tears when they saw me around the resort.

'I'm sorry you're upset,' I said. 'I'm sorry if it's spoilt your holiday.'

And I was. It was bad enough that I was floating around in tears without seeing other bikini-clad women sobbing on my behalf.

And then she spat out, 'I'm not crying about *you*. I'm crying for *me*. I wish it had been my husband who had been dragged out of the sea, *dead*.'

On a scale of inappropriate things to say to someone whose husband had just drowned, this woman went beyond anything imaginable. On reflection, I wish that I had pushed this self-absorbed princess into the pool and sat on her, thereby giving the local pathologist another drowning victim to slice open, but I didn't. I sat down beside her.

Through angry sobs, she explained that just after Christmas, her husband of 25 years had announced that he had been having an affair with one of his employees, a younger 'exotic' woman and he was leaving to set up home with her. This had come as a bolt from the blue. There had been no sign of his infidelity: they had recently celebrated their 25th wedding anniversary, been on holiday with friends and enjoyed a lovely family Christmas. She had come to Barbados at the suggestion of friends who thought she would have a nervous breakdown if she didn't take a holiday.

Pool Woman's anger towards her cheating husband was of nuclear proportions. I sat and listened as every vile, bile-laced insult she could muster poured out of her. With the selfishness of deep grief, the anger of the wronged and absolutely no knowledge of my situation back in London, she told me that I was lucky that JS was dead. *I* would get my husband's share of our property; *she* would have to give this dirty cheating rat half their home. *She* would lose her job and her income as she worked for her husband at his business, whilst the 'slut' was going to remain on the payroll. The list of hardships this woman would have to suffer came thick and fast, each one far worse than anything I would encounter as a widow. She had even banned her husband from attending their son's wedding. Her son agreed with her that they would be better off if his father was dead.

So there we were, both suddenly without our husbands, but worlds apart in our grief. Her grief was fuelled by a feeling of abandonment, the knowledge that her husband had stopped loving her to the point where he was prepared to walk away from his wife and their home, and into the arms of his mistress. Is it any wonder she felt betrayed and rejected, angry that her marriage had failed?

I have no sympathy for the woman by the pool. She was a rich, spoilt bitch, toxic with hate and without an ounce of humility, a woman whose anger was fuelled not just by the loss of her husband, but by the loss of her lifestyle and her status as the wife of a successful man, but my contempt for her does not mean that I have no sympathy for the divorced, that I don't acknowledge that when a marriage ends there is grief. 'They chose to get divorced! I didn't choose that my husband died!' is often the response from widows angered by articles where divorcees have claimed, 'My divorce was like a death.' Well, actually, no it isn't. Death is death and divorce is divorce, but both bring with them grief. Not all marriages end by mutual consent; sometimes there is no slow winding down of love and affection. A friend of mine told me how on the Saturday night her husband snuggled up to her and their new baby on the sofa and said, 'We're so lucky to have all this, aren't we?' The following Monday, she was standing by the stove making spaghetti bolognaise, when her husband came home from work. His response to her question, 'Good day?', was: 'I'm leaving you.' Just like that. Out of the blue. She thought he was joking, so she turned round to face him and he repeated it. He'd been having an affair. Some years later, her partner collapsed and died whilst reading a men's fitness magazine in WHSmith. After I was widowed, I remember her telling me that her divorce was far more traumatic than her partner's death. JS was also widowed and divorced, and though he wanted a divorce, he used to say that divorce was worse than death, because with death, 'You just have to get on with it, you have no choice, whereas with divorce, you watch someone else getting it on with them.'

The widowed look at the divorced and the divorced look at the widowed, and each think that they have it harder than the other. I'm still not sure who, if anyone, is right, because when I wake up from one of those dreams where JS has left me for another woman, where he has looked scornfully at me, climbed over a wall to get away from me, is happy in his new life without me when I am weeping and pleading with him to come home, I feel far more wretched, more lost, more abandoned than the dreams where he has died. JS's assertion that watching other people make a new life with your old spouse feels – at least in the dream – far more painful than the finality of death.

I still want to slap that woman by the pool though.

FEAR AND CLOTHING

I've always been a worrier and ten years ago when I was first widowed, my anxieties grew beyond all proportion. The second time I was widowed, I was virtually certifiable. More recently I have been physically ill when my new partner was uncontactable for two hours. I cannot live like this. I need to find a way to stop. My aim is to become warrior rather than worrier. ~ **Jay**

Way back when, I met a woman whose life was ruled by emetophobia: an intense and irrational fear of vomiting. So severe was her phobia, to limit her chances of getting food poisoning, every day for every meal she ate the same thing: two crispbreads, mushroom paté, a packet of plain crisps and a bottle of water drunk through a wrapped straw. Phobia Woman rarely went out for fear of seeing someone be sick or sick splattered on the pavement, was unable to watch any TV dramas in case one of the characters chundered on screen and claimed that even seeing or hearing the words 'sick' or 'vomit' made her gag. She did everything she could to control her environment, but her mind had other ideas and constantly reminded her of her greatest fear.

Along with a man who was terrified of hidden asbestos and a young lad who feared seeing one of those waving 'lucky' cats you see in Chinese takeaways, I managed to persuade Phobia Woman to leave her house and come to the pub. I had to open all the doors for her, she couldn't drink and she sat with her hands on her lap the whole time looking anxious and miserable. Although sympathetic to her plight, I spent the entire evening fighting the devil on my shoulder who was urging me to tell this poor woman about my abandoned studies into vomiting ferrets at St George's hospital to see how quickly she reacted…

The point of this early (and you are probably thinking totally bonkers) digression, is that Phobia Woman told me that I would be surprised at just how often you notice vomit-related incidents, in the same way you suddenly notice red Ferraris if you are thinking of buying one. Apparently, it's known as Perpetual Vigilance. I suspect her psychiatrist told her that. I knew her in 2002, but a decade later, I still can't see a pile of vomit outside a kebab shop without remembering her.

Perpetual Vigilance may go some way to explaining why over the last 18 months, my world seems to have been filled with people having something to say about holidays.

Pre-Holiday from Hell, I thought it was just hairdressers who chirped, 'Going away anywhere nice on holiday?'

Wrong!

All manner of people at all times of the year have asked me if I was going on holiday/had gone on holiday/knew anywhere nice to go on holiday/told me in great detail about their fantastic holiday/ their neighbours' disastrous holiday or bored me rigid with because they were so tired and stressed ('I feel as if the whole family has sat 15 GCSEs. We're totes exhausted!'), they needed a holiday.

Then there are those who on hearing that I've been bereaved/ depressed/ill/tired, etc. suggest brightly, 'You know what you need?' and before I can say, 'A good night's sleep without upsetting dreams?' they prescribe a holiday in the sun. It's fun to see them squirm with embarrassment when they remember what happened, especially if I remind them that, twice in the last few years, I've gone on holiday and come back with one of the party having died (one dog, one husband) whilst having fun at the beach.

'I no longer do holidays abroad,' I'd announce in the same prim, determined way I wrote that I would *never* wear another bikini.

I could no more imagine me getting on a plane to go somewhere warm and sunny by the coast, than I could imagine donning a helmet with a torch and squeezing myself through cracks in a dark, water-filled cave.

Except now I am going.

Not potholing – I'd only go down a cave if there was a champagne bar and Alastair Campbell in shorts running it – but on holiday. In a few days. To Portugal. With Gorgeous Grey-Haired Widower.

There had to be negotiation of course: GGHW wanted to go for ten nights, I wanted to start with five, so we compromised on seven. I couldn't face flying from Gatwick, so we're going from Heathrow and although I was happy to stay by the coast, I didn't want a hotel right on the beach. I made one rule: on no account was GGHW to go swimming in the sea, not even a bob around in the shallows in a pair of Speedos.

I knew that going away was never going to be easy, that it would be a milestone, but whilst I imagined I might collapse on the X-ray machine going through security and find myself on the conveyer belt along with a pile of hand-baggage, or begin hyperventilating at 33,000 feet wondering if a body was being carried in the hold below, I completely underestimated how difficult the run-up to this trip would be.

I had it all planned: new start, new suitcase, new bikinis, perhaps even a few new dresses.

I bought a rather spiffy suitcase from Selfridges – bright red, light but strong, made from something NASA uses for its rockets. I'm going to Portugal, not the moon, but I bought it because I wanted a fresh start and it was lovely and rather swish for a box on wheels.

The day after my purchase, I became filled with despair at what I'd done. It was expensive! I didn't need a new case! I loved the old one! It had been a loyal and faithful case and I had traded it in for something modern and flashy. GGHW suggested I took the new one back. I wished I could, but it was too late. I'd got the man in the shop to take all the packaging off so I could take it home by wheeling it along Oxford Street.

Stung by regretting my new suitcase decision, I veered between using my old bikinis (not The Bikini of Death, *obviously*) and buying new ones. In the end, I decided on a new and old combo and, treating myself, went to über-stylish swimwear emporium, Heidi Klein, and bought a couple in the sale. As the assistant was wrapping them up, she asked me where I was going. I told her and then launched into what had happened last year, where it had happened, etc., etc. I haven't had that sort of verbal diarrhoea for months, and as I prattled on I kept thinking, 'Bailey – shut the f**k up!' but I couldn't stop. It was a Saturday afternoon in a busy swimwear shop in Knightsbridge. I'm sure that the entire shop didn't want to hear how you could go on holiday and drown. I'm sure the assistant didn't want to hear it either; I'm guessing it doesn't do much for the holiday mood of their customers. I left the shop hating myself for behaving like that. I felt I'd gone back to the days when no one was safe from hearing my story.

Everything about the run-up to this holiday has been depressingly familiar, almost Groundhog Day. Try as I might, I have not been able to avoid the natural rhythm of planning a trip: organising a dog-sitter; sorting out the holiday wardrobe; buying sun cream; booking a pedicure, a bikini wax and so on. These pre-holiday preparations have brought everything back – the countdown to JS's death. Of course, I could ditch the personal grooming, but if buying a new case and a bikini doesn't change anything, manky toes and a bikini line hurtling towards my knees wouldn't either.

The last week or so has been as bad, if not worse, than the run-up to the first anniversary of JS's drowning. I've been getting more and more anxious and tearful to the point where when I flicked a caterpillar away from the front door with The Hound's ball launcher a little more forcefully than I intended, splatting it against a window with a resounding thud, I crouched over its fat, lifeless body and sobbed, 'I'm so sorry. I didn't mean to kill you. I'm *so* sorry.'

That's just bonkers isn't it?

I've cried on buses and in the street. I got teary looking through old currency kept in an envelope. I found JS's holiday wallet, something which must have come back from Barbados, but which I've never looked at. The ordinariness of its contents floored me: a receipt for the car we hired less than 24 hours before JS died; bills from the few meals we had before that fateful Sunday morning.

I'm not crying for JS or JS and me any longer. I'm crying for the woman who the week before her last holiday abroad bought new bikinis and sun cream and got a Brazilian and a pedicure and looked forward to sitting in the sun, drinking wine, but who ended up wearing a bikini as her husband died in front of her.

I wandered through Fenwick's a couple of days ago and remembered going there to buy a sunhat just before I went to Barbados, excited at the thought of going on a holiday both JS and I badly needed. I cried as I left the shop and walked along Bond Street, reflecting on how completely oblivious I was to the tragedy hurtling towards me.

I don't feel sorry myself now; I've still got a lot of challenging legal and financial issues swirling around me, but, on balance, I'm grateful to have a good new life. But when I think back to the woman who went on holiday full of hope and fun and faced hell, I feel overwhelmed with grief for her and that is why I weep.

I want to go away and sit in the sun with GGHW, to eat outside in the evening, sharing a bottle of wine. We will do those things. But right now, as I write this, rather than having one life and wanting to live it, I'm filled with fear.

Everyone tells me that I will have a good time, that everything will be fine. That the hurried will I made won't be needed. That the top-level travel insurance I have taken out is just a precaution. That no one I love will die abroad, or will die at home when I'm abroad.

On one level, I believe them.

But on another?

I know how quickly paradise can turn into hell, and changing my suitcase or buying a designer bikini won't erase that as easily as I'd hoped. Like Phobia Woman, I've done everything I can to reduce my anxiety, but, infuriatingly, my mind has other ideas.

POSTCARD FROM THE EDGE

*My husband, Gavin, died suddenly and unexpectedly nearly two years ago, of an undiagnosed heart condition. He was also away on business in China at the time. So the whole issue of being abroad made a traumatic event even harder. Anyway, to cut a long story short, I work for myself and took on a client that is based in Seoul, and in December, I travelled there. I had huge reservations before going: What if I die, too, when I am away on business? What if the plane crashes? I'm leaving my two children (both under five) back here with my parents. If I die, they are both orphans, etc., etc. In the end I decided I had to bite the bullet and do it; I couldn't stop living, because of this fear. Gavin would have HATED me to miss such a wonderful opportunity. So I went, and I felt proud of myself, and it kind of reaffirmed to me that I have to get on and do these things. **Charlie P**

Sitting around the pool on holiday in Portugal, I came to the following conclusions:

1. Unnaturally skinny women, particularly rich, groomed-to-an-inch-of-their-bleached-teeth, Ralph Lauren-type women, look better dressed than undressed, especially if their butt is so flat they exhibit severe bikini-bottom droop when climbing out of the pool.

2. It doesn't matter how young, fit, tanned and exotically foreign a man is, budgie smugglers are stomach churning.

3. If you are young and female, even if you are not conventionally pretty, you can get away with wearing just about anything, irrespective of your body size or shape. I wish I had come to this conclusion 30 years ago.
4. I'm relieved that I never had a dolphin tattooed around my belly button, as now it would be unattractively drooping, rather than energetically leaping.
5. That I am living every day as if it's my last, which, in my case, isn't a good way to live.

I had a **WONDERFUL** holiday. Note the capital letters, bold and underlining. *That* is how great it was.

The weather was glorious, the food delicious, the surroundings fabulous and Gorgeous Grey-Haired Widower was just as gorgeous overseas as he is in the UK, other than on the last day when he did that typical 'Brit Abroad And About To Go Back Home' thing, i.e. he tried to accelerate his tan and ended up the spitting image of a humongous boiled lobster.

It's always a worry the first time you go on holiday with someone; sometimes you see a completely different side to their personality and far from coming home with your relationship strengthened, you look at them at the luggage carousel back in the UK and wonder what on earth possessed you to go away with this alien in the first place.

In a life before marriage, I went on holiday with someone who at home appeared to be the opposite of everything he despised in his father, who was narrow-minded, grumpy and wildly right-wing, the sort of man who would announce at the dinner table that he hated foreign food because it was 'mucked up grub'. We went to Spain. I don't know if the aircraft cabin pressure scrambled his brain or just that the stress of going away with me caused him to revert to type, but the moment we landed he turned into his father: he hated Spanish food, hated the Spanish, hated the ex-pats who crowded the English bars we went to because he hated the Spanish bars, yada yada yada. Perhaps he would have been happier in Greece, but I never found out because I dumped him.

Anyway, this time, GGHW and I got there and back in one piece without any mishaps, which was a relief to both of us as not only had *my* last holiday ended in disaster, I can now reveal that GGHW's last trip out of the UK involved a family member ending up in hospital and taking a flight home under medical escort.

I was so anxious and wound up before I went, it was only at the end of the holiday that GGHW confessed that he had had two worries: either that I would pull out just before we were due to leave, or that I would arrive and completely freak out.

Neither of those things happened, but there were a few initial wobbles. At one point, my anxiety shot so high I nearly broke into the emergency Valium tablet someone gave me when JS died, and which I carry with me. I didn't use it because I was worried that it might react with the travel sickness tablets I had taken and form some strange hallucinogenic drug cocktail.

The days were filled with sunshine, a little sightseeing and lots of laughter, and the evenings saw us sipping drinks before dinner at sunset. They were perfect days.

But the nights?

They were dreadful. At times, *truly* dreadful.

The dreams that have plagued me on and off since JS died, and which have been more on than off over the last few weeks, accompanied me to Portugal. I don't remember all of them and some of them slipped away from me the moment I woke up, leaving me with heart hammering, panic-stricken. But others were vivid: I was on my knees, inching along a steel girder hundreds of feet above the ground, only to slip, clutching at the metal with my fingertips until I couldn't hold on any longer and down I went; trying to dodge a reversing articulated lorry (a Royal Mail lorry, should you be interested), which eventually pinned me to a wall, crushing me as I felt my breath ebbing away.

When I wasn't dying, I was in my house, but it was no longer mine. I'd walk through the door and find someone else living there. Confused, I'd plead with them that there had to be some mistake, that this was my home, that *they* had got it wrong, not me. And then I'd wake up, in a state. To calm myself down I'd get up, go to the loo just for something to do and remind myself that it was all just a dream and go back to bed, when another bizarrely upsetting scenario involving my death or some loss would emerge.

I only had one JS dream and it was very odd and totally different from the heart-hammering sort. A man who looked either like a tramp or someone from ZZ Top (long hair, beard, unkempt) was in the dream. If I could smell in my dreams, I would say he probably reeked of Special Brew and stale pee. You get the picture. At some point, I realised this man was JS. He was talking and, though it sounded like him, it was the incoherent ramblings of someone clearly mentally unwell. I remember thinking, 'He's gone nuts! It's not my fault he left after all! He didn't know what he was doing! None of this is my fault! He's ill!'

And instead of waking up feeling panic-stricken, I felt relieved. None of this was my fault!

Lying in the dark, I never really defined what I might be at fault for: that I didn't make a big enough fuss, withhold his glasses, fling myself in front of him, all to block his path to the sea? That my last words were shouted at him (accompanied by finger wagging) as if he was a naughty child, 'BE CAREFUL! I MEAN IT!' so he just thought I was nagging rather than genuinely worried? Or going on a holiday that I arranged, that I pushed for because we were both so drained from a difficult year? That my screams and my feet tickling and my pleading couldn't bring him round when they dragged him out of the water and on to the beach? That part of me had given up on him in the ambulance before we even got to the hospital, because I knew he was dead, that, despite everyone's efforts including my own, it was all futile? That I have had to begin to carve a new life for myself, and that new life includes new love?

My conscious mind admits no guilt – I did all I could and I have no choice but to keep living and I intend to live well – but clearly, at some deeper level, guilt is swirling.

Poolside in Portugal, in an attempt to calm my mind on some unconscious level (get me, going all spiritual!), I abandoned my normal practice of reading a chapter of a book, mentally annihilating the holiday garb of all around me and then snoozing with my sun-hat over my face, and decided to listen to Eckhart Tolle's *The Power of Now* on my iPod. The problem was, as this little gnome-faced guru (who, incidentally, I think talks a great deal of sense) was encouraging me to stay in the present moment and focus on the here and now, my mind kept wandering to thoughts such as, 'Where are we going to eat tonight?', 'Did I put sun cream on the backs of my knees?' and 'Was the house insurance up-to-date when I left?'

So I gave up being spiritual and went and watched the football in the poolside bar, where I met Eddie, a larger-than-life character who was at a conference for people who made electrical things: switches and junction boxes and so on.

Eddie and I got talking about football and about business and at some point I used the phrase, 'My late husband.' Eddie said that I was young to be a widow (which pleased me, the young bit, not the widow bit obviously). He asked what had happened. I briefly told him and then he said, 'A thing like that must make you live every day as if it's your last.' I agreed, but when I went back to my sun lounger I started thinking, 'How would I live if I knew this day was my last?'

Magazines often pose this question to celebrities and the answer is usually along the lines of watching the sun go down with a bottle of vintage wine having spent the day with their nearest and dearest, or blowing all their money on a Porsche and blasting along the coast. But when I thought about my last day, I realised that if I wasn't lying in a darkened room with shock, I'd be at the computer typing out instructions for my funeral and passwords for online accounts, making sure my will was up to date and everyone knew who got what and on what condition. I'd be checking that there were no dirty knickers in the laundry basket, that the drawers were tidy and that The Hound had enough food. I'd make it clear where the spare keys were kept and what I wanted done with my clothes. In other words, I would want to make everything as easy and neat and tidy as possible for those left behind. But the sad thing is, perhaps I would be so busy getting everything in order, I would run out of time to tell the people I love that I loved them.

Those who have faced enormous change in their life through death, illness or accident sometimes claim that post-disaster, they have a much more relaxed approach to life, that they have realised what is important. GGHW is one of those people, a man who can see an upside in the most dire of situations, a man who doesn't get all stressed out because the hotel room doesn't have the right balcony, or stockpile teabags at breakfast in case they run out because a large family on the next table stick five bags in each of their four teapots.

I admire him for it.

But that's not me.

The night before the morning JS drowned, we were having dinner at our favourite restaurant in Barbados, The Lone Star. The woman next to us started choking – proper emergency choking – and after she had vomited into her napkin, we got talking. I don't know what we were talking about, but I do remember JS saying to this woman, 'My wife worries about everything.'

And now I worry even more about the fleetingness of our life here on earth.

I have always embraced life and taken opportunities. I have always, even as a child, had a fear of getting to the end of my life and feeling that I have wasted it. We all know, in theory, just how quickly and unexpectedly life can end, but until you have witnessed it, felt it in your bones and lived and breathed it every day, you cannot really understand it. Now, I am even more anxious to make the most of everything, to get everything in order.

GGHW and I had some lovely meals, but more than once I caught myself thinking, 'What if this is the last evening we have together?' GGHW doesn't say, 'It won't be,' because he knows as well as I that he can't make that promise, but he does say, 'We'll have wonderful memories.' But I miss the innocence of sitting having a wonderful meal, with a wonderful man looking at spectacular scenery and not having that nagging little thought in my mind: 'This could all be over in a heartbeat.'

One of the things Eckhart Tolle said was that his anxiety about life got to such a degree that he could no longer live with himself and at that point, the point when he was (to use my ugly phrase, not his) 'all anxioused out', he finally found some peace.

I feel that I am getting to that point, that I can no longer stand worrying, that I must just slow down and let life unfold. Because living every day as if it's your last is a lovely idea in theory, but in practice, it's so exhausting, I need another holiday.

FRIENDS AND NEIGHBOURS

I remember someone saying to me in about the first week that I would find out who my friends were. I thought at the time that it was an incredibly harsh thing to say. I have since realised that it is true. I also realised in grief that a lot of my friendships were dependent on my efforts. I ran out of energy, I care(d) little about anything, I let them go. If people weren't able to offer me what I needed, I just let it go. Some still say, 'If there is anything we can do, just ask,' or, 'you must come round for dinner sometime, just let us know when,' but they never actually offer or invite. I smile, say 'Thanks,' know it is empty, and I let them go. Sometimes I feel sad about that, but nothing can be done about it. The rocks are still there, and mine are really great. And what I have realised is that there are new friends! A lot of the people in my life now are new and have become friends with me since 17th January 2010. They are friends with me on the basis of who I am since that awful day, grief and all. In a way they have unknowingly helped me establish a new life and a new identity. ~ **Sophie Day**

Recently, I've been thinking of what I've lost in the last one year, seven months and 20 days since JS drowned.

I've lost the ability to sleep at regular times, any desire to cook, a ridiculous amount of money on legal and accountancy fees, the motivation to re-start my writing career, peace of mind, my memory, any form of routine in my life and the ability to concentrate for more than a nanosecond.

JS and I worked together, but as it was impossible to carry on the business without him, I've also lost a job I loved for 24 years and, with it, part of my identity. Now, when people ask me what I do, I don't know what to say. 'Grieving' hardly counts as a profession, does it?

I've lost the feeling of safety that being in a good marriage gives you, the knowledge that even if you've been apart during the day there is someone there at night, *every* night, even if some nights you have to listen to endless grumbling over how bad the round of golf has gone, or worse, watch a slow-motion re-enactment of every good shot using a rolled-up umbrella. How I long to stand in my kitchen with a glass of wine, waiting for dinner, whilst JS yet again takes me through the complexities of the seventh hole on some goddamn course or other.

I've lost the rhythm of my life, the certainty that weekends won't be spent alone, that there will be a roast dinner on Sunday night and always someone to watch football with. That on Monday the working week starts and on Friday, it finishes. That if we didn't go to watch Arsenal play in London at the weekend, we'd be at the beach in Kent.

I've lost the fun of shopping. Any purchase is now accompanied by worry that the cost of the little frippery I've bought would have been better kept for the day the roof needs doing, or the heating bills come in, or I'm so fed up I decide to buy a camper van and live in it with The Hound. And that last part has a ring of truth to it. I *am* fed up for all sorts of reasons. Fed up and often lonely. The sort of inner loneliness that even having hundreds of friends wouldn't solve.

Which is just as well, as in the last 20 months, I've also lost friends.

Despite outward appearances to the contrary, I am one of the least sociable people you could meet, assuming that I actually left my house in order to meet you. I'm told that as a child I could be found lying on my bed reading during my own birthday parties, and probably had parents all over the village where I lived thinking that I had severe constipation, because at kiddies parties I would sit on the loo for ages, just to get a breather from passing an orange under my chin.

As an adult with a job that required constant socialising, I spent a great deal of time moaning to JS that I didn't want to go to [insert event]. He would sigh and say, 'You know you'll have a good time when you get there, you always do,' to which I'd grumble, 'No I won't,' only to have a *great* time, promising to take out to lunch or invite to dinner someone I'd only just met.

Between us, JS and I had a wide circle of friends stretching back decades.

These friends came to JS's funeral. Over and over again, my hand was clutched by misty-eyed mourners who assured me that they would be there for me and that if there was anything they could do, *anything*, I only had to ask.

Where are they now?

Some I never heard from again. They disappeared as if abducted by aliens.

Some let me down, big time. It was totally their fault, not mine and no, I won't forgive them. I *did* ask for help and they scurried away, terrified that they might have to change the habit of a lifetime and put someone other than themselves first.

Some continually said that they were thinking of me, but did nothing. There comes a point when thoughts are useless and action is needed: thoughts don't get a casserole made or the grass cut or The Hound walked.

Some tried to reach out to me, but, uncomfortable with my raw grief and unable to handle it, said things that at the time I found hurtful, but on reflection were just their clumsy attempts to make me feel better. They felt rejected, I felt pissed off and told them so.

Others didn't realise just how exhausting grieving can be. They would ring and say cheerily, 'When are you going to come over and see us?' not realising that it was a Herculean effort to negotiate the route from the sofa to the kitchen, let alone get in the car, check it had petrol, set up the Sat Nav and negotiate my way through London traffic. I didn't go, and they stopped inviting me.

Some, I realise, were sucked into the drama of the situation and loved the attention that it brought. 'Gory Hunters', I used to call them. The equivalent of people standing around a road accident, gawping. They faded away, probably to swoop down on some other disaster and feed off the bones of misfortune.

Others behaved inappropriately; I hope they now feel embarrassed about using my grief to unburden themselves of their own relationship issues.

Of course, some 'friends' fitted into several of the above categories: they didn't do anything, they revelled in my misery, they sat on my sofa, made stupid remarks, drank wine and unburdened their soul, and that was even *before* the funeral.

But there are others who have genuinely tried to reach out to me over and over again, and I have shunned them, ignored their endless calls, left their emails and letters unanswered, declined their invitations and hidden behind the front door when they have called round in an attempt to contact me, even clamping The Hound's muzzle shut for fear he would bark and give the game away.

It was comforting to know that those people were in the background, but now they have dwindled away and I don't blame them. What I have only just begun to realise is that as well as wanting to support me, some needed me as part of *their* grieving process. I couldn't help them as *my* grief was too overwhelming.

I've had several messages in the last few months from people who have tried to be there for me, who have genuinely cared and who have shown me nothing but kindness and patience. All these messages have been along the lines of: 'We have done everything we can to keep in contact with you. We understood you needed some space. We gave it to you. We won't contact you again, but if you'd like to contact us, we'd be thrilled to hear from you. We hope you are finding your feet and are happy.'

I've been on the verge of picking up the phone and saying, 'Let's meet up!' but something has stopped me.

It's got nothing to do with seeing Gorgeous Grey-Haired Widower: most of the time I am on my own and he is with his family and there are 45 miles between us.

Some of it is because I have always been a loner, albeit one who needs to know that there are people around, which is why city life suits me: lots of people, lots of interaction, but only for brief periods. But the other part is because I know that my lovely, patient friends just can't win.

Sometimes I no longer want to talk about what has happened or the problems (practical and emotional) I am still having dealing with my husband's death. I don't mind talking about these things with those who have experienced spousal bereavement, but those who haven't can never really understand what we are going through, however hard they try. But selfishly, when I am feeling down and overwhelmed, I don't want to talk about their lives: problems with noisy neighbours, the truculent au pair, their irritating husband or the cat's hairball problem. These problems make me want to scream, 'Shut up! You haven't got a clue you self-obsessed cow!'

And yet we can all be self-obsessed, can't we? Even widows. At times, *especially* widows.

My poor friends. They can't win.

I don't want to talk to them about me, except when I do want to talk about me.

I don't want to listen to their (by my standards) insignificant issues, except when I want their problems to take my mind off my own problems.

But perhaps the time has come to get back in touch with some of these friends. I don't know what I'm going to say, how I'm going to explain my withdrawal from 'society', but I suspect that they are the sort of people who won't need an explanation, they'll just be glad to see me.

Not all my post-death friendships have been turbulent.

I have some amazing friends who have stuck by me through thick and thin and, make no mistake, I have been hard work to be around for much of these last 20 months. JS's close family and my brother and his partner have also been absolute rocks.

In writing this, I've been thinking about what it is that has made these people such stars. Friends such as Big Bird, The Grammar Gestapo and Jan haven't lost a spouse, but they were unafraid of my grief. They didn't try to make things better because they knew they couldn't. They didn't make a hysterical song and dance out of what had happened, even though they acknowledged the enormity of JS's death. Big Bird (who moved in for weeks after JS died) was never afraid to tell me to 'Grow a pair' when I was cowering in fear of the future. When I had wallowed in grief for too long, The Grammar Gestapo would laugh and say in that wonderfully self-aware way she has, 'Can we bring this conversation back to being about me?' Jan's constant quest for the perfect handbag and her leather goods fetish reminded me of fun times stretching back to when we were nine-year-olds. I needed that. These people (and there were others) had an inbuilt gift of making life feel as normal as it could be in a totally crazy time. And because they treated me pretty much as they had always treated me, I felt sort of normal and was happy to talk to them about normal things: a lost job, internet dating, spineless ex-husbands.

But what of the friends I have lost? I expect some of you are thinking that they were never real friends in the first place, so good riddance.

I agree.

To a point.

There's a 'but' coming, but you knew that, didn't you?

These women were part of the patchwork of my life, the occasional meet-up over a glass of wine after work to hear how their children were, whether their mother was driving them mad or they've still got a ban on having sex with their husband because they suspect he's having an affair, but are too afraid to ask him. We popped in and out of each other's lives, never demanding too much of each other, but with the understanding that should the chips be down, we'd be there for each other.

I was there for those friends.

I would drop everything and clear the diary to see them when they had yet another crisis over a dog or a man or some health issue. It's what friends do.

Except when the chips were *really* down, when someone died rather than just got a lower grade in a GCSE than expected or they mucked up a contract at work, they didn't do the same for me. My grief had to fit in around their lives.

The rational me realises that even when I was planning my own death to get out of what seemed an interminably wretched life, others had commitments and lives to lead. But if Big Bird could just move in with me, Jan sort out the care of her children and jump on a train from Newcastle to London for me, my brother get on a plane to Barbados at a moment's notice to be with me and The Grammar

Gestapo make as much time in her packed diary as I needed to listen to me, why couldn't others?

But still, I look back and wonder how they are getting on, how their children are, if their husband *was* having an affair and so on.

The problem is, if I did get in touch with these women and we started back on our old meet-up-and-gossip-over-a-drink routine, I'd be sitting there thinking: 'You weren't there for me, were you? You let me down.'

And that's no basis for a relationship of any sort, is it?

HOMESICK

I personally refuse to think of grief as some sort of monster. I refuse to give it this sort of mental power to terrorise me. I think of it more like a need to vomit now and again; until you actually vomit, you won't feel better. So as with grief, you go through the motions, you roll with the punches, until your mind and your body are purged and begin to recover and feel better again. ~ ***Angela***

Thirty years ago, having just turned 18 the month before, I left my Northumberland village for a new life in London.

I intended to go to Sheffield University to study Physiology, but abysmal A-level results kyboshed that plan. The university promised to keep my place open for a year on condition that I re-sat one exam, so that was what I planned to do.

But when friends started buying kettles and duvets (or Continental Quilts as we called them 30 years ago) for their rooms in Halls of Residence, the thought of being left behind became absolutely unbearable. To add insult to injury, whilst I was lying in my room listening to Genesis, feeling wretched that I wasn't bright enough to be the owner of my own kettle and a set of Brentford Nylon sheets, friends who had far worse grades than me managed to secure a place at uni through the clearing process.

At the last minute and in a panic, I started ringing round universities, only to find out that yet again I had been left behind: all the places had been taken. Thames Polytechnic in Woolwich, south east London, could offer me a place to study, but not a place to live.

I jumped at it.

I was so desperate to leave home, I would have jumped at the chance to study sheep sh*t on Stornaway, especially if I was snug in my Continental Quilt drinking tea made with water boiled in my own kettle.

I really don't want you to get the violins out, but whilst the parents of my friends were packing up the car with the aforementioned bedding and household equipment, motoring across the country to deposit the fruit of their loins in some centrally heated room with a canteen on the ground floor, I was a forlorn little figure who got on the train, alone, at Newcastle Central Station, my belongings packed into one enormous, red, nylon roll-bag, my teddy tied to one side and my squash and badminton racquets strapped to the other. There was no room for a kettle or duvet.

At Kings Cross, I tried to get on the Northern Line to make my way to London Bridge, but the escalator had broken. I was tired, lonely, a bit frightened and my bag was too heavy to carry far. I stood at the top of that motionless escalator and as commuters swarmed around me, I sobbed my heart out.

A small Indian man carried my bag down the stairs and helped me on to the tube. Even 30 years on, the man, who saw me stranded in the crowd and came to my rescue, remains one of the most touching acts of kindness I have experienced.

I only stayed in the digs I had organised for one night: the owner of the house came back from the pub with a bunch of his friends and sat on the end of my bed (and that of another girl staying in my room) telling the leering drunken crowd, 'These are my little girls. Come and see my lovely little girls.' We screamed at them to get out and then barricaded the door, staying up all night before slipping out unannounced early the next morning. There was police tape across the road. There had been a murder.

You can put the violins away now.

Please.

Despite a seriously shaky start, I had a wonderful four years (one year on placement at University College, London). I loved my course, the people on it and being away from home. I eventually got my own kettle and a duvet. I flourished. Academically, I found my feet and discovered that I was much brighter than my exam results suggested: away from the tensions and dramas of home I was able to concentrate. I also had my first big love affair, one that endures to this day: I fell hopelessly in love with London.

Of course, it wasn't all plain sailing. There were times when I was ill or fed-up or worried or overwhelmed and during those times, I became *terribly* homesick. The feeling of wanting to run home totally engulfed me and I'd long to go back to Northumberland and walk through the front door. I could see it all: Mum and Dad would be there welcoming me, the lights would be on, there would be chicken soup and Shepherd's Pie for tea, everyone would be delighted to see me. Back home I would be safe, secure, soothed.

Quite why I thought my leaving home would turn us into the Waltons overnight I have no idea; it was certainly a triumph of hope over experience. The life I was imagining no longer existed and hadn't done for some time and it made me sad. Sad and disconnected, homeless even. I cried buckets every time I left.

Even by my usual standard of ramblings, musings and digressions you must wonder where this is going; what dredging-up tales of student days and lecherous landlords has got to do with grief.

Stick with it.

My husband loved looking at houses. Throughout our marriage, we were forever trudging up a path clutching estate agent's particulars. I hate looking at houses so much, I'd love to use one of those home-finding companies who (for a price) whittle a hundred homes down to a shortlist of three. I'd go on *Location, Location,*

Location, except Kirsty Allsop is too bossy for me, so perhaps I could do something with Sarah Beeny. I *love* Ms Beeny.

But I digress.

What usually happened was that whilst I stood stony-faced in some clearly unsuitable (price/location/bad atmosphere) property that we had no intention of buying, JS would be discussing the cost of running the heating system, or worse, browsing the books on the owner's shelves. It was always a surprise to the estate agent that we didn't put an offer in, such was the enthusiasm JS had shown for, say, the under-floor, temperature-controlled wine-rack.

I started becoming more vocal in my opinions of these houses. 'You have a lovely house, but I'm afraid it's not for us,' would trip off my tongue as we were ushered out. JS thought that I was rude, that I wasn't playing the game. I said people would rather know the truth.

One particular house we saw was spectacularly unsuitable for us.

As we left, I said to the owner, 'You have a lovely house, but I'm afraid it's clearly not for us.'

The owner thanked me for being so honest. I shot JS a smug 'Told you so,' look. Actually, I was lying. I didn't think the house was lovely at all. It was boxy, modern, split-level and there were so many cream tiles on the open plan layout it felt like living in an empty swimming pool.

Outside, JS said, 'I love it.'

I said, 'I hate it.'

We never discussed it again, until a few weeks later, JS got a phone call. He was jubilant. 'They've accepted the offer!' he trilled.

It transpired that without my knowledge, JS had put in a cheeky offer on the house. Crucified by a huge bridging loan after their last buyer pulled out, the vendors had accepted it. To say I was upset is an understatement, especially when JS – never one to be told what to do – wouldn't back down. He loved the house and he was going to have it. He said that if in a year I still hated it, we'd move. I still hated it in a year, but he refused to move. The compromise was that we would make changes and we did, although I moaned incessantly for *years*.

That was in 1996. The house is now a far cry from the minimalist 'one massive erotic painting and an oversized blue suede sofa in the living room' style it was when we viewed it. It's not my dream house, but it's pretty close. And it's in London and I feel about London like *SATC*'s Carrie Bradshaw felt about New York.

We still looked at houses of course, because that's what we did. I'd say, 'I don't want to move, I love this house!' JS would look smug and say, 'I knew you would, eventually.' And we'd laugh and I'd tell him that even though he got away with buying a house without me, he must never do it again, knowing full well that he was the sort of man that might.

It has been a very happy house. A house which, when I came in through the front door, cosseted me from the outside world. A house in which we had parties and dinners and lunches and fun. A house filled with energy. A house I looked forward to coming back to.

Not just a house, but a home.

My life has changed dramatically in the last 21 months. This journey through grief takes some strange twists and turns, and I have been surprised by the latest one.

Thirty years ago, I used to imagine that everything would be rosy if I could just get home. It never was. Time and time again, I fell for the fairytale, only to be crushed by the reality.

And it's happening all over again.

Out of the blue, I can suddenly feel unbelievably, breathtakingly homesick. I'm swept by a longing to go home. It's quite definitely homesickness, the same feeling I recognise from the days when I first left Northumberland. Like Dorothy in *The Wizard of Oz*, I am engulfed by a feeling of desperately wanting to go home, of *needing* to get home.

It takes me over so completely, for a split second I forget I *am* home.

And then the bleakness descends, that same feeling of sadness and disconnection I felt as a teenager, when I acknowledged the gulf between fantasy and reality.

Where I live is no longer a home. It's just a house.

The eighteen-year-old girl standing at the top of the escalator carrying the back-breaking bag, sobbing, frightened, lonely and overwhelmed at the thought of the future, is now 48.

And she's just as scared and longing for home.

And, like 30 years ago, that home no longer exists as she remembers it.

And even though she is living in a lovely house with lovely things in a lovely area, she feels homeless.

And sad.

Spirit-crushingly, soul-destroyingly sad.

Dorothy got home.

Will I ever feel truly at home again?

LIFE, DEATH AND LAUNDRY

*It's funny the things we keep, from toothbrushes to breakfast cereals. I still have Tony's aftershaves next to my things on the shelf; some clothes still hang in the wardrobe. More bizarrely, I had to recently make myself bin some ginger ale that was two years out of date, but which was bought when he was going through chemo in the naive hope it would reduce his nausea, and some frozen kippers that I kept for an unsavoury amount of time. ~ **Emily H***

I hate clutter. Piles of stuff around the house make me feel over-whelmed, out-of-control and claustrophobic, which is somewhat of a problem as I am a naturally untidy person, perfectly capable of turning a room from pristine to pit within seconds.

Putting stuff in cupboards doesn't really solve my Clutter Fear either; a bit like the hair dye on my roots, it simply masks the reality. *You* may think I have tidy rooms and dark hair, but *I* know what is rammed behind the doors just as I know what grey lies beneath the dye. I also know that at some point I'll have to deal with both these issues.

Even other people's clutter can have me hyperventilating. I recently had a peek into Gorgeous Grey-Haired Widower's loft; it was packed with stuff. I felt quite ill just looking at it, which was completely irrational because it wasn't even my stuff. When I was told that there was another loft, equally as jammed to the rafters, I became quite hysterical and had to hit the sherry bottle to calm down.

Truth be told, these days I am in danger of becoming a hoarder myself, though hopefully not in the same league as those who appear on television programmes about extreme hoarding, the sort where someone living in a huge house is confined to the downstairs toilet because they haven't thrown out any newspapers, soup tins or even kitty-litter for two decades. It's both sad and yet fascinating to watch the Environmental Health team go in and start removing what any 'normal' person can see is filth and junk, whilst the hoarder, anxious and desperate, tries to dive into the skip to retrieve old copies of *The Times*, now rigid with dried cat urine.

Before my husband died, I used to watch these programmes and wonder how on earth anyone could get themselves into a position where they became emotionally attached to a plastic bag full of till receipts. It was only *after* JS died that I noticed a link between the hoarders. In each case, the hoarding started after a loss: a parent, a child, a spouse, a home. The hoarding may have escalated unchecked beyond the initial loss, but loss seemed to be the starting gun followed by depression, anxiety and OCD. Hoarders feel trapped by their possessions, yet fear their loss and the safety and comfort they represent.

I now understand this hoarding behaviour in a way I never imagined I would.

When JS drowned, I was convinced that by about the six-month anniversary of his death, everything would be sorted. I don't mean that my grief would be sorted (if only it could be that easy!), but that JS's estate and businesses would be wound up, his clothes shipped off to any homeless men that needed Armani suits and Hermès ties, and his golf paraphernalia listed on Freecycle. I had plans to finish the decorating that had been started before he died, clear out and close down the office-storage facility and get back to writing the book that my publishers were waiting for.

Have I accomplished any of those tasks I set myself in the first six months?

Next month it will be two years since JS died and I haven't even washed the last sheets he slept in at home; they are *still* in the laundry basket along with his dirty washing: a golf shirt, a T-shirt, boxer shorts and some mismatched socks. There wasn't much laundry because it was done before we went on holiday. Speaking of holidays, JS's suitcase is still unopened. It stands in his study next to his desk. I haven't even taken the luggage tags off. I read about someone opening their suitcase and finding a colony of lizards inside. When I eventually get round to opening it, perhaps I had better open it in the garden, just in case some scaly beast slithers out.

But I digress.

I wouldn't want you to think that for two years I have slept between the same unwashed sheets. Grief does weird things to folk, but even for me that would be taking weirdness to a whole new level. I think it was around the three-month post-death point that a friend tried to change the bed, whereupon I flung myself on the sheets and clutching them like a lioness protecting her cub snarled, 'Leave them alone.' The ridiculous thing was that by that point they didn't smell like JS, they just smelt of my sweat and tears and whatever wildlife excrement The Hound (now sleeping with me) had rolled in. A compromise was reached: the sheets came off, but they were put into the washing basket on top of JS's laundry, all to be washed another day, a day which two years down the line has yet to arrive.

Nothing has moved, nothing has been cleared, nothing has been thrown away other than a couple of golf videos, a tube of Deep Heat and some fish oil capsules, and only then because they began to ooze smelly gunk.

Do I go to the washing basket, bury my head in the sheets and underwear and sob? No, I don't. I open it, get out my washing and then seeing the sheets, aka The Divide of Death, feel depressed, frustrated and angry with myself that I don't seem to be able to fire up the Bosch and load the bedding into its drum along with a capsule of Persil Bio. I feel the same about JS's wardrobe, his bedside cabinet, his golf clubs. The list is endless. Others have said that I will know when the time is right, that one day I will wake up and simply fly through the house in a whirlwind of black bin bags and charity sacks. I am not so sure. I have previous form dealing with the possessions of lost loved ones.

It is ten years in March since my friend, Karen, died. Little did either of us know when she walked out of the office we shared that she would never be coming back. After she died, I guarded her desk in the same way I protected those used sheets. No one was allowed to sit at it, *everything* had to remain just as Karen had left it: her hairbrush matted with golden-blonde strands of hair; Post-it notes with scribbled messages stuck around her computer screen; a smudge of pearly pink blusher on her phone handset. At first, it was comforting to come in and see her things left exactly as she left them; it felt as if she had just popped out to M&S for a prawn sandwich. Then things changed. Karen's abandoned hairbrush was no longer comforting, but a brutal reminder of the gap she left in our lives. I started to dread the emptiness of our office and yet I couldn't bear to even move a pencil in her desk-tidy.

It took five years to clear out Karen's things and only then, because it was forced upon me as we moved offices. Right up until the burly removal men arrived, I longed to have an English Heritage Blue Plaque on the wall outside the office and her desk listed as a site of historical interest. For once, I'm not joking.

Just before Christmas, I tried to start decluttering JS's things. Websites advised using the mantra: 'If it's not beautiful, useful or sentimental, chuck it.' The problem was, I found the most ridiculous things sentimental.

I started with the best of intentions. If I couldn't clear out JS's wardrobe, paperwork would be no problem, surely? I bought several recycling sacks from a company that promised (for a fee) to shred paperwork in the street using a shredder on a lorry. I was ecstatic at just how easy it would be and started to work my way through files of financial information with gusto, tossing letters, receipts and bank and credit card statements into the sack.

But what I have here? The receipt for a meal we had at that lovely restaurant! I'd completely forgotten we'd even been there. Perhaps I'll just keep it to remind me. And look at this entry on the Amex statement. It's for that Fawlty Towers-style hotel we stayed in! The one next to the prison where the heating kept us awake and sweating all night, and I had a strop because they kept trying to fob me off with a flat champagne cocktail. I couldn't remember its name, but now I can. What if I forget it again? I'd better keep the statement, just in case.

And so it went on…

Despite constantly being sidetracked, the sacks filled up, but then I thought, 'What if I've missed something? What if there is something important in there? When it's gone it's gone. I'll never get it back!'

I sat in front of the television and sifted back through all the rubbish I had thrown out. I found new things I wanted to keep, nothing legally important, just more memory joggers.

A few days later, I did *exactly* the same thing all over again.

The sacks are still in the house.

Forget the 'big' things like JS's clothes, shoes and sporting equipment; I am compelled to keep things I don't even want to keep: the boarding pass from British Airways for the nightmare flight back to England without my husband; the return train ticket from London to Gatwick when JS joked with the guard that we would be coming back together, 'Unless something terrible happens.' We collected hundreds of matchbooks from the days when hotels and restaurants gave them out. I find these matchbooks incredibly painful; each one reminds me of happy times and the sort of life I no longer live. Throwing them away feels as if I am throwing away my old life and I simply can't do it. I feel trapped by the possessions associated with my past life. I may not be physically confined to the downstairs bathroom with towering piles of junk around me, but mentally I feel trapped. I know others trot out lines about memories being kept in your heart, not your home, but I seem to need proof that my old life existed: We did this! We did that! We went here! We travelled there!

I'm sobbing as I write those last few lines, because I realise that the only person I'm trying to convince of my past life is me. Only two years and yet it all seems so long ago and far away and so utterly alien from the life I live now; it feels as if those 22 years of living and working and travelling with JS, half my life, were a figment of my imagination.

JS did exist, he must have done.

I have his bank statements to prove it.

MONEY MATTERS

I spent weeks going through paperwork needed for the solicitor, pension provider, etc., finding important papers, then losing them on a daily basis, until in the end I just wanted to scream and get off from the merry-go-round (nothing merry about it!). ~ **Deena**

Is there anyone who has been widowed who hasn't worried about money? If so, I've yet to meet them. There might be widows reading this whose bank balance is overflowing with zeros, and those whose bank balance is below zero, yet I would bet my last pound that in the early days of bereavement, even the richest widow felt their gut twist when another bill landed on the doormat.

I want to be honest from the get-go here. I'm going to write about my struggle with money, but I would hate you to think that I am writing this by candlelight, my hands blue with cold in my fingerless gloves, a hot-water bottle on my lap under a coat which I wear all day to save putting the heating on, occasionally pouring another cup of tea from the Thermos flask beside me as I don't want to keep boiling the kettle and risk high electricity bills. I'm not going to pretend to you that when things get so cold in the house I go to bed with The Hound and an electric blanket, even if it's during the day, or that I give myself a limit of £20 a week for groceries in Sainsbury's, an amount so strict that if I get to the checkout and find if I have overspent by even a pound, I will infuriate those behind me by asking the assistant to remove something from my shopping.

I don't do those things *now*, but I did do them after JS died because in the first year of widowhood, I had absolutely no idea how I was going to survive financially, and I was terrified. Like many Londoners, we were cash poor but asset rich, our wealth tied up in bricks and mortar. You know those tiny announcements in the paper informing you that Lord Peter Pocklington of Ponsonby left an estate valued at £3million? What you don't realise – at least until you are knee deep in death-related paperwork – is that the figure on paper bears very little resemblance to the cash in the bank, and that whilst Lady P may well be weeping in a country mansion worth several million (or a terraced house in Chelsea), EDF Energy want money now, not when Ponsonby Towers is sold so that the widow Pocklington can move into a McCarthy and Stone assisted-living flat.

I have always had a complicated relationship with money, which is odd, because thankfully I have never been truly 'below the poverty line' poor. If I wanted something I saved up for it, if I couldn't afford it I didn't buy it, and if I needed more money I took a job, or another job. To me, money isn't about being able to afford the latest handbag or the newest car. To me, money equals freedom, the freedom to be able to say to the travel agent, 'Get me a flight home, tomorrow, whatever it takes,' when you have finally been given the green light to leave the island where your husband drowned.

As I child, I loved counting the money in my Thelwell piggy bank, something I did several times a day. When I graduated to a Building Society account with a blue-covered savings book, I'd often deposit small sums to ensure that the balance was always a rounded figure, something that gave me great pleasure every time I looked at it. It was a sad day when I had to make a withdrawal, and I would do anything rather than deplete the coffers. In later years, I remember discussing with JS and my brother (who has no such monetary hang-ups) what we would do if we won the lottery. JS fancied a new car, my brother a house, but when it got to my turn to 'spend' my winnings, my brother said he knew exactly what I would do: put it in the bank and stare at the balance each day.

I never wanted to have to stay in a relationship because I couldn't afford to leave, and even during my marriage I always had what I called my 'F-Off Fund', a sum of money squirreled away so that if I ever needed to leave and do my own thing, I could. As our living arrangements and our working lives were so tightly connected, it felt important for me to have this safety net.

My neurotic relationship with money wasn't helped by JS's attitude to it, which varied from 'Splashing the Cash' to 'We're Doomed!' sometimes within the same day. When we bought our first flat, the financial fall-out of JS's divorce (which included a hefty settlement for his ex-wife and provision for his children to be able to buy property when they were older) left us several hundred thousand pounds in debt and wracked with worry. As JS wrote in some correspondence I found after his death, everything he had ever worked for, saved for and inherited had been wiped out, which was devastating for a man of 44, and something I only appreciated when I was widowed at 46.

Hard work and hustle grew the company, but the rollercoaster financial nature of our business and self-employment made it hard to plan ahead. Whilst one month JS would be dragging me to look at a house that I felt we couldn't afford, the next he would be full of gloom that the sales figures were lower than expected, or a client of ours was planning to open their own UK-based office and sack us.

As well as the good times, there were many years when I took a nominal salary from the company to cut costs, and there was a large loan against our house to keep the business solvent. Things were tough, and I'd wake up in the night to find JS wide awake, sweating with worry, which would then keep me awake, sweating with worry. Things were very difficult in the last few years leading up to JS's death. We had investments, a lovely house in one of London's most desirable areas and a cottage at the coast, but when it came to going to Barbados – our first holiday in four years, and only then because I was insistent that we went away because JS needed a break and some sun – I paid half and JS sold some shares to pay the balance.

In Charles Dickens' book, *David Copperfield*, Mr Micawber states that: 'Annual income twenty pounds, annual expenditure nineteen (pounds) nineteen (shillings) and six (pence) result happiness. Annual income twenty pounds, annual expenditure twenty pounds ought and six, result misery.'

The problem was that after JS died, I had absolutely no idea as to what either my income or my expenditure was. My ever-present money anxiety and the feast/famine nature of our work could have been one of the reasons that JS kept his financial cards close to his chest. This lack of knowledge made me feel insecure, and periodically I would raise the matter; he'd tell me that I had nothing to worry about, that he would put together a spreadsheet so I could see our income and expenditure. Despite chasing him continually, it never happened. It was humiliating to sit in front of a panel of financial and legal advisors after JS died and have so many gaps in my financial knowledge when they asked me to detail my outgoings. I could tell them how much we spent on food or dry cleaning, but not what Council Tax we paid or how much our Broadband package cost. JS had done all the bill-paying online, and without the passwords, little physical paperwork and the Data Protection Act stopping me getting the information I needed, it was hard to get a handle on my financial position. I was a modern, financially independent woman who ran my own business and submitted my own VAT returns and paid Corporation Tax, and yet I didn't know how much our house insurance cost. Actually, as it turned out, I discovered that we had no buildings insurance, but that is a tale for another time. Holiday insurance took care of JS's body being repatriated back to the UK, but as JS refused to face up to the fact he might one day die, he had no life insurance and because he was self-employed, no regular pension provision. We had a small mortgage on the London property that came with life insurance, but a few weeks before JS died, I had paid it off in full with some money I had come into. I didn't want to; I kept the money in the bank for months because I liked to know it was there, but JS badgered me and became angry because I wouldn't use it to clear our debt. Fed up of his nagging, one day I walked in to Barclays bank and paid off the mortgage.

So when I saw posts on bereavement sites about people depositing large life insurance cheques into the bank, getting a regular income from their husband's pension or a 'Death in Service' lump sum, I felt aggrieved. I was terrified I was going to lose the house. I seriously considered walking into my local Tesco to ask them for a job and began all manner of money-saving ideas. I started to grow my own salad, a disaster because in spite of spending money on compost and slug shields and plastic covers for the pots I bought, my yield was three tiny tomatoes and I couldn't tell the cut-and-come-again salad from the weeds. I turned off the energy-hungry halogen garden lights, only to drive into the garage one day and see a lake of water: I had turned off the freezer as well as the lights and ruined hundreds of pounds of food. To make the heating more energy efficient, I contracted an electrician to fit a new thermostat in the hall. This box of electronic wizardry was guaranteed to reduce my bills. They went up. I couldn't understand it and turned the base temperature even lower. Still the bills remained high so I switched the central heating off at the boiler. It was a year later when Gorgeous Grey-Haired Widower took a look and discovered that the thermostat had been wired incorrectly; the heating was never automatically switching off when it got to the right temperature. I cut out coupons, I saved water, I sat in the dark, I cancelled all but the most basic TV package and on top of the grief about JS dying, I was cold and miserable.

JS used to despair at my F-Off money; he'd tell me that I'd never need it to use it, that whatever happened, he would make sure I was financially OK. I used to say that it was vital that I had my financial independence. In a sense, we were both right: as it turned out, JS did make sure I was looked after, but in the short term, the F-Off money I had saved should I ever need to walk out of the house was used to help me stay in it.

TWO, DOWN, WAY UP!

*I long to tell Mark what my life is all about now, what has happened, where I have ended up, and ask him if this is what he thought my life was going to turn out like when he chose to end his. Is this what he was thinking when he wrote me his suicide letter, that this is how I was meant to 'move on'? - **Emma S***

It is an undeniable fact that the unexpected and untimely death of your spouse changes you. Some widows and widowers have done amazing things after they were bereaved: built their own house from scratch; travelled around the world; reached the top of Kilimanjaro clutching a picture of their husband. It makes me very proud of them and their achievements, whilst feeling somewhat depressed that if *I* had to give examples of what I have achieved in the two years since JS died, I could only dredge up minor things such as learning how to change the halogen bulbs in the kitchen and filling my car with petrol, something JS always did for me.

I have changed, of course: I am considerably sadder, poorer, grey-haired and generally more of an anxious, sleep-deprived, snivelling wreck than I was when JS was alive. Those are just a few examples. I have a list as long as a fresh roll of Andrex of such changes. But there is one thing that hasn't changed since JS died: my love of making plans.

Rats are incredibly bright creatures. They quickly learn how to negotiate a maze and differentiate between tasks that give them a reward (a tasty morsel) or disappointment (no food and an electric shock). Clearly, I have an IQ lower than a rat, because it doesn't matter how many times my plans go to pot, how many times I'm left standing in the wreckage of some carefully constructed itinerary or even after the ultimate plan-gone-wrong, my husband dying on holiday, which annoyingly *completely* altered the restaurants I had booked from the UK, the clothes I was going to wear and the day-trips which were set in stone. I never learn. Like some bright-eyed, brain-dead Weeble, I pop back up after a thwarted plan and chirrup, 'Never mind. I have a plan…'

In more than two decades, poor JS never really got to grips with my plan-fetish. A simple evening out with friends in another part of London would have me planning the route, the time we had to leave, what to wear, even down to quizzing JS as to where we would park the car as the walk from vehicle to venue influenced the height of the heels I intended to wear. This is all very sensible a day or two before said event, but such planning would begin the moment the invitation arrived, even if this was *weeks* in advance. The more planning I did, the more likely the evening would be cancelled because of some last minute dog squits/migraine/food poisoning issue.

Once, I even started making notes about the Christmas lunch I planned to cook…

In July.

Woody Allen said, 'If you want to make God laugh, tell him about your plans.'

I'm not a believer in God, but if I was, I'd be pretty proud of myself for giving him so much to laugh about over the years. So, it won't surprise you to know that I had the first few months of 2013 all planned out. And it also won't surprise you that it all went horribly wrong.

At the end of last year, I was invited to give a talk about my *Planet Grief* blog at the March 2013 annual general meeting of the charity WAY – Widowed and Young. WAY is a self-help group that offers emotional and practical support to men and women widowed under the age of 50 (there is a group for the over-fifties called WAY UP) as they adjust to life after the death of their partner. WAY has more than 1,400 members across the country, and around 180 delegates were due at their AGM in Edinburgh.

I gave the idea of speaking about five minutes thought. The date of the conference was 2nd March 2013, which would mean I would need to travel from London to Scotland on Friday 1st March, which was only two days after the two-year anniversary of JS's death on 27th February. This was hardly a reason to decline to speak. I'd got through the first year anniversary in some style; surely, that first year was the hardest? See, I even had my emotions planned out.

I accepted the invitation to speak and planned to start preparing my talk in January.

Early in January, I fell ill with something more than a cold, but less than full-on flu. I felt wretched, but unfortunately, my very limited local support network was either also ill, on holiday or not close enough to lob a bottle of Night Nurse and a box of tissues over the garden wall.

Forty-five miles away, immune-suppressed Gorgeous Grey-Haired Widower became really quite ill, so ill he needed to be whisked to Addenbrooke's Hospital in Cambridge by ambulance where he spent a few days in the High Dependency unit. I lay in my bed feeling not just ill and worried about GGHW, but horribly, terrifyingly vulnerable and alone all over again. When JS was alive and I was poorly, even though he went to work during the day, he would regularly ring me to see if I was OK, if I wanted anything bringing in and, whilst no cook, he could recall the entire ready-meal selection at M&S to tempt my virus-sodden palate. But the biggest comfort was knowing that he would be coming home. Isolated and ill, my anxiety levels began to rise.

Nothing on my list of January tasks got done.

GGHW came out of hospital. I recovered sufficiently to go and look after him, but not sufficiently enough to say I felt well.

Appointments that had been postponed were re-fixed.

It was now February. My plans were in chaos, but there was still time to rescue them. The January plans would have to be squeezed into February. I felt better. I was taking something called 'Daily Immunity', which was packed with herbs and vitamins. It was expensive so it had to work. I was back on track. I made a new plan.

I fell ill, *again*.

The diary had to be cleared, *again*.

Sewage from the block of flats next door started coming onto my property. Day after day, men with tankers and pumps arrived whilst they tried to work out the run of crumbling Victorian drains under the streets of north London.

My anxiety levels shot through the roof.

Stuffed with cold, I sat down to prepare my talk for the WAY AGM. I thought of my old introduction in the days when I gave talks to schools: 'Hello, my name is Helen Bailey. I'm a writer of children's books, mainly teenage fiction…'

Clearly, I needed a new intro: I would be speaking to widows and widowers about bereavement and blogging, not a group of schoolgirls about boys and snogging.

I typed a new introduction: 'Hello, my name is Helen Bailey. I'm a widow, I'm a member of WAY and I write a blog called *Planet Grief.*'

Then I sat back and looked at what I had written.

And *completely* freaked.

I couldn't believe the difference between the two introductions, of what had happened between them and how different my life had become.

The last time I spoke in public (other than at my husband's funeral) was to 300 schoolgirls in Kent on 17th February 2011. JS drove me to the school that morning and picked me up from the station later that afternoon. I remember ringing him from the train and telling him that the talk and workshop had gone down well, and him laughing and saying, 'Of course it did! I never doubted it wouldn't!' At the station, I slung my laptop case into the boot of JS's car. Work was over. I was about to go on holiday.

Ten days later, JS was dead.

Staring tearfully at the screen, I started to resent the fact that I had agreed to talk at the WAY AGM. I began to resent *everything* to do with widows. I wanted to talk to bright-eyed, eager schoolgirls, not hollow-eyed, grief-stricken men and women. I'd been a member of WAY since shortly after JS died, but I hadn't been to any events. Now, I didn't want to be a member of WAY. I wanted the whole widow thing to go away.

Desperate for a get-out, I hoped that my cold would turn into something more sinister requiring hospitalisation, or that there would be such bad weather that I was forced to cancel my trip to Scotland. If I cancelled my talk, I'd also cancel my WAY membership, stop the blog and delete all the internet bereavement sites I use. 'It wouldn't be running away,' I told myself. 'It would be leaving grief behind and getting on with my life.' Meanwhile, the sewage continued to rise, Thames Water continued to let me down, my cold got worse, but not bad enough to cancel and the second anniversary of JS's death approached.

Ah yes. The second anniversary.

I had intended a more low-key event than the first anniversary, but I did intend to do something, even if it was just going in to town to buy myself a little present and meet a friend for lunch. But as the date got nearer and I got more and more fed up of the whole widow thing and how all the plans I made failed, I decided not to make any plans at all. It would just be a day like any other. After all, it wasn't as if I forgot what had happened on the other 364 days, was it?

Big mistake. Big, *big* mistake.

February 27th arrived. I was still under the weather and still had sewage issues. I was stressed over unresolved and expensive legal problems. A close friend of mine, someone who has been supportive over the last two years, was diagnosed with advanced and inoperable oesophageal cancer. I was anxious about my talk because every time I started to rehearse it, I was reminded why I was giving it and to whom, and it made me sad and scared. I wasn't afraid of forgetting my words, I was frightened of collapsing in a sobbing, snotty heap in front of the audience. I did a lot of reflecting and, after lots of sobbing, I went to bed for the afternoon, not to sleep or because I felt particularly ill, but because I wanted to shut out the world in a way in which I haven't done for some time. I dragged myself up for a swift, early dinner with Mike the Bike, my accountant who is also a friend, but as I went around the house pulling down the blinds before going out, I saw the lights come on in the street outside as the sky darkened. It reminded me of sundown that first evening after JS died and the overwhelming feeling of bewilderment and terror, alone in a paradise that had turned to hell. Two years! How could it possibly be two years since I last saw JS! I crumbled again. I had planned to leave the events of 27th February 2011 behind me, but my brain had other ideas.

So, a year in advance I made another plan, which was to plan something for 27th February 2014.

Two days later, I made it to Edinburgh, but not without hiccups. At a coffee break on the first morning I suddenly felt the same 'I don't want to be here!' thoughts overwhelm me. It wasn't about running away from doing my talk – once in Scotland I was committed, and from past experience I knew that by the time I stood up, the nerves would begin to damp down – it was about the enormity of the situation, of what I had been through, of what I was still going through, what we were *all* going through.

The committee had thoughtfully arranged a quiet room, a space away from the main conference where delegates could go if they felt overwhelmed. I never imagined needing such a room, but at that moment I had to get away. I slipped inside.

Sitting quietly in the room was someone I shall call Curly Girl because of her gloriously springy hair. As I sobbed, Curly Girl put aside her own need for time-out and comforted me. Shortly after, Kentish Lass came in. She simply saw me and hugged me. No explanations for my tears were necessary. Those two widows held me up as I felt I was falling down. Later that day over a drink, Denise, the lovely Queen of Herts whose husband committed suicide, shared with me the trials and tribulations of her house move, something I am thinking of doing. She was a beacon of hope, of encouragement, of warmth. Far from wanting to run away from these people, I felt enveloped by them. I am not the sort of person to feel proud of being a widow, that's just not me, but I was proud to be associated with these ladies and the other men and women I met over the weekend. Yes, there were tears, but there was laughter and lively debate and dancing as well as time for reflection. Edinburgh was a fabulous host city and I truly had a wonderful time surrounded by amazing people.

GGHW and I flew back to London on Sunday 3rd March. We flew British Airways. Two years before on that same date, I boarded an overnight BA flight from Barbados to London, leaving my husband on the island. He didn't come home for another week.

In the last two years, I haven't climbed a mountain or built a house and I do beat myself up about how little progress I think

I've made, but when I sat on the plane on 3rd March this year and thought back to the 3rd March 2011 flight I made, never could I have imagined I would have any sort of a life, let alone one which included flying to Scotland to speak at an AGM full of widows and widowers, who, far from being the hollow-eyed zombies I anticipated, were just as eager and interested to hear what I had to say as my schoolgirls used to be.

I came back to London and, the next day, I started to clear out JS's office. There had been a major shift over the Edinburgh weekend. Yes, I am still anxious, overwhelmed and frightened, but I truly feel ready to start a new phase of my life.

SHARP DRESSED MAN

*I am at three years, three months and eleven days. For me, the pain, in some form will always be there, it is just that I am coping and managing to live with it. My wife made a list of things she wanted to give away to family and friends – mostly jewellery. No problem doing that even though the process hurt, since these were her last wishes. I am currently looking at a bookcase full of her study stuff. No use to anyone, but I can't just put it into a skip. I suppose, in my head, we will always be together hence why I can't get rid of any of her stuff. ~ **Chris J***

JS and I were together for more than two decades and in all that time, we rarely had a proper argument. We *never ever* had a real humdinger of a row.

There will be those reading this who think that either I am:

A: Telling lies or,

B: Since my husband's death, I have rewritten the past and beatified JS, who is now to be known as Blessed Saint John of Highgate.

Before you have visions of the two of us smiling adoringly at each other over the table for 22 years, may I take a moment to give you the Oxford English Dictionary's definition of an argument:

Noun: An exchange of diverging or opposite views, typically a heated or angry one.

Do you see the word 'exchange'?

Therein lies the clue to my astonishing opening statement. There was rarely an *exchange* of views, because at the first hint of trouble between us, JS would walk out of the room/restaurant/pub/car/house.

If he was angry with me he'd walk out, and if I was angry with him, he'd walk out, so eventually I adopted a 'There's no point in trying to argue with a man who'll walk out' approach, so I'd walk out first. At times, there was a lot of walking out one way and another. When eventually we were back in the same room, whereas I can be spectacularly angry one minute (usually fuelled by tiredness and low blood sugar) and completely fine the next, JS would mope around with a strained look on his face for days, sulking in heavy silence. Eventually, his demeanour would irritate me and unable to help myself I'd say something like, 'Are you still angry or just constipated?' at which point JS would flounce out again.

If for some reason he couldn't walk out (say we were in a plane at 33,000 feet), he'd completely shut down and refuse to speak. I did once order him to stay in the kitchen so we could talk about something that I felt was important, and, to prevent him leaving, stood in front of the door waving a fish slice in what I hoped was a menacing manner (I was frying crab cakes at the time). JS opened the oven door, put his head in and started examining the lights and the element, totally ignoring me.

Of course, on reflection and with the startling clarity of hindsight, I realise how unhealthy all this was. I'm sure if I read out the opening of this chapter to a relationship therapist, he or she would have said we should get couples counselling immediately, which of course would have been futile. Even if I managed to get JS through the door, he'd quickly walk out again. In any case, whatever I think now, I didn't then, or if I did, life was much too exciting and full to have time to dwell on it for long.

The trip to Edinburgh to speak was a turning point on my journey across Planet Grief: two years and two months after JS died, I have put the house on the market. It's a positive step, though positivity doesn't mean that I don't go to bed with a pile of

House Beautiful magazines and the *Rightmove* app, full of excitement at the thought of a fresh start, only to wake up tearful and completely crushed by the thought of leaving my lovely home full of memories. I feel incredibly sad that it has all ended like this, that instead of JS and me closing the front door to start a new chapter of our lives together in another house, I will be leaving alone.

I've been de-cluttering and clearing with such manic vigour, I'd make a grasshopper on speed look lazy. Once I started, there was no stopping me and despite my careful research about where JS's clothes should be donated to, having made the decision to let them go, they had to go *straight away*, into the car and off to somewhere with easy parking (Londoners will understand). The North London Hospice shop in East Finchley was the recipient.

The mind is a peculiar living computer. I couldn't bear to load JS's clothes into black bin bags – maybe subconsciously it felt as if I was throwing JS away, or perhaps that's reading too much into it – so I went to the local pound shop and bought lots of large, tartan, zippered laundry bags and used those instead. Some months ago, when I cleared the few clothes JS had at our cottage in Broadstairs, I nestled a perfectly good purple top of mine in amongst his clothes when I took them to the charity shop. I couldn't bear his things to go without something of mine to keep them company. If you haven't been bereaved you will think this strange. If you have, you'll understand.

After JS died, a good friend of ours described him as 'urbane'. This wasn't intended to be an English lesson, but the OED's definition of 'urbane' describes my husband perfectly: 'Elegant and refined in manners; courteous, civil; suave, sophisticated.'

JS's wardrobe was exactly how one would imagine an urbane Englishman to look: beautifully cut suits, linen jackets, crisp shirts, cashmere jumpers, stunning silk ties; everything exuding understated elegance, all neatly stored. If I died suddenly and someone had to go through *my* clothes, I'm ashamed to say that in my pockets you would undoubtedly find a wide selection of items including but not limited to: pooper scooper bags, sticky sweets, a Tampax dislodged from its wrapper, used tissues and bucket-loads of biscuit crumbs. I once opened an A4 ring binder at the start of an important presentation to find a fossilised sausage sitting between the clasps, said sausage having been kept back from a railway breakfast some weeks before 'in case of an emergency'. It must have been at the bottom of my briefcase, the binder acting as a giant pair of tongs, scooping the banger out and displaying it for everyone around the boardroom table to see. JS was considerably tidier, the only things I found in his clothes were neatly folded lens cloths for his glasses, the odd clean tissue and, in his evening suit pocket, a wrapped toothpick and his business card.

JS loved clothes. His sartorial elegance was even mentioned in the eulogy at his funeral, but this (along with his summer job at *Vogue*) gave him an unshakable belief that he knew what was fashionable and what wasn't. And whilst the urbane Englishman look suited JS, it didn't mean it was fashionable. As I carefully folded his clothes and laid them in the laundry bags, I remembered one of the few almost real arguments we had. It was about clothes.

We were watching a programme where some nerdy Heavy Metal fan who couldn't get a girlfriend, despite soaking himself in Lynx, was transformed into a babe-magnet, just by cutting his hair and ditching the Iron Maiden T-shirt. JS took one look at the sanitised man and pronounced that the stylist didn't know the first thing about fashion. 'He's put him in a cardigan!' JS sniffed. 'He looks ridiculous.' 'Cardigans are trendy,' I countered. JS became riled and insisted that cardigans were not and never had been fashionable. My riposte was that if you were a whippet-thin rock god, they were, citing a recent cardigan wearer, Alex James of Blur, as a prime example. JS wouldn't have it. In his opinion, 'That man' (the stylist) was an out-of-touch idiot for using a *cardigan* – the word was practically spat out. 'That man,' I said, 'is Dylan Jones, the editor of the men's fashion magazine *GQ*.' The argument was getting heated. 'Well,' snapped JS. 'In that case, he shouldn't have been given the job. He knows *nothing* about style.' It was unusual for us to have such a heated exchange, and in another change from the usual routine, instead of walking out, JS picked up a newspaper and sat with it in front of his face, refusing to further debate the issue of the day: Cardigans: Yay or Nay?

After JS died, the undertaker in Barbados asked me to choose some clothes for my husband's journey home. I couldn't think straight and, quite frankly, Coffin Chic had never before entered my mind. The undertaker suggested I chose the sort of clothes JS would have worn had he been travelling home in a seat in the cabin, rather than in a coffin in the hold, but, I was advised, he must not wear a belt or shoes.

No belt or shoes!

It was inconceivable that JS would get on a plane without either of those things. I felt I was sending him home only half-dressed. After discussion with family back in England, I chose an outfit and then suddenly remembered underwear. JS *had* to wear pants. There was no way he could come home commando, he wasn't a 'swing free' type of guy. The pants were delivered to the funeral directors with the instructions that they must make sure JS was wearing a pair of underpants on the plane.

I became obsessed with those pants. I even emailed the undertaker to confirm that JS would be in his coffin wearing pants. Looking back, after two autopsies, one each on either side of the Atlantic, various other tests and a four-thousand mile flight for repatriation,

I wonder whether JS was wearing *any* of the things that were so heartbreakingly picked out for him, let alone his underpants. I didn't see him back in the UK. I wavered about it until the undertaker in London gently suggested that after all the tests, the length of time and the compulsory embalming, it might not be a good idea. JS could have been dressed in anything. Or nothing. Someone might even have pinched the pink polo shirt he should have been wearing.

Ah, the polo shirts. JS loved polo shirts for casual wear. Wherever we went on holiday, he would buy another one embroidered with the name of the resort we stayed at or the golf club he played at. Personally, I think that holiday shirts should stay on holiday. I found it strange that JS would wear something saying *Port Royal Golf Club – Bermuda* whilst shopping in north London, but occasionally some stranger buying a loaf of bread would spot a badge and cry, 'Hey! You've played Port Royal! Me too!' at which point JS and the stranger would talk about the complexities of the tenth tee or whatever, which further strengthened his love of the shirt and logo combo.

I kept all JS's ties and a few other items of clothing, and his suitcase from Barbados remains packed, but whilst I thought it would be the posh suits and smart jackets which would upset me, it was the piles of polo shirts that I found the most distressing. As well as the newer shirts, he'd kept faded, shapeless ones for painting and gardening. Decades' worth of shirts were there. As I took them out one by one, they told a story of a man and his golf and his travels, of *our* travels, because my life with JS was also woven into the history of those shirts.

I haven't written about the inquests, one in Barbados and one in London, both almost two years after JS died. I haven't written about them because, despite the conclusions of both inquests, you could torture me by waterboarding and to my dying day I will never agree that JS ignored the official warning signs not to go into the water.

I was there from start to finish and my experience of the event simply wasn't how it was portrayed in the court documents. I am certain, that the *only* warning that JS ignored was a warning from me, a concerned wife who had heard of the dangers of that stretch of beach via other guests. I asked JS not to go for a swim, I warned him of the dangers, but he brushed aside my fears. My final words shouted to him were, 'Be careful! I mean it!' as I jabbed my finger at his retreating form. I remember suddenly feeling embarrassed that I had shouted after JS as one would shout at a naughty dog and wondered what the other sunbathers on the beach must think of such a heckling wife.

JS walked away from me and my warnings into the sea and, minutes later, as I watched from the beach, to his death.

I've been angry at many things these last two years, including other situations that I had warned JS about and which he ignored, but which now I am having to deal with. But I have never been angry with him for dying, because although he might have ignored my fears, he didn't intend to die. He was a stubborn, proud man who didn't like to be told what to do, a man who always thought he knew best even when he didn't, but he balanced his stubborn nature with great charm, generosity, kindness and humour. JS didn't go into the water to spite me or prove a point, but because he wanted to, and he always did what he wanted. But as I moved those polo shirts from cupboard to bag, looking at the logos and remembering the life we had together, which whilst not perfect, was a wonderful one, a flash of anger tore through me and I said out loud, 'Bloody hell, John. You really went and ruined everything, didn't you?'

He wasn't there to respond.

But I know that if even if he had been alive to witness my anger, he'd have been out of the door and to the golf club, like a shot, probably wearing a polo shirt.

RISING FROM THE ASHES

I had a feeling that Luke was around me for the first few weeks; in hindsight I think this was part of the horrible process of trying to figure out first-hand what happens to people, and why. Fate? Afterlife? So many questions. Then I got his ashes and everything came crashing down around me. The scientist in me was back – this is what he was reduced to, this was him. So I carried 'him' around (a whole stone) in my bicycle pannier or rucksack for a month until I got a bad back and came to the conclusion that that tub of ash wasn't actually 'him' anymore. ~ **Sophie Day**

When I was a child, I went to a relative's funeral – a cremation – and, as is usual, the family invited everyone back to the house for something to eat and drink. There may have been a few strangers there too; I once met a woman at a funeral who confessed that she didn't know the deceased at all, but wanted to pay her respects, presumably by taking advantage of the free food and drink laid out in the bar of a nearby hotel. It was the third funeral that week she'd been to, the last being for a farmer who had been crushed to death against a wall by one of his cows, a man for whom she had no sympathy as she felt he should have known to get out of the way when the herd came into the yard for milking.

Anyway, there I was, at this funeral, probably gorging myself on sausage rolls, when the phone rang, something that signalled lots of whispering and the room thinning out.

'Where has everyone gone?' I asked.

I remember being told in a hushed voice that the ashes were ready to be scattered in the garden of remembrance at the crematorium, and realising for the first time, that whilst we had been sitting on the sofa eating, drinking and swapping stories, our relative's body was being burnt to a crisp, something which rather curtailed my appetite.

Over the last few years I have often thought back to that time, though to my shame I am not completely sure whose funeral it was. I have remembered it because in hindsight, I wish that we had scattered JS's ashes at the earliest opportunity.

Talking to older widows, it seems that scattering some of your husband's ashes on the ninth hole of the local golf course, taking some to New York because he'd never been but had always wanted to go and making the rest into a diamond ring or paperweight, is a relatively new phenomenon. It used to be that if you were cremated you were interred, scattered in a garden of remembrance or put in an urn and kept on the mantelpiece.

As part of JS's refusal to acknowledge that he was mortal and therefore guaranteed to drop off his perch at some point, he would never discuss what he wanted doing after he'd died. A shrug of the shoulders and an off-hand muttering of 'Do what you like, I won't care,' has not been helpful to me. Alive, you may think that giving your relatives carte-blanche to dispose of your remains gives them freedom of choice, but I can assure you that at a time when you are dealing with grief so great, even deciding whether to have ham or cheese in a sandwich is a major decision, it's an added burden you could do without.

So let me pause for a moment to give a public service announcement: *Let everyone know what you want done with your dead body.*

OK, so I may have phrased this slightly oddly – I don't mean that if the postman calls later you should open the door and announce,

'I want to be cremated and my ashes sent up in a firework over Wimbledon Common,' as you're signing for a Special Delivery. What I mean is, don't be squeamish; let your loved ones know what you would like done with your remains. *Please*. I'm putting it on record that I want my ashes scattered on Stone Bay beach in Broadstairs, and so that there is no confusion as to *where* on the beach, I shall be drawing a little map and putting a red arrow to mark the spot.

So, JS was cremated, and without any clear instructions from the deceased, I decided that as he was a London man through and through, I wanted his ashes (and those of Rufus) scattered at the top of Parliament Hill on Hampstead Heath, overlooking London, a spot we both knew well.

A few weeks later, walking The Hound through a wooded area on the Heath, I remembered JS saying how much he loved the walk through this wood, how first thing in the morning when the cobwebs and leaves were dusted with frost it looked like a scene from a fairytale. I scrapped Parliament Hill and decided on Fairytale Wood.

The crematorium wrote to me to say that JS's ashes were ready for collection. If I wanted the cremains scattered in the garden of remembrance, I might like to consider a rose bush or a plaque in the garden; there was a range of options detailed on an attached list. I'd dismissed the idea shortly after the funeral, but now I found the grounds around the crem extraordinarily peaceful, and knowing that JS was up there, albeit in a box, I visited regularly. I decided that I wanted his ashes to be scattered in the garden of remembrance.

Weeks later, I decided against the garden of remembrance. Other than the fact his funeral had been held there, JS had no links to East Finchley, plus, Rufus' ashes wouldn't be allowed.

I went back to the idea of Hampstead Heath, this time a memorial bench. JS's ashes could be scattered around the bench. There was a long waiting list, and I couldn't choose the spot.

Instead of looking over London, with 790 acres it was entirely possible that 'his' bench could be somewhere he'd never been or overlooking the toilet block by the café.

One year after JS's funeral, the crem wrote to me asking if I had made a decision. I popped into the office brandishing the letter. 'Please could I have more time?' I asked. The lady told me I could. 'He's got plenty of company on the shelf,' she said cheerily.

I don't know why I didn't just bring him home, even though I hadn't decided where to scatter him.

Time marched on. Every so often, the crematorium would get in touch with me, but still I dithered. Consulting family members just added to the confusion as everyone had different ideas or didn't want to discuss it.

The golf course at Embleton in Northumberland, the spot where we had planned to scatter Rufus' ashes before JS broke down whilst standing in the dunes clutching the box and said he couldn't let him go yet? I didn't want JS that far away from me. The beach at Broadstairs we both loved so much? Someone said it was weird that JS had drowned and yet I was taking him back to the sea. The garden at his sister's house in Hertfordshire was a possibility, but what if the family moved? I had a memorial stone erected at The Emirates Stadium, home of Arsenal Football Club, but it was inconceivable to scatter his ashes there: the cleaners around the stadium would have swept him up and bagged him within hours, and however much I told myself that the ashes weren't JS, that they were just bodily remains, even I couldn't stomach the idea of him being thrown into the back of a Geesink Norba dust cart and taken to Islington's refuse depot.

I still liked the idea of the crematorium, and went there several times a week. I debated taking Rufus' ashes up bit-by-bit in my coat pocket, secretly scattering him next to JS.

But was this about me and what *I* wanted? JS had said to do what I liked, but surely it was about what *he* would have wanted?

The only thing I was clear about was that I didn't want his ashes split up – a bit here, a bit there. In another irrational thought, I felt it was akin to his legs being in one place and his arms in another.

Two years after JS died, the crematorium wrote to me again.

I emailed them explaining I had still not made a decision. Please could I have more time? 'No problem,' they emailed back.

Remember how certain I was that I didn't want the ashes split up? I still couldn't decide where I wanted the ashes, but now I was certain that I wanted to keep some of them to be made into an hourglass – a large egg-timer – which could sit on my desk. This would be perfect! Not only would the ashes be useful, it would be as if JS was telling me to get on with my life, a permanent reminder from him that time does run out, and to make the most of every minute. I told myself that JS would like this, that he would appreciate being useful after he had gone. I spent hours on the internet researching where I could get one made, looking at antique ones, wondering how I could replace the sand with ashes. I now look back and wonder if I was truly bonkers.

Eventually, it wasn't that the crematorium ran out of patience, but of space. I received a letter stating (very kindly) that if I didn't arrange collection of the ashes within 30 days, they would be scattered in the garden of remembrance.

Two years and four months after JS died, I fired up the little Fiat, motored to St Marylebone crematorium, parked outside the office and went in. As I pushed their ultimatum letter across the counter, I burst into tears, something the staff were clearly used to, given the speed a box of tissues appeared.

Naively, I had imagined that I would just sail in and be handed the ashes, but because I hadn't been given any instructions as to how I wanted the ashes dealt with (closed urn, urn for scattering, etc.), JS hadn't been 'bagged up' and there was a wait. I stood there looking at a cabinet filled with knick-knacks: urns and keepsake boxes and 'diamonds' which could be made out of your loved ones ashes, but no egg timers, and yet again wondered how on earth all this had happened.

Eventually a woman appeared carrying a green cardboard box.

'I've got a bit of a daft question,' I said through tears. 'I've seen a programme about pets being cremated and some places just give the owners back any old ash. How do I know this is my husband and not someone else?' I didn't want to be sobbing over the wrong ashes.

I was shown a label that had accompanied JS all the way from Barbados to East Finchley. There had been checks at every stage. The label of death meant that the dust in the box was definitely my husband.

I signed some paperwork.

'Do you need a bag?' the woman asked, as if I was at the checkout in Waitrose.

'Yes please,' I said.

The green box was put in a green plastic bag.

Other widows had warned me that ashes are heavier than you expect, but still, I was surprised at the weight of the bag.

As I was leaving, a man came in and said to the ladies behind the counter, 'I've come to collect my mother.'

I got into the car, put the bag on the passenger seat, composed myself and said out loud, 'Time to go home, John.'

We'd only just moved off when: PARP! PARP! PARP!

The ashes were heavy enough for the car to detect someone was sitting in the passenger seat without a seat belt.

I stopped, leaned over and clipped the belt across the bag.

A few metres further along, I couldn't stand the fact that I had JS in a box with a seat belt on. In amongst everything that seemed wrong, *this* was something I could put right. I stopped, put the bag in the boot and drove off, but had *another* change of heart. I couldn't possibly have my husband in the boot of the car. What was I thinking? I stopped the car again, and got the bag out of the boot. I considered putting it on the back seat, but JS *hated* being in the back seat, and I couldn't imagine him ever sitting in the back whilst I drove. So JS went in the foot-well of the front passenger seat. It wasn't ideal, but by this point I had pulled out of the grounds into traffic, and it wasn't going to be easy to stop suddenly to play 'Pass the Ashes'.

I (we?) arrived home.

Before JS died, if I'd had to write a scene where a widow brings home her husband's ashes, I would have made it quite dramatic: the widow coming through the door clutching the urn to her ample bosom and saying through tears and with a sad smile, 'You're home now, darlin'. Safe back amongst those who love you,' and putting them in pride of place on a table or a mantelpiece surrounded by photos and candles. I did actually meet someone who took their brother to every family party, even having a place-setting for him. This brother had been dead for 25 years.

JS's return home was rather less dramatic. I made a fuss of The Hound, put the bag on my desk and made a cup of tea, and then, deciding that I might as well go the whole way, opened the box. Inside was a plastic bag filled with what looked like cat litter. I stared at the grey and white granules for a moment, and then, through the plastic, poked it a couple of times. It felt crunchy, the sort of mix of fine sand and ground shells you find on a beach. I didn't feel upset. I didn't feel anything because it was impossible to believe that it had come to this, that JS's powerful physical presence should be reduced to a plastic bag of powdered bone sitting in a cardboard box on my desk in my study, that he should walk out of the door holding a suitcase and be carried back in, in a green plastic carrier bag.

I put the lid on the box, put the box back in the bag and put the ashes in a wardrobe.

FOUR BIRTHDAYS, THREE YEARS, ONE BLOG

I was on a course with work yesterday with lots of people who know nothing about me, and I am sure never imagined that I am a widow, and we were doing something about 'personal brand'. The facilitator was asking us what our first impressions of him were, and then what we thought his first impression of us was. I said, 'Quiet, but if I have something worth saying then I say it,' or something like that, and he agreed, but he also said that I was always smiling and rarely had a smile off my face. This is the person I want to be; a person that other people think is smiley and friendly, and if I can be smiley at the moment, then I can be smiley forever, and that is a GOOD thing. ~ **Linz**

In a moment, I'd like you to do a little exercise for me.

Don't panic!

I don't mean the sort of exercise that involves jumping around in camel-toe revealing thrush-inducing Lycra, more of a cerebral exercise, but not the type that used to make me break out into a cold sweat at school with the words: *Two trains on parallel tracks are travelling towards each other. If one train…*

Those were the sort of questions I couldn't answer for obsessing over what sort of trains they were – was it a trick question? Was one a new train and the other a steam loco? – or worrying about getting the answer wrong, failing the exam and ending up in the local fuse factory, soldering the ends on to fuses whilst wearing a hairnet, lonely because my friends had swanned off to university to become big cheeses in industry with expense accounts and Audi Quattros.

But I digress.

No, what I would like you to do is to imagine a guest list for a party you might have given before the Grim Reaper gatecrashed your life. Now, imagine the guest list for a party you might (if you weren't exhausted/grief-stricken/broke) throw today.

And then compare the two lists.

I recently came across a guest list for a birthday party I threw for JS some years before he died. It was a significant birthday, but the Birthday Boy was in no mood to celebrate. He grumbled about getting older, moaned that he didn't want a party and, other than choosing the wine, showed absolutely no interest in the planning whatsoever, claiming that his role was simply to turn up.

You may be thinking: 'What sort of wife holds a party for her husband when he clearly didn't want one?'

I'll tell you what sort of wife, one who wasn't going to let her husband get away with being a party-pooper *ever* again.

Ten years earlier, JS had taken the same anti-celebratory stance, proclaiming that he would ignore any birthday that ended with a zero and shunning my suggestion that we should do something significant, such as throw a party.

The day dawned, a card and a gift were given and everything was low-key, just as Sir had ordered. Except that men can be more complicated than I'd realised, and JS was irked that I had taken him at his word.

'But you said you didn't want a party!' I bleated, confused.

'I didn't mean it!' he retorted and flounced out to go for a drink with his friends, whilst I sat in front of the TV with an M&S microwaveable curry feeling wretched.

At various points over the next ten years, the fact that I had done nothing for his birthday was occasionally raised in an accusatory manner, so for this one, JS was having a party and he was damn well going to enjoy it.

And he did.

It was a joyous event with a band and a magician and a room filled with balloons and friends and family, a lunch at The Oval, home of Surrey County Cricket Club, because although as a member of the MCC JS tended to go to Lord's, his introduction to cricket was as a young boy when his father took him to The Oval.

JS gave a speech. He said something like, 'My wife said that I should hold a party now because I might not live long enough to see my next big birthday...'

Oh, how we laughed. But in persuading JS to have a party I had said exactly that. Over the years we had lost so many people dear to us – some very young – and I was acutely conscious of making the most of the life we had whilst we could live it. *Carpe diem* and all that. Of course, I am now even more aware of the fragility of life, but unfortunately most of the time I am too stressed, anxious, tired and overwhelmed to seize anything other than the sherry bottle and a packet of Frazzles, let alone the day.

For some time after the bereaved have crash-landed on Planet Grief, we are certain that whatever we are feeling is unique to our situation. On internet bereavement sites I see posts from recent widows and widowers asking the same sort of bewildered questions I used to ask: is it normal not to be able to sleep? Has anyone else had constant heart palpitations? Will I *ever* be happy again? With the experience of over three years of widowhood I can answer with some certainty: Yes, yes and eventually, at your own pace, yes, even if a deep seam of sadness remains.

One other question that regularly crops up is, 'Has anyone else lost friends?'

I have not been good at keeping in touch with those that have reached out to me. Now that the fog of selfishness that is part of the bereavement process is finally clearing, I am ashamed of my behaviour. A dear friend wrote to me recently in the depths of his own bereavement (he lost a child) and said that he and his partner had tried to reach out to me many times, but I had shut them out. They had been very hurt, but now he understood.

I thought I had put the subject of friends to bed.

And then I found the list and compared the old list with a hypothetical new one.

This time round I wouldn't need to hire a huge room at The Oval, I could have the party in a four-man tent on the lawn with a couple of picnic tables. But what really got me wasn't how many people had fallen by the wayside, it was wondering that if JS were to walk into my garden party, how many people he would recognise? Just like his beloved Arsenal, since JS died, Team HB has changed. There are the core people of course: friends and family who have remained strong in the hurricane of my grief, but there are children that have been born since he died, children who had only just been born and now are little people with strong personalities, new friends and those that I now consider part of my cherished extended family. And if JS queried why certain people were missing, I'd tell him, 'They weren't friends. They were parasites.' Sadly, Andrew, one of the steadfast ones, someone who brought me protein shakes when I couldn't eat, who did all he could to help me having lost his wife when he was young, would not be at my imaginary party. He died last month.

It's three years since I first started writing my *Planet Grief* blog.

Last Saturday, it was JS's birthday, the fourth birthday without him.

I had lunch in a restaurant with some of JS's family, and then went back to a house in Hertfordshire to release a balloon, the tradition I started on his first post-death birthday and which I have continued since. JS loved this house and his family living in it and saw it as a sanctuary from the strains of his life, a constant reassuring presence through good times and bad. I first went there and met his family in February 1990. The moment I walked in, I felt like JS did, enveloped by kindness, warmth and family life. I loved going there: some of the happiest moments in my life have involved sitting in the garden eating egg sandwiches as children and dogs rushed around. I still love going there, but there is a dreadful, yawning gap when I'm at the house and JS isn't, and I expect there always will be.

Two other family members lost too soon shared their birthday with JS, so we stood in the garden and continuing a tradition I started on his first 'absent' birthday and which formed the basis of the first post I wrote for *Planet Grief* exactly three years ago, released three balloons into the sky, one for each departed loved one. As the balloons raced upwards, I vowed to make sure that the children who will never physically know their grandfather know all about JS and what sort of a man he was. A man who enjoyed the good things in life, but for whom the greatest pleasure of all was spending time with his family.

CONFESSION

*I got home around noon that day and heard sirens blaring outside of my place and had a moment's thought about my mum. I was making lunch for myself, only to be interrupted by a neighbour saying there had been an accident and I needed to come. My partner wouldn't let me, she just knew. So she went ahead, and I made sure I got my new $200 jeans out of the dryer; I was determined they were not going to be ruined. We do the strangest things when entering denial. Mum was killed that day right outside my front window. ~ **Dr Toby Silverton***

Have you ever done something so shocking, so out of character, that the memory of your behaviour is branded through your very being in the way the word 'Brighton' runs through a stick of pink-and-white rock?

Before JS died, the worst thing I ever did was steal a re-usable sticker from a boy called Paul Attwood at primary school. We both had sticker sets – I had a garden scene, he had a farmyard – and whilst I had no desire to populate my beautiful garden with sheep or pigs, I coveted Paul's little wellington-wearing farmer boy, who I thought would be the perfect addition to my garden tableau. Despite repeated attempts to get him to swap his boy for one of my daffodils, Paul refused.

So I stole it.

In those days, we sat at old-fashioned desks arranged in blocks, and I was inkwell-to-inkwell with Paul. I saw Farmer Boy lying on Paul's desk, waited until he was distracted, and then by using my exercise book, leaned over and flicked the sticker into my inkwell and began to sharpen my pencil on top of it. As we were packing up to go home, Paul realised that his sticker was missing. We all hunted around, but no one thought to look in my inkwell. Last out of the class, I fished Farmer Boy out from underneath his blanket of wood shavings and squirreled him away. I would be about five or six years old, but I have a vivid memory of being appalled at what I had just done, of feeling frightened that I had been so dishonest. When I got home, I stuck Farmer Boy onto my garden scene, only to find that the proportions were all wrong: even as a six year-old I knew that pink water-lilies were not supposed to be four times the size of a human head, and the addition of a minute plastic boy in black wellingtons didn't enhance my beautiful garden, it made it look ridiculous. I took Farmer Boy back to school and dropped him on the floor in the classroom. I can't remember whether Paul found him or not.

It's a funny story and a touching one, but I can honestly say that the event stuck with me because of the feeling of being shocked at my behaviour. It was the first time I recognised that my mind and my body took over, 'making' me behave in a way I didn't recognise. I never stole anything again, ever; I became nauseatingly honest, even getting my parents to take me to the police station to hand in a pound note I found in the street.

Nine months after JS died, I wrote a blog post called Getting in a Lather (see page 182). It's strange that out of all the posts I have written in the last four years, this one post has needed revisiting twice, firstly to confess that 'Mac' was GGHW, and now, to explain the following paragraph:

When I was taken back to the hotel room shortly after JS's death was confirmed in hospital, I would have put money on me running around the room like a headless chicken wearing a bikini (now that's a bizarre image), screaming, banging the walls, trying to throw myself off the balcony onto the terrace below. But, of course, I didn't. I remember someone telling me how amazingly strong I was, how calm I was being, how other tourists who had lost their partners on holiday had cried hysterically. I remember thinking: Am I supposed to cry? How am I supposed to react? *Perhaps in another post I will tell you how I reacted. I still find it difficult to comprehend how in such circumstances the mind does everything it can to grab onto some shred of normality. Certainly mine behaved in a bizarre (and at the time) inappropriate way, a way that for months made me ashamed.*

I have never written about this 'bizarre, inappropriate' behaviour before, about what happened when I walked back into the hotel room for the first time after JS died, specifically when I walked into the bathroom.

I have never told anyone what happened, what I did.

Until now, well over four years later.

When I got back to the hotel, the police were waiting for me: two officers. I went up to our room (my room?), and someone suggested that as the police were going to interview me, I might like to get changed. I think they said something like, 'You might be more comfortable in some clothes.'

I walked into the bathroom. The maid hadn't cleaned it. It was just as we had left it only a couple of hours before. The bathroom smelt of deodorant and sun lotion and that sweet, warm perfume that pervades the Caribbean air. It all looked so normal, so far removed from having just seen my husband drown and end up navy-blue on a hospital gurney.

And I laughed.

And as I laughed, I pumped my fists.

I would like to say that for a moment I thought that nothing had happened, that walking into the bathroom had been like waking up from a bad dream, and I was laughing from relief.

Perhaps. I would like to think that my laughing and fist pump was some sort of nervous reaction, that vomiting outside the hospital and laughing in the bathroom were both involuntary reactions to trauma. Undoubtedly. But whereas pouring your breakfast into a flowerbed having witnessed your husband die is quite understandable, laughing is not. Why am I crying now, as I write this, and yet laughed back then?

In an attempt to work out what happened in the bathroom, I have tried to recreate that laugh hundreds of times, but never come even close. I can tell you what sort of laugh it wasn't: It wasn't the sort of laugh that bursts out when you're watching a great sitcom. It wasn't hesitant, nervous laughter or polite laughter. I didn't snort or cackle. It wasn't the sort of joy-filled laughter at The Hound, when he begs me to play ball with him, or the type of sarcastic laugh accompanied by the phrase, 'Yeah, right.' I don't know what sort of laughter it was. It lasted perhaps a second. It was followed by years of tears.

I didn't tell anyone about what had happened because I was confused and ashamed, and because I wanted to work out why it had happened. I now know that I will never really understand why I laughed as I walked into the bathroom, so now I just accept it. Acceptance dilutes the confusion, but the shame remains.

I didn't write about the incident because however gifted a writer is, there is a huge capacity for the reader to misinterpret the words on a page. Can you imagine someone newly bereaved reading that in the moments after my husband died, I laughed and pumped my fists? No, I can't either, or at least I couldn't.

And now? Now I realise that our brain works in mysterious ways, and that sometimes we are, literally, out of our minds.

And what about all the stuff earlier, about Paul Attwood and the sticker I stole?

Think of the sticker-story as the support act, as a comedian's warm-up man preparing you for the main event. Because the page is my stage, and even with acceptance over that moment in the bathroom in Barbados, I sure as hell couldn't walk out onto the stage and announce, 'Have you heard the one about the woman who laughed at her husband drowning?'

PUPPY LOVE

We lost a dog in very tragic circumstances a few years ago. It took me two years to get over the death of my lovely dog, so god knows how long it's going to take to get over the death of the love of my life, but it is definitely happening, inch by inch. ~ ***Angela***

There was something that JS only revealed to me after we were married, something so disturbing that had he mentioned it that day when standing by the photocopier in the one and only dress I owned I first clapped eyes on him, even Cupid would have admitted defeat and gone to sling his arrow of love somewhere else. But then I suppose it would have been odd for a boss to introduce himself to a temporary agency secretary with the words, 'Hello. I prefer cats to dogs.'

Had JS been upfront with his domesticated pet of choice, I might have taken a completely different view of him. As it was, I assumed that he liked dogs because he owned one, Crofter, a loveable but rather badly behaved Border Terrier with a habit of jumping up at the office staff and ripping our tights.

I suspect that my disdain towards cats had its roots in my childhood. Whereas in our house, my mother ensured that our dog enjoyed a social status higher than any human inhabitant, cats were looked on as pests, furry menaces who trespassed in our garden, killed the song birds, crapped in the flower beds and tormented the dog, who would hurl himself at the patio doors until we let him out, only to run in the wrong direction.

In student digs in London, I endured two years of broken sleep by what at first I thought were the blood-curdling screams of someone being murdered, but later discovered was gang-warfare between the local tom cats who patrolled the large council estate at the bottom of our garden. A friend's cat suddenly turning feral and flying at her face added mild fear to my dislike; a visit to a household with cats who walked across the kitchen counters, anointing everything including a cheese sandwich with cat hair (or worse), added disgust. My anti-cat attitude made it all the odder that I once chose to share a flat with a woman who owned two cats. I don't remember these moggies' names, just that the flat always stank of dirty cat-litter trays and plates of fish-based food, even when the litter tray was clean and the plates were cleared away. It wasn't the smell that got to me: anyone who has been on the receiving end of a flatulent dog has no right to complain about a bit of stale salmon. No, it was the unpredictable way these cats operated that rattled me. One moment, they'd be winding themselves around my legs, softly purring, the next flying at me hissing and screeching, rapier-like claws extended, shredding my skin and my M&S fuchsia-pink towelling dressing-gown.

So, like I say, if JS had told me from the get-go that he preferred cats to dogs, both our lives would have been very different.

JS did love dogs, just not all dogs, and especially not large, slobbery dogs that did massive poos and left fur everywhere. And there we had common ground, because whilst I love dogs, I couldn't live with a large slobbery dog either. I once knew a woman who owned a Boxer, a gorgeous-looking hound, but whose good looks were accessorised by strings of white drool dripping from its slobbery chops. She spent half her life rushing around clearing dog-slobber off the furniture, and the other half shovelling poos off her lawn, the size of which looked as if they had dropped out of a pony's bum.

But, as usual, I'm digressing.

Throughout our marriage, the whole Cat v Dog debate became something of a running joke between us. My position was that cats were useless unless you lived somewhere with a mouse infestation, and even then a cat would only catch a mouse if it felt like it, not to order. 'Have you ever heard of a mountain rescue cat?' I'd say, 'or guide cats for the blind?' JS was forced to admit that there were no hearing cats for the deaf, or bomb disposal cats. Sometimes, we'd be at a football match and see the police dogs lined up, barking menacingly, and I'd ask him to imagine whether a line of police cats meowing would deter the opposition from making a run towards the home supporters. Exactly.

JS's defence of cats seemed to rest on the fact that compared to dogs they were low maintenance and didn't need to be walked, a strange position to adopt given that JS loved dog-walking.

After his divorce, JS used to say forlornly, 'I miss taking Crofter for a walk.'

I wanted a dog, JS missed his dog, dispatches from his previous home seemed to indicate that Crofter was becoming more of a tie than a pleasure, so we decided to offer Crofter a home, only to discover that the dog had already been re-homed without JS's prior knowledge, an act that incensed him, though in retrospect a Border Terrier was undoubtedly better off living on a farm than a top-floor flat in central London.

Re-homing poor, displaced Crofter and getting a new puppy were two entirely different things, and it took years of vigorous campaigning by me before we got Rufus, a feisty red male miniature dachshund.

After Rufus died, JS wanted another dog *immediately*. He couldn't bear the gap in our lives. He didn't want to just go out for a walk on Hampstead Heath. He wanted to go for a walk with a dog, *our* dog.

I didn't want another dog. I love dogs; I'm obsessed with dogs. Before Rufus died it was inconceivable to me that I wouldn't want another dog. But after the initial shock of losing him calmed down, I began to relish the freedom of being dog-free. It was a joy to be able to go away for the weekend without organising dog care before we went, or worrying about how the dog was getting on whilst we were there. To accept a last-minute invitation to dinner after the theatre because we didn't need to get back 'for the dog' was liberating. We went to Australia, and instead of the last hour at home anxiously briefing the house sitter about every nuance of the dog's personality and digestive system, we just shut the door and went. Make no mistake, JS loved Rufus, but the nitty-gritty of dog-owning, the thinking ahead and the organising fell entirely to me, and I wanted a break.

I found life without a dog easier. JS found it depressing.

He said, 'You really wanted a dog and I didn't but we got one and now I do, so now it's *my* turn to get what I want.'

JS promised that he would be entirely responsible for this new dog. He would feed it and walk it and take it to the vets. He would arrange a dog-sitter if we needed to go away. There was no need to fear losing the freedom of being dog-free I had come to love: if I wanted to go out for the day, JS would stay in. He promised not to feed the new dog prawn crackers or poppadums from the sofa and then say (not entirely good naturedly), 'Will you stop that dog from staring at me?'

Rufus had been very much 'my' dog. This new hound would be entirely his.

Eventually, I caved in and agreed to another dog on all the conditions outlined above. After several lengthy interrogations as to our suitability as owners by the breeder and her husband, we were put on their waiting list. Finally, a litter of six puppies arrived. On our first litter-viewing, one fat little fellow raced towards us wagging his tail. He jumped on my knee and starting playing tug with the strap of my camera. I have a video of the exact moment that this pup chose to own us; on the footage, you can hear me shrieking, 'Could you be our puppy?' and JS laughing. We called the pup Boris, after Boris Johnson, because a picture in the London Evening Standard of BJ scowling looked just like *our* wrinkly-faced, flat-nosed Boris in the newborn photographs the breeder had emailed.

Boris was due to be brought home from the breeder's on 30th December. A couple of weeks before he arrived, some friends of ours invited us to their New Year's Eve party outside London.

'We'd love to come,' JS said.

'What about the pup?' I pointed out. 'We're only getting him the day before.'

'Can't your brother look after him?' JS asked.

'He's in Northumberland,' I retorted, my stomach plummeting at the thought that we hadn't even brought the puppy home, but already JS was reverting to type.

'Is there anyone else we could ask?'

'No.'

'He'll be alright, won't he?' JS pressed. 'He'll be sleeping anyway.'

'You are joking?' I was aghast.

'OK, so what do you propose we do?'

'Stay at home with our new puppy?' I rolled my eyes. JS rolled his back.

I can't tell you how upset I was over this exchange. It was every-thing I feared, but once this gorgeous little bundle of fur arrived, it was to get worse. JS came to puppy classes, but refused to get down on the floor to do the exercises; he didn't want to get his suit dirty, but he wouldn't wear old clothes. The trainer's instructions for everyone to cheer manically and throw their arms around as their pups came towards them in an exercise, saw JS standing with his arms folded, muttering that everyone looked 'ridiculous'. He had promised to do all the house-training, but if Boris was circling and sniffing and I pointed it out, JS would say, 'I'll just finish this and then take him out,' but was annoyed with *me* when a ten-week old puppy didn't wait and squatted on the carpet. I took over the house-training, repeatedly going into the garden in all weathers, day and night. Once, I asked JS to keep an eye on Boris whilst I had a bath, only to come down to find JS sitting at the computer with his back to the action, a pile of steaming poo on the carpet, several damp patches, and Boris happily munching on the corner of a rug. JS swore blind that all the mess had been there before I went for a bath, but I hadn't noticed.

Not long after Boris arrived, I said, 'Remember, I'm out for the day on Saturday.'

'I'm playing golf,' JS said. 'It's an all-day thing, a competition.'

'You've known for months I was out this Saturday.' I was angry. 'Who's going to look after the dog?'

'Oh, so because you want to go off shopping with your friends, I can't play golf any longer, is that it? Well, *I'm* not cancelling.'

This was so unfair. JS was behaving like a small child who had promised his parents he would look after a puppy, only to immediately lose interest.

I was so angry, I couldn't speak. It was usually JS who did the walking out, but this time it was me who went up to the bedroom. I wasn't only angry with JS, but mad with myself for not going with my gut instinct and saying 'No' to having a dog.

I lay on the bed and cried.

JS came in with Boris in his arms and stood at the end of the bed.

'Right,' he said. 'I'm not putting up with this. I'm going to ring the breeder and tell her I'm bringing him back.'

I carried on sobbing. I think he thought I was immediately going to say, 'Don't!' but I didn't.

JS tried again. 'If that's want you want, I'll take him back.'

When I didn't rise to it, JS went in for the kill. 'So, if you really think that someone else will love this little fellow more than us, that someone else will give him a better home, a better future, then fine, I'll take him back right now.'

And of course, it wasn't as simple as that. I knew that if we kept him that little pup would want for nothing, that he would be loved and looked after until the day he died. The problem wasn't that I wouldn't love him, but that I would love him too much.

Of course he wasn't going back. Boris, aka 'The Hound', grew in to the most wonderful dog: gentle, good with children, full of fun, but still very much a stubborn, nose-to-the-ground hound with selective deafness.

A fraction over two years after we brought Boris home, JS died. The dog I was reluctant to own became my *only* reason for getting up in those first dark months. Some days I'd want to stay in bed and block out the world, but I'd hear a little grumble from the side of the bed, and look down to see Boris impatiently shifting from one paw to the other, waiting for his walk. Swinging my heavy legs out of bed, I only had to say, 'Come on then, let's go,' and he'd rush to the front door and wait, tail wagging. It was impossible not to raise a smile, however fleeting and faint. Some days, it was the *only* time I smiled. Together, we roamed Hampstead Heath for hours, sometimes alone, sometimes with other dog-walkers I knew or strangers I met. I'd walk and cry and scream at the sky, and when I started writing my blog, *Planet Grief,* I'd walk and think about what I wanted to write, what I *needed* to write. In many ways, Boris saved me.

Did Boris grieve for JS? I'm not sure. Sometimes, he appeared confused, but in the early weeks before the funeral, it *was* confusing for the little fellow. He would be thrilled when visitors arrived, only for the house to be filled with weeping and wailing humans uninterested in playing ball with him. Certainly, there were no 'Greyfriars Bobby' moments: he didn't sit staring at the front door waiting for JS to come home as he used to, or stop eating. He did rush up to JS's car in the street and stand beside it wagging his tail, but then again, the car was a sign we were going somewhere exciting. No doubt picking up on *my* chaotic emotions, Boris became anxious: he was quicker to bark, whine and howl, and started being uncharacteristically destructive in the house. I've always shown far more patience with animals than I can ever muster for humans, and Boris has never *ever* been mistreated, but once, when I came home, tired, desolate and lonely, and found that he had managed to open the catch on the sideboard and pull out and chew everything he could reach, dragging stuff through the house, I screamed at him, 'JUST GIVE ME A BREAK! JUST GIVE ME A GODDAM BREAK YOU STUPID HOUND' whilst throwing some of the vandalised items towards him. He cowered, I slumped to my knees on the carpet and wept, and then felt a little warm body wriggle onto my lap and try to lick my face. I sat there rocking, holding him, weeping into his dampening fur saying, 'I'm sorry. I'm so sorry, Bozzy.' It was the first and only time I'd behaved like this, and I was ashamed. In the future I made sure that whatever the state of the house behind the front door was when I came home, I never reacted that way again. Gradually, Boris – and me – got our equilibrium back.

As I write this now, Boris is curled up on a chair by my desk, sleeping. He has known Gorgeous Grey-Haired Widower longer than he knew JS. As I look across at him, I can't help but wonder if

JS walked into the room right now, whether he would greet him as a stranger or as a long-lost friend.

Friend or foe, whatever the reaction, the thought of it makes me sad.

A ROSE-TINTED LIFE

G died suddenly and unexpectedly just over two years ago. I completely understand that feeling that for the first year that we could have just got back to where we left off when he suddenly vanished from our lives. Now, I sometimes feel if he walked back in, I would have to say, 'You don't just walk in here, like nothing's changed. Look what I've had to endure on my own these last two years… etc. etc.' I regularly feel anger; it wasn't his fault he died, so I feel guilt for this anger. But my god, it's tough being the one left behind to deal with the aftermath. ~ **Charlie P**

I am shocked at the number of people I have known that have died. Seriously shocked. Of course, I don't know whether I have known more than the average number of dead people or fewer, because I don't know what the average number is for a woman of my age. I could give you the number I came up with, but you might then start counting up your dead friends and family and comparing it to my list, and I really don't want this to become sort of competitive Death-Off where you sit back and think: 'I've known more dead people than her!' and feel wretched about your lengthy list, or start freaking out that your list is unusually small and, instead of feeling grateful, begin to worry that you are due a few deaths to even things up. So just take it from me that when I flick through my old address book, I'm sad at how many people (of all ages) are no longer alive. I'm also struck that my feelings towards them are frozen at the point that they died, that my relationship with them in death is as it was in life, unchanged by time: Karen will always be young and smiley with never a bad word to say about anyone; Don, quiet and thoughtful; Alistair, warm and witty; Lance, full of fun and so on. But when it comes to my husband, my relationship with him has continued after his death; it has changed and become far more complicated than when he was alive.

During a bereavement coaching session, I remembered an incident which I had forgotten for years, but which since JS died, I have thought about many times. When I first recalled it, I told the tale as if I was recounting a story about a lovable but exasperating child. The incident went like this: JS and I hadn't been together very long – perhaps a year – when we went to New York for a trade show. One evening, the trade association held a dinner at the New York Hilton, after which there was a moneyless 'casino'. I was having a great time frittering away my cardboard chips, when out of the blue, JS turned to me and said, 'I'm not putting up with this. You obviously don't want to be here, so we're going.' I had no idea what he was talking about. Perplexed, I told him that I was fine, that I was enjoying myself. JS seemed annoyed. 'You've made it quite clear that you don't want to be here, and it's obvious to everyone around us. We're going.' He stalked off towards the cloakroom. I followed him.

I remember walking back to the Intercontinental Hotel wondering what on earth had happened. I put it down to this: I have the sort of face where if I'm not smiling, I look as if I'm annoyed or the world is about to end. Time and time again over the years, complete strangers have come up to me in the street and said, 'Cheer up!' when I have been perfectly cheery. When I first met Gorgeous Grey-Haired Widower he used to say to me, 'What's wrong?' and I'd say, 'Nothing's wrong!' because there really wasn't anything wrong, not the sort of 'Nothing's wrong,' women say when they mean that *everything* is wrong. GGHW now knows this 'Oh woe is me, the problems of the world are weighing on my shoulders look' is my default facial expression, and no longer asks me if I'm OK several hundred times a day. I did try to walk around constantly smiling, but catching my reflection in shop windows, I realised I looked as if I was walking around with a lemon up my bottom.

Back to New York.

We walked back to the hotel, JS fuming, me trying to jolly him out of his mood: 'I was fine! I'd be great at poker! My face would always look as if my hand was crap!' JS sulked for a while, but I don't remember giving it another thought until when, 20 years later, I told Shelley the story. Now, I don't look back on that evening and its outcome with affection or even wry exasperation. Now, I am irritated at JS *and* myself. Someone or something – not me – had upset JS (and he took offence very easily), and instead of saying that he wanted to leave, to take responsibility for prematurely ending the evening, he blamed me. I put up with it. I didn't challenge him beyond the initial exchange in the casino; not only that, I accepted that somehow I was to blame. I knew that JS had behaved badly, but it didn't worry me or upset me; it was, 'Just JS.'

Fast forward a decade or so. I had a serious bout of depression that took everyone, not least me, by surprise. I can pinpoint when it (and the crippling agoraphobia) started, but not when it ended, but certainly there was at least 18 months of hell. If I couldn't understand what was happening to me, JS certainly couldn't, and his reaction to my tears was to turn cold. I remember very early on, perhaps a week or so after it started, sobbing in the hall and him just standing in his coat, his bag over his shoulder, looking at me. I said to him, 'I just need a hug!' and still he stood there. I cried that if I saw a stranger in the street in such distress I would go up to them and put my arms round them (and I have done), but my own husband wouldn't. He said, 'You're being ridiculous,' but he didn't comfort me. He walked out.

One morning, I begged him not to play golf because I was so depressed and frightened. It was the only time I had asked him to change his plans because of my illness, and I found it humiliating to do so, but he refused. This was at the point I was so terrified of the dizziness I was experiencing, I'd shuffle down the stairs on my bum and crawl from room to room because I was terrified of falling down when I was alone. It wasn't so much that I was frightened of my own mishap, but I had visions of falling and crushing Rufus. Like I say, I was depressed.

JS's birthday was in June, and I remember steeling myself to go into a shop (which took enormous courage in those days) and queuing up to get him a birthday card. By the time I reached the till, my anxiety felt unmanageable, so I dropped the card and bolted out of the shop. On the day of JS's birthday, I told him why he hadn't got a birthday card; he seemed fine about it. The following February, I gave him a Valentine card, but there was no reciprocal card or gift. Nothing. February 14th came and went completely unmarked. Eventually, I asked him about the (uncharacteristic) lack of a card. His response? A petulant, 'Well, you didn't get me a birthday card last year.'

I am sure if you could set up a celestial web-link to wherever JS is now, he would have a very long list of things that he found annoying about me. It is interesting that some of the things that Gorgeous Grey-Haired Widower clearly finds irritating about me are things that used to irritate JS. It would be impossible not to work and live with someone for a quarter of a century and *not* have bad times. I *was* difficult to live with when I was depressed: *I* couldn't understand how I had gone from confident girl about town, to someone who sat in pain because she daren't go to the toilet on her own at a football match for fear of going through the crowds alone, or who one minute could fly on Concorde across the Atlantic by herself, but the next couldn't cross the road without holding on to the traffic lights for fear of falling, that's if I even managed to make it outside. JS didn't cause my breakdown (there were multiple factors which piled up one on top of another), but his attitude to it certainly added to the pressure. When I came home from the doctors and told JS that the doc had said that I was very depressed, JS said, 'Well, we've got to go to New York at the weekend, so you'll need to be better by then.' I wasn't, but we went. There was no room in his life for weakness, for vulnerability, either for himself or to be tolerated in others. I'm all for the mantra, 'Get up, dress up and show up, however you feel,' but surely there are times when you should be able to say, 'Actually, I've had enough. I can't do this,' without being made to feel as if you're letting the side down.

I said at the beginning that my relationship with JS has changed since he's died, that it has become more complicated. There are many instances I look back on with a new perspective: remembering how JS bought our house without me knowing was at one time funny, but feels less amusing now. Being whisked away by a bank official for a separate 'interview' when it became obvious that JS hadn't made me aware of the ramifications of signing a business loan form he was cajoling me to complete made a good story, but it should never have happened, nor should his fury that I dared to ask the bank whether we could lose our home if I signed it (we could), when he had assured me we couldn't. There are so many stories, but it would do no one any good to make a list of them, least of all me. They flit through my mind and when I remember them I no longer raise my eyebrows and think with a smile, 'That's JS for you.' I think, 'How dare you?'

In hindsight, I made far too many excuses for behaviour that now I would not tolerate. It wasn't that I didn't challenge him – far from it – but in my mind I always absolved him of blame: he was tired; he was worried; he didn't deal well with emotions; I wasn't acting logically; I was hysterical; I hadn't made myself clear or more usually, that's just the way he is. And of course JS was incredibly charming, exciting to be with, decent and wonderful company, so the bad times were always, *always* dwarfed by the good.

Except in the last year. The last year was tough. There were money and business worries, and JS was particularly difficult to live with, or should I say, we found it particularly difficult to live with each other. Because in the last year or so, I had stopped making excuses for him. I was no longer the wide-eyed girl in her twenties who thought JS knew it all. I was in my mid-forties and had been through a great deal (though the worst was yet to come), and I saw JS for what he was: a human being full of the faults and foibles we all are, not the man who I thought could do no wrong and whom I had put on a pedestal nearly 25 years before. I was tired of issues being swept under the carpet, of decisions being made without my knowledge, of blame being apportioned everywhere other than where it lay. I was tired of walking on eggshells so as not to bruise JS's fragile ego. So, I started saying calmly but firmly, 'No John, *you* were the one who…' or, 'Sorry John, but I won't agree to that and it's not just your decision to make.'

The worm had turned and JS didn't like it one little bit. The sadness is that when we went on that much-needed holiday to Barbados, the tension faded away and, as I have written about before, I looked across at him on the sun lounger and thought to myself that I had been worrying about nothing, that things were just as they had been in the good times. We both were happy and relaxed. I know we were because, unlike being at home, we talked.

And then, against my advice, JS walked into the sea and drowned.

There is one final story which sticks in my mind and which I have to share. One evening, I was watching TV and JS was in the next room. Something came on, I forget what, but I thought that he would like to see it. This was in the days before you could pause/rewind live programmes. I shouted for him to come and take a look. 'John! John! Come here! Come quickly!' He didn't come. Afterwards, I went through to him and asked him if he had heard me shouting. He said he had. 'So why didn't you come through?' I asked. 'Because no one tells me what to do,' he replied.

There is a perception that once people have died, you only remember the good in them, and that their flaws fade into the background as if death hands you a pair of rose-tinted spectacles. I wonder if for me if it has been the reverse, that I spent over two decades wearing rose-tinted specs, but that on JS's death, I lost them.

It was definitely easier to live wearing rose-tinted spectacles.

MR BLUE SKY

I remember after a few months, a very caring friend said, 'I think we've got the old you back.' I wanted to bite her head off and say that 'she' will never be back. Now, after nearly four years, I can honestly say that there are still traces of the old me. I consider myself to be still grieving, although not so intense. After 36 years together I don't think that will ever go away. ~ **Sue Smith**

The third summer after JS died, some friends invited Gorgeous Grey-Haired Widower and me to their house for a little soiree. It was one of those last-minute impromptu affairs where we all bumped into each other, the late August weather was lovely and they said, 'Do come over for drinks and nibbles later. Six o'clock suit you?'

It suited us very well indeed, particularly me, as it gave me no time to start worrying about all the usual things I worry about when someone invites me to something well in advance.

I blame the worrying on my mother (don't we all?) whose illnesses and state of mind in my childhood meant that plans were often made, but almost always cancelled. As an adult I understand this, but as a child I would look forward to an outing only to be told on the day that we weren't going because 'Mum isn't well,' or that we were going but without mum because 'Mum isn't well,' and so I'd be out, but worrying about Mum being at home ill. If it wasn't Mum's ailments that scuppered our plans, it was some other family member that was ill, or, much more worryingly, our dog, a dachshund called Rusty. It got to the point that a neighbour called our various problems the 'Bailey Bug'. In the end we didn't even tell anyone what was wrong with us, we just said, 'We've got the Bailey Bug.'

It wasn't only the Bailey Bug that caused our family's plans to alter, it was the weather or the traffic or my mother's low blood sugar. Whilst others were heading off to the coast on a summer's day, we stayed at home because it was bound to be either too hot in the car, or the traffic would be chaos, or taking in to account the length of time we *might* be stuck in the traffic in a car that would *definitely* be hot, this could mean we wouldn't be able to eat at a reasonable time thereby threatening a metabolic crisis involving bingeing on Dextrosol glucose tablets.

Fast-forward 40 years and I have turned into my mother, complete with emergency sugar supplies and the same breed, colour and sex of pet dog.

A planned event has me worrying about whether I will be ill on the day (anything from waking up with a headache to Ebola, depending on the state of my anxiety at the time), The Hound will be ill (I couldn't leave him) or whether inclement weather (rain, fog, ice, snow, high winds) will cause chaos both on the roads and in my bowels. Of course, as any self-help guru will tell you, what you focus on you attract, so invariably I *do* get a stinking cold or wake up with a crashing headache or a bout of IBS. It's a shame I've spent more time worrying about my health than imagining a life married to Thierry Henry.

I don't remember a time that I wasn't anxious, waiting for some disaster to happen. As a child, I vividly remember lying in bed waiting to hear the start of ITV's *News at Ten*. I was convinced that if there were only nine chimes of Big Ben or eleven, my parents were going to die. As the chimes started in the room below my bedroom, my stomach would be in knots until the sound had got to, and stopped at, ten chimes. My night-terrors were not over, because, having seen an advert where a television left plugged in overnight burst into flames, I worried that my parents had gone to bed and forgotten to unplug the telly and we were *all* going to die, the dog going first as he slept downstairs. I walked to school worrying that my mother was going to die during the day, and walked home worrying about what I would find when I got back. The *Protect and Survive* nuclear adverts of the 1970s had me begging my parents to build a radiation-proof bunker in the back garden. I wonder whether I've lived with anxiety for so long, it's become as natural for me as breathing? I've stockpiled water and tinned food in case of the Millennium bug, bought enough rock salt in summer to last a small village the entire winter and stashed away face masks (bird flu) and sick bags (norovirus) along with the sanitising hand-gel.

It can't all be nurture, as my brother had the same upbringing, albeit four-and-a-half years behind me, and he has the sort of gung-ho attitude that I admire, but am unable to replicate. Extremes of weather or a bout of diarrhoea do not merit a change of plan, just a check that the car has enough anti-freeze in its radiator and a dose of Imodium.

JS also had this stoic mentality. However he felt or whatever the weather, his attitude was that you had to get up, dress up and show up, and if something had gone wrong, shut up. I mention this last one as, even if I did manage to drag myself off the sofa Nurofened up to the eyeballs, put on a swish frock and totter out, undoubtedly on arrival I would reply to my hosts polite enquiry of, 'How are you?' with a long list of ailments including the date the first symptom started and a detailed description of the progression of my illness. The phrase, 'Good journey?' as our coats were taken would see JS smiling and saying, 'Yes, thank you' as I launched into tales of near misses with lorries on the M25 and the state of the toilets in the motorway service station.

Poor man. I never really realised until he was dead just how much he had to put up with when he married me.

But I digress.

Six o'clock came. We trotted over the road clutching a bottle. It was a lovely evening putting the world to rights over champagne and snacks with witty, interesting people who I've known for years. The summer before he died, JS and I had sat in that same garden, with the same people at the same time of year. I have a photo of us all, squinting into the evening sun. The only difference between that evening and this one was that instead of JS sitting beside me, it was GGHW.

The next morning, I saw one of the people who had been at the soiree the night before.

She said, 'It was so lovely to see you last night. After you left, we all said that finally we've got the old Helen back. You haven't changed at all.'

Her words were kindly meant, but they jarred with me. Why? Wasn't to come out of the other side of this tunnel of grief unscathed something I had always strived for? Didn't I feel irritation, contempt even, towards widows who years after losing their husband were still proudly wearing the badge of widowhood, unable or unwilling to move forward into a new life? Of course I've changed because of what happened that dreadful February morning! How could witnessing the distress and then the death of the man I loved not have left its mark long after the condolence cards were packed into a shoebox? JS's death couldn't be just smoothed away, a new love simply slotting into his empty seat in the garden and life carrying on as before.

These people are kind and were very fond of JS, and I have no doubt that this comment only meant that they were happy to see me happy, but one of the side effects of JS dying seems to be that I am more sensitive. I feel any emotion more deeply than before, the highs being higher and the lows that much deeper. I am both happier than I was when he was alive and yet far sadder. I am calmer but angrier, stronger yet more readily moved tears, and I can feel all these emotions within moments of each other.

A few days ago, I was pottering about in the kitchen, snacking on some M&S sausage rolls, the really delicious 'handcrafted' ones sprinkled with poppy seeds, when ELO's *Mr Blue Sky* came on the radio (somewhat ironic, given that it was dark outside). It's such a happy song and one that reminds me of my teenage years. I turned up the volume and I danced and I laughed and I sang along. I felt deliriously happy. Life was great! The future looked rosy. Even The Hound's arthritic leg was improving. And then, within seconds, I was sobbing with the same intensity that I'd laughed moments before. I felt soul-crushingly destroyed, as if I'd never be truly happy again. Life was a struggle. The future looked full of misery and death. And then I became angry, angry about everything, so angry that I wanted to drop a sausage roll on the floor and jump up and down on it.

Before the song had even ended, I was done. Spent. The storm had raged and now it was over. There was no more hysterical laughter, crying or anger. I could eat a sausage roll without wanting to murder it under my slipper.

Perhaps I did have these highs and lows before JS died. Perhaps JS came back from golf one day, and looking through the window saw me massacring a sausage roll whilst listening to rock music, but by the time he'd cleaned his clubs and come into the house I was serenely floating around with a feather duster. If so, I don't remember being like that, but we don't always see ourselves how others see us, and JS is no longer around to ask.

I suspect that I have changed more than anyone – including me – realises. But here's a thought: perhaps these peaks and troughs of emotion even each other out into making me a much more balanced person than I was.

Now, that *would* be an unexpected bonus of grief.

SUICIDE IN SPRINGTIME

The stigma and awkwardness on someone's face when I follow the words that I am a widow with 'my husband died by suicide,' well, it's a bit like a slap in the face every time. Don't get me wrong, there are plenty of experiences of suicide, just not the method and circumstance of M. Then I think of the man that was, and this is just another thing that I can put down to being 'unconventional'. He was like it in life and he certainly seems to have been like it in death. It's one of the things that I loved about him, yet at the moment, it is something that is smacking me in the face at every turn... and quite frankly, making me feel more alone with every smack of the face. ~ **Emma S**

A red-penned note in my diary last week reminded me that it was the anniversary of the death of my late husband's first wife, Kay. When JS was alive, I needed no prompt that we were approaching the anniversary. At the beginning of every March, JS's behaviour changed: he became preoccupied, morose, snappy and withdrew into himself. Any reference to the emerging bulbs in the garden or the blossoming of the cherry trees in the road would have him muttering darkly, 'I hate spring. Nothing good ever happens in spring.' I remember staying at a holiday cottage in Northumberland and through the window, watching a group of lambs in the field over the road running up and sliding down a mound of earth, over and over again. I laughed and called them 'crazy lamb chops'. JS said darkly, 'People go crazy in spring.' In writing this, I looked into which season had the highest rates of suicide. Spring.

I knew that Kay had died in March, but I didn't know *when* in March, just that it was around the spring equinox. Twenty-two years of enduring Moody March, and yet I didn't find out the actual date until after JS's death. Why didn't I just ask him? Why didn't I say, 'Look, I know you find the run up to Kay's death difficult. Is there anything I can do?' I married a man whose first wife had died, and yet never in the twenty-odd years we were together did I ever ask him about her. Ever. Never even when we were sitting in an office in Barbados in May 1996 as JS clutched his divorce certificate and Kay's death certificate, waiting to get our marriage licence.

'How weird is that?' I can hear you say to yourself. 'What was wrong with you woman?'

In hindsight, it was bonkers, but when I first met JS in 1987, I was young and I was his employee and I was warned off the subject. Barely had I typed my first letter as a temporary secretary when his PA, Katie – an elderly woman built like an east German shot-putter on steroids who wore her long grey hair in a bun and her glasses on a chain – confided to me in whispered tones that JS had a 'tragic' past, because his first wife had 'killed herself', but that it must never be mentioned as JS didn't like the subject being brought up. Katie had had a colourful life and, though it later turned out that most of the outrageous stories she told were pure fantasy, she was right about JS's reaction: if Kay was mentioned, the shutters came down; he would change the subject, clam up or simply pretend to be deaf. JS *would* mention her, briefly, but on his terms: When a friend got a VW Beetle, I learnt that JS and Kay had one and had taken it abroad; I tried to get rid of an old guitar that had been in the cupboard for years and which I believed was JS's, but was told it was going nowhere as it was Kay's. Once, JS started crying in the car on the way to work when Don McLean's *American Pie* came on the radio. I asked him if he was OK and he said, 'It just reminds me of K…' He didn't even say her full name, but pulled himself up short and asked what meetings we had in the diary that day. He never expanded on these snippets of information about his past, and I never pressed him. I am not the jealous type: whilst friends quizzed their boyfriends over old loves, torturing themselves with every new detail, I had no burning desire to know more about a woman who was in the past. JS could surprise me though: at his birthday party and giving the roll-call of people he had loved and lost, he mentioned Kay's name. There were people there who thought of JS as a good friend and yet had no idea that he had had been married three times.

I wasn't jealous of Kay when JS was alive, but after he died, during the early months when I believed there was another life being lived in parallel to this one, I was *furious* that someone who had taken her own life and left JS was now reunited with him before me. How dare she get him back now! She had had her chance to be his wife and by her own actions she lost her life and sentenced JS to years of guilt and torment, the legacy of which could make him difficult to live with. Guilt? Torment? Other than Morose March, how did I know he suffered when he refused to talk about it? I knew because after he died, I was told that the JS before Kay's aspirin overdose and subsequent death from complications was not the same man as after it, that he had never really recovered from the guilt that he could have/should have done more. There were so many stories that swirled around Kay's death, but it was only after JS died that I finally learned the facts. JS didn't want to talk about it, and whilst he was alive, no one talked about it either, including me.

JS kept a handful of small boxes and files in a cupboard at the top of a run of built-in wardrobes in our bedroom. I never went up there, not because I feared what I might find, but because of the threat of humongous spiders. But after he died, there were missing documents that needed to be tracked down. Aside from the files of paper there was an old box file. I flipped it open, and there on the top, was a purse, a cheap little old battered purse, the sort with an old-fashioned clasp. Inside was a bus ticket, a handful of change and some rings, the sort of folksy rings I imagined someone in the 1970s who drove a Beetle, played a guitar and listened to Don McLean might wear. Under the purse was a photograph. It was the first time I had seen a picture of Kay, and I looked at it without any feelings at all: no sadness, no curiosity, nothing. I was telling a friend about it recently. She asked me what Kay looked like, and even though I had looked at the photograph for a minute or so, I couldn't tell her. I have a good memory for faces and details, but I had no recollection of the face in the photograph, not whether she had short hair or long, she was smiling or scowling, not even whether the photo was in black and white or colour.

I didn't carry on looking through the boxes when I realised that there was nothing relevant to the information I was looking for; JS is still too alive in my mind for me to go through his personal paperwork without it feeling like a violation of his privacy. I will keep them of course, for future generations to look through, should they want to, when I am dead and gone. For now, they are sealed back up and safely stored.

It still seems strange to me that I could know someone for almost a quarter of a century, not just know them but live with them and work with them and be their wife, and yet know so little about such a big part of their previous life. JS didn't want to talk about his past and I was too busy living in the present to worry about it. But now, thinking back, it all seems very odd.

Very odd and very sad.

JEMIMA

I went to the cemetery and they were digging a new grave near James. I feel so sorry for those poor people who are just starting out on this journey and have lost their loved one. ~ **Linz**

After JS died, I was walking The Hound on Hampstead Heath and, suddenly overwhelmed with sadness, stopped to sit on a bench in front of Kenwood House. At some point, the elderly lady next to me asked if I was OK. I told her that no, I wasn't, that my husband had died. Those were the days when any kind enquiry had me pouring out every detail of JS's death to complete strangers, many of whom I never saw again, possibly because whenever they saw me and The Hound, they turned and walked in the opposite direction to avoid becoming embroiled in another sob-fest. The elderly lady told me that she understood my pain: she was also recently widowed after fifty-plus years of marriage. As lovely as this old dear was, I remember thinking that despite her saying she understood my grief, she couldn't possibly do so. I was young and she was old. An elderly widow is not an oddity, a young one is. And then she said, 'You're still young. You still have the chance to meet someone else, to start a new life, to begin a new chapter. I'm too old. I don't have that hope for the future you can have.'

I smiled and made comforting sounds, but privately, I was incensed. Didn't Old Widow realise that there was no hope for either of us, but unlike her, I didn't have fifty-odd years of memories to comfort me? My husband had drowned, not got old and conked out. We all conk out at some point, and hers had followed the natural ageing process and died because it was his time to go. How dare she compare her loss to mine!

But now, four years later, I understand what she meant. We may have been disgusted by the thought of a new relationship during the early months or years after our partners died, but the fact is, that most of the men and women who were widowed around the same time as me have gone on to form new relationships: some have even re-married and had children. For those who haven't found new love, some are perfectly happy, albeit in a new context of happiness; others still harbour a hope that one day they will one be part of a couple.

A few months ago and in her late eighties, after 62 years of marriage to her husband, Hugh, my Aunty Betty died after a short illness. Recently, I asked my mother (my aunt's sister) how my uncle was coping. Uncle Hugh had told my father that despite the family being around he felt lonely, and that without his beloved 'Bet', he had nothing to go on for.

When I was a child, Aunty Betty made me a fabulous ragdoll that I christened, Jemima. Aunty B was an excellent seamstress, and Jemima was perfect, right down to her wide eyes and the slight smile on her lips, carefully embroidered by my aunt. She had a day dress with matching lace-trimmed pantaloons, a nightdress and thick, brown plaits held in place with red ribbons. Jemima is one of my prized possessions, and she now sits on top of a chest of drawers in the master bedroom of my cottage in Broadstairs. Sometimes I wonder about what will happen to Jemima when I die. I don't have any daughters to pass her on to, but I'd like her to stay in the family and not be stuffed in a black bin bag and taken to the charity shop along with bobbly jumpers and odd socks when I'm gone. I want her to go to my second cousin Eliza, Aunt Betty's granddaughter. I know Eliza will look after her and make sure Jemima always wears her pantaloons with her day dress.

I hadn't been to the cottage since Aunty Betty died. I took our bags up to the bedroom, and there was Jemima on the chest of drawers facing the door, but instead of looking at me, she was bent over, her head on her knees as if she was doubled up in pain. I lifted her head, but she collapsed again. I thought of my Uncle Hugh, widowed and lonely at 92. Downstairs, I could hear Gorgeous Grey-Haired Widower moving about: putting the heating on, opening the shutters. When I met that elderly widow on the bench on Hampstead Heath, I was furious with her for suggesting that I had some hope of a new life ahead of me, whereas she had only despair. She was right though. I couldn't see it at the time, but she was right.

I held Jemima and sobbed. I sobbed for my Aunty Betty who I will never see again; for Uncle Hugh who is old and alone even in a room full of his family, and for everyone who has lost someone dear to them, however old they are, however long they have known each other. Because the fact is, it doesn't matter whether you have been married for six days or 60 years, the pain of loss is searing and unrelenting. The difference is that widowed at 92, you have little hope and no energy to start that new chapter.

THEY SAID WHAT?

Someone suggested I might like to take up pottery. When I asked why pottery in particular, she said she had been thinking of the movie Ghost. ~ **Helen B**

When I asked some of my tribe of widowed friends to share with me their tales of what not to say to the newly bereaved, I was inundated with anecdotes that made me wince, laugh and shake my head with sheer disbelief that people could be so thoughtless. As tactless as some of the following quotes are, I have always been of the school of thought that I would rather people say something than nothing at all, however misjudged their comments. A few weeks after JS died, a neighbour, on seeing me in the street, put her head right through an open car window in an attempt to avoid me; walking past her protruding butt rather than her face was far more hurtful than anything she might have said to me, and I had a strong urge to pinch her bum, in anger, not in jest. Death is difficult for us all, and most people are simply at a loss of what to say and search for some common ground or (what they perceive to be) the silver lining in a dark cloud, often with cringeworthy results.

Personally, I've never minded the whole golf/football widow thing, even though my research for this book indicates it is a source of irritation for most of my tribe. I simply take it as a turn of phrase used by people who don't know any better. But when the Death Diet caused my weight to drop below seven stone (not a good look at 5 foot 8), I went nuclear at a friend who told me that she loved it when her husband was away on business, because she could cook meals using ingredients he refused to eat. 'Why don't you start cooking things that John wouldn't eat when he was alive?' she suggested. I will also never forgive the local travel agent who, when I went to see him to get some paperwork about the Barbados trip he'd sold us, asked me, 'Is it back yet?' Genuinely confused as to what he was referring to, I asked him what he meant. 'It. You know. On the plane.' He looked as if someone was manually extracting faeces from his constipated bottom and the penny dropped. 'You mean, is my husband's body home?' I corrected him. A few weeks later whilst waiting to see the doctor, we both realised we were sitting next to each other in the waiting room. I said 'Hello,' and reminded him who I was. He got up and walked out of the surgery muttering that that he had 'forgotten something'.

Even widows get it wrong: I've had widows say things to me such as, 'You must feel it's difficult to keep your head above water,' or, 'I expect you are drowning in a sea of paperwork' and so on. Things that upset me then don't upset me now, and I can laugh rather than be outraged.

So here, in their own words and obtained with the promise of total anonymity, are examples of what *not* to say to a widow:

'My sister (always the Drama Queen) said she was finding it very hard to cope with my husband's death. "People avoid me in Waitrose because they don't know what to say to me!" she sobbed.'

'Once, on a bad morning at one of my daughter's soccer classes in the winter, another mom asked me how I was doing and I said, "Pretty shitty." "Why? What's going on?" she asked. A valid question really, even though she knew about my husband. But I couldn't help answering, "Oh still kind of stuck on the whole husband dying thing."'

'My mother knew that G and me were going through a rough time when he died, but that we were hoping with counselling we could work through our problems. With a house full of visitors, she cornered me in the kitchen and whispered, "Look at it this way. A divorce would have been much more expensive."'

'I was telling someone how I kept bursting into tears in the shops, in my car and so on. She said, "Oh, I know what you mean. I kept doing that when our rabbit died."'

'I told a parent at the school gates that my husband had died. She asked how he had died and when I said, "Suicide. He shot himself," she said, "Are you sure?"'

'I had to return to the hospital where my husband had died. The nurse commented that I had lost weight. When I told her how much she said, "That's impressive! Do you feel more energetic?"'

'One guy said to me after I told him I was widowed, "Oh, but you're better now?"'

'As everyone left after the funeral, someone said to me: "Oh that's good, everyone's going, you'll be able to get back to normal now."'

'We were working out funeral cars and someone said, "I want my partner to come with me, you need your partner at a time like this." "Yes" said I, "Mine's the one in the hearse in front."'

'The first counsellor I saw six weeks after P's sudden death and four months pregnant with his child, started quizzing me on what I was going to tell our child about his father. Errr.'

'After my first husband split up with his second wife, he was feeling sorry for himself and said, "It's easier for you, you don't have to picture him with someone else." I replied, "No, you're right, I can picture the last time I saw him instead, on a trolley, cold, dead."'

'At six months: "I bet you think there's something wrong with you, you haven't met anybody yet." After six months: "Haven't you met anybody yet? You need someone to go to the theatre with."'

'When I stopped work: "So you've now given up work and are living the life of the idle rich?" Me: "See that camellia bush over there? That's where his ashes are."'

'This was a corker: "Bad things happen to you to teach you to be a better person." Really? I'd love to know what my then twelve- and ten-year-olds had done that was so bad.'

'About two to three weeks after D died, I had a call from a "friend". She said, "You doing anything fun today?" I said, "No, I'm very down today, very upset." She said "Oh? How come? It's really sunny 'n' everything."'

'I instantly (and often) got the "Well at least he didn't leave you" line. Within a couple of days, my mother-in-law assured me it was much harder for her daughter whose husband left her.'

'Said to me three weeks after by a neighbour, "I must say you do look good on it." My answer? "I would have rather joined Weight Watchers or Slimming World." She never spoke to me again.'

'At the "ham tea" after the funeral, still in the widders weeds: "Oh T (friend) is a golf widow and you are a real one" – like it was a fun coincidence and we'd all say, "Small World!" (Poor T was mortified).'

'"Going out again with your new friends? You really are living the dream."'

'At an anniversary party last year, a stranger sitting at the same table as me (with her husband of 40+ years) says, "Are you the woman whose husband died young?" Me (uncomfortably): "Um, yes. He was 47." Her: "Now, tell me, how long were you married?" Me quietly (conscious of others listening in): "18 years." Her: "Fffft, my niece's friend was married six months and was pregnant when her husband died. You were very lucky. Very lucky. You shouldn't complain." Uh ok. I actually hadn't said a word before you grilled me.'

'Comments I got ranged from, "Why do bad things always happen to you?" and, "Well at least you've got your daughter" to, "Oh, I'm so jealous. I wish my husband would die then I could start again."'

'Not my story, so I can't name her, but one of "us" was asked by the milkman if she needed as much milk now her husband was dead.'

'The benefit of having a large gap between my kids' ages is you get some diverse shit said to you. Re: my eldest (17 when his dad died): "At least he had his dad for all his childhood." Re: my youngest (seven): "At least she hasn't TOO many memories."'

'I remember going to the JobCentre to sort out the widow's bereavement payment, and the lady saw my form and shouted, "Angela! I've got a bereavement!!" Just the sort of attention I wanted to attract!'

'On a date, in the early months, the date said that he knew just how I was feeling after the death of the man I worshipped for 23 years – he compared my loss and pain to his symptoms when he had glandular fever.'

'One of my widowed friends lost her husband at the end of November. She later received a Christmas card with the "Mr and" crossed out.'

'Just recently, a friend was bemoaning the fact her friends were having to deal with elderly parents dying, and said how much better it was for those whose parents died young as they didn't have to worry about care homes, etc. She got a glare and a bit of a mouthful.'

'I went to the Building Society to deposit my husband's pension (lump sum) into my account. The lady said, "Oh, how lucky you are, having that amount." Not really...'

'My sister-in-law told me she had been a single parent too, you know; her husband had been in the army.'

'My best friend (having an affair) complained about her complicated life and envied me the freedom widowhood brings.'

'Six months after my husband died, my brother told me to "stop feeling sorry for myself and get over it." He kinda got a mouthful and has not spoken to me since. Both my mother and my sister "envied the love I had had," and that "I was very lucky." Two husbands, both dead from cancer, does not feel lucky.'

'I bumped into an ex-colleague in the supermarket a few weeks after the funeral. We had a catch up and on hearing my "news" he announced I was in a better position than him, as he was getting a divorce and at least I didn't have to split everything!'

'Having been widowed twice, on my wedding day to my third husband, a "friend" held my hand, looked me in the eye and said most sincerely, "I'm so pleased you're not afraid of scoring a hat trick."'

'A teacher at my daughter's school caught me outside when I was waiting for her and asked me, "What are you going to do about money now you're a widow? I expect you'll struggle? Do you get any benefits?" Now, bearing in mind I'd barely spoken to the woman, I turned to her and said, "Why? Are you offering a loan?" She shut up.'

'At the funeral, someone said, "I suppose you'll be moving to somewhere smaller." I live in a two-bedroom house. How much room did they think I needed or how much did they think my husband took up? My mum intervened and said, "Yes, she's going to live in a burrow."'

'When I was out on a girls' night out, an acquaintance, on hearing that I'd been widowed (by then about three years) and not seeing anyone asked me, "What do you do for sex? Are you a lesbian?" I was gobsmacked.'

'My favourite was the "friend" who sympathised as her husband worked away for three nights every week, and felt it appropriate to tell me that her daughter (my son's age) was already in tears over it, and "god knows how we'll cope if it increases to four days!"'

'My aunt told me at two weeks that I'd be ok as my husband's best friend was still single. That's ok then – sorted.'

'Within the week of Steve dying suddenly and unexpectedly, I met a neighbour out walking her dog. She said, "I am so sorry to hear about your husband. Was it gang related?" then in the next breath, "Don't worry, you are a very attractive girl you won't be on your own for long." Steve was a six-foot black guy so I guess that's why she thought gang related – as you do!'

'The one that sticks the most is my mother-in-law shouting to me in the kitchen at my daughter's birthday party (19 days after he died), "You having any more kids T?" Me: "I doubt it. My husband seems to have died." Her: "You'll be okay. You'll meet someone soon."'

'The most spectacular one I had was at a party where I ended up sitting on a sofa between two other people. I didn't realise they were a couple until the girl leaned over me to say to him, "This is the one I told you about whose husband died."'

AND NOW

Life for me is very different now; it is over four years for me and sometimes it feels like I just saw him, and others, like he was never there at all and I made him up. I think I'll always feel that, somewhere in a parallel universe, I am living the life I was meant to, and this one is somewhat of a substitute. But, I'm here and surviving and in many ways, experience happiness every day. It's just different. ~ **Emma A**

During a bereavement coaching session, my coach, Shelley, asked me to imagine my life in the future, perhaps five years on. It was about four months after JS's death, and so I just sat there sobbing and rocking and slurping tea, totally unable to face tomorrow, let alone another five years. This was too broad a question, so Shelley narrowed her focus. 'Darling, where can you see yourself living?' she asked. 'Tell me about where you would like to live, what your surroundings are like, how you feel living there.'

This was more like it! I knew *exactly* the answer to Shelley's question. I would be living in central London, probably somewhere off Marylebone High Street, in a stylish flat entirely decorated in tasteful neutral tones filled with fresh flowers and scented candles. Hanging on the walls would be a mixture of JS's English watercolours and more contemporary work I'd purchased since his death, the odd sculpture dotted here and there, and books, *lots* of books. I imagined holding little soirees for friends to whom I would serve tasty morsels purchased from nearby delicatessens as jazz softly played in the background. I'd spend my days writing, reading, floating around art galleries, possibly doing another degree in something like psychology. In the evening, I'd go the theatre and walk back through the West End to my little nest. My key words were: serene, cultured, stylish.

Now, for a woman who at that time could barely remember her own date of birth, and couldn't see beyond the next hour without becoming hysterical, this future fantasy of jazz, snacks and sculpture in Marylebone was quite impressive, wasn't it? The thing is, over the years I *had* thought about the sort of life I might eventually lead when I found myself on my own. As JS was 19 years older than me, I had always assumed that I would be widowed, though I reckoned around the age of 70, because JS had grown old and conked out, not at 46 because he'd drowned.

It is now well over four years since JS died, and am I in my tasteful, fragrant, central London flat listening to jazz whilst whipping up a plate of canapés for pre-theatre nibbles with friends? Am I heck! I'm in a large old house in Royston, Hertfordshire (only 40 miles from London, but a world away, Planet Royston if you like) living with The Hound, Gorgeous Grey-Haired Widower and his two sons. Instead of jazz in the background, there is the noise of doors slamming and cars coming and going and phones constantly bleeping. As for tasty morsels, according to the three male inhabitants of this house, there is no dish that can't be improved by adding garlic bread and lashings of tomato ketchup. I never know who is coming or going – or what pouting poppet's shoes will appear by the front door overnight – and the entire house smells of a hamster cage sprayed with Lynx. There are rooms that I dare not venture into because of the smell, the mess and the darkness, the logic of a young male brain being, 'Why open curtains that are just going to be closed again later?' I banned takeaways from being taken into the bedrooms because I was fed up of waking up to the smell of chicken madras on the landing, but plates still mysteriously disappear, only to reappear on top of (not in) the dishwasher. It's impossible to know whether someone is dead in their bed or sleeping off a hangover, as even The Hound going mental when he sees the neighbourhood cat through the window, fails to rouse them. I never realised one pair of trainers could infuse an entire house with a toxic stink of sweat and testosterone, or how much meat men can eat.

I'm still not entirely sure how it happened, how the vision I gave to Shelley with such clarity and certainty could have veered so spectacularly off-course.

I don't regret moving from the London house, not for one second; it was time to go. All the redecorating and rearranging of furniture wasn't going to turn 'our' house in to 'my' house. GGHW and I both needed a fresh start, and we spent months discussing various permutations of house, location, timing and occupants. In the end, we decided that the two most important things were for us all to be together, and not to disrupt the boys' lives any further than they already had been. So we bought a house, and I moved out of London and headed up the A1(M), and GGHW moved house and stayed within the same postcode.

The process of selling my house wasn't as painful as I had imagined, although I absolutely hated seeing the 'For Sale' sign outside and, for the first week, kept the blinds closed in the hall all day. I was completely sure that I was doing the right thing, and felt excited rather than frightened when the house sold. In a bizarre coincidence, my buyer was a lovely woman who had been widowed some years ago, and who had written a book about how walking her dog on Hampstead Heath had helped her heal. Months before, I'd downloaded it onto my Kindle and read it, sobbing, in bed.

We exchanged contracts. I was still sure I was doing the right thing.

About ten days before moving, I had to visit the new house to meet a man about some dog-proof fencing. I sat in the car on the drive and felt overwhelmed. What was I thinking? What was I doing? Tearfully, I told GGHW that I wanted to pull out, that it didn't matter who sued me for the collapse of the sale of either property, I wasn't moving and they would have to physically drag me out of the house to get their furniture in. When I realised that there was no way out, I considered 'pretending' to be too mentally unwell to proceed to completion; I'd read on the internet that a house sale had fallen through for just that reason. It was a desperate time.

But of course I didn't feign a breakdown, and the nearer it got to moving day, the more detached I became and the less the house felt like mine.

There were a few hitches further along the chain: twice, the completion date which I'd been assured couldn't be changed was, but just under six weeks from accepting an offer, the removal men moved in for two days and I moved out.

Before finally closing the front door there was something I needed to do. I had kept back from the packers JS's and Rufus' ashes. Alone, I walked through the house hugging the boxes in my arms, remembering the good times and saying 'goodbye' out loud, to every room. And then two years, five months and three days since JS drowned, and almost 17 years after we moved in, I said to the boxes in my arms, 'Come on you two, it's time to go.' I closed the front door for the last time, put the two sets of ashes on the passenger seat of my car, strapped them in with the seatbelt, and drove away.

And here I am, in Royston. I don't miss the old house at all (except my kitchen, I loved my kitchen), but boy do I miss London. Royston has many things going for it including lovely neighbours and a strong sense of community, so it's not that I don't like living here – far from it – it's just that I'm a London girl, and when I go to London, I now feel as if I'm in some kind of location limbo, neither a tourist nor a local. Just as I used to tell taxi drivers and shop assistants and random strangers at bus stops that I had been widowed, I now find myself telling those same people that up until recently I'd lived in London for 31 years. I'm still shell-shocked that my life after JS's death is so different from my life before it, and it's taking time to adjust to. I genuinely can't get my head around why this household gets through so many toilet rolls or biscuits, or why damp washing is left in the machine for days. Having seen a very expensive piece of vintage 'artisan' cheddar being slapped between two slices of Mighty White and rammed in the toaster, I now buy mega blocks of plastic cheese, as no one (but me) seems to notice the difference. GGHW suggested that I squirreled away my own supplies, but this reminded me of my student days when I shared a house with four boys and had to hide food under my bed to stop them finding it.

JS's suitcase is still packed and in the spare bedroom, his golf clubs are in the garage, and his ashes (and Rufus') have yet to be scattered. I finally took my rings off, and had my engagement and wedding ring merged into one 'dress' ring to wear on my right hand. JS said he was going to buy me a yellow diamond for my fiftieth birthday, so I had two small 'stacking' rings made to sit either side of the new ring; one is set with nine tiny yellow diamonds and the other with five, symbols of our wedding anniversary, 9th May. It's JS's fiftieth birthday present to me, or that's how I like to think of it.

Despite the loo rolls and the cheese and the stinky feet and missing London, life is good in ways that over four years ago I could never have imagined. It's not all rainbows and puppies, but then that's life, widowed or not. There are still times where I feel knocked off my feet by all that has happened, and I suspect that will always be the case, for *all* of us. The other day, GGHW and I were debating whether grief is finite, but the feeling of loss isn't (which is my view), or whether you grieve forever (which is his). We agreed that the end of the day, the semantics of grief versus loss don't matter; they amount to the same thing, which is that we miss someone we love, and that there will always be an emptiness in our lives that our spouses are no longer here to see their children grow up, to take part in family celebrations and to reminisce over the decades of shared history we had together.

A few weeks ago, GGHW and I were walking back home late one night, having been out to dinner with friends. It had been a lovely evening, but as I walked home, I realised that four years ago I had never met any of these people, didn't know GGHW or his family and had never even heard of Royston. I suddenly felt soul-crushingly lonely and homesick, right back on that alien landscape of Planet Grief where nothing felt or looked familiar. I looked up at the sky, inky black and studded with stars over Royston Heath and thought, 'JS, come back, please! The big experiment is over. You can come home now.' The feeling didn't last long, but for the few moments it did, my despair was raw. And then I walked through the gate and up our drive, and into the house which smells like a curry-eating male rodent's nest, and sometimes looks like one too. GGHW went into the kitchen to make a cup of tea whilst I let The Hound out for his last wee of the day. We stood chatting, waiting for the kettle to boil and The Hound to give a single 'woof' to be let back in. It felt so gloriously normal and comforting and right. It felt like home. *Our* home.

It's not always easy living in a home that came together through sudden death. We all carry the burden of grief, and we deal with it in different ways. The lads will only ever have one mother, but I hope that they will come to see me as an older sister, someone who will always love them, look out for them, want the best for them and fight their corner with and for them, however much we drive each other nuts at times. A moment ago, one of them wandered into my study (even though it's supposed to be out of bounds when I'm working), and asked how the book was going. I told him that I was writing the final chapter, but that I was finding it difficult to know how to end it, that there was so much I still wanted to say. He stood and thought for a moment and then said, 'Why don't you just write: And they all lived happily ever after.'

A FINAL REASSURANCE

I wish I could go back and make my newly widowed self believe what others told me back then. Now, it is me who tries to tell new widows: this is not the end of your happiness. There is every chance for a new kind of happy again. With a new partner, or on your own. You CAN do it! ~ ***Marieke***

Writing new material, reviewing and editing old blog posts and re-reading every one of the thousands of comments left on *Planet Grief* in the last four years was far more painful and emotionally draining than I had anticipated when I agreed to write this book. I was first approached with the idea of publishing it about a year after JS died, but I felt that it was too soon, that I was still in the thick of bereavement, still crazy with grief. In any case, *Planet Grief* was never started with any intention of publication; it was started to help me – and others – heal through writing and sharing our experience of bereavement. Later, the opportunity cropped up again, but by that point I was fed up with anything to do with death and wanted to leave it all behind me. Finally, the right combination of timing and a publisher/editor who I count as a good friend and someone I trust completely, came together, and I agreed to write the book.

I have never had any doubt that JS would approve of my publishing this account of my grief, despite its deeply personal nature. I have tried to be as accurate as my memory and my diaries permit, but if JS took a day-return trip from Heaven to Hertfordshire to comment on the narrative, I suspect he would vehemently dispute my recollection of some of the events during the 24 years we knew each other. I hope that he would feel, on balance, that the book has reflected him in death as he was in life: dignified, decent and gracious, a man with a kind, open heart and an infuriatingly stubborn mind.

It has been heartbreaking to look back on my grief as it unfolded, and to re-read the words of those whose lives had also been ripped apart by death. At times, my writing was agonisingly familiar to me: the depth of loneliness coming into the garage late at night or dragging the wheelie bin out into the street will remain with me, but I look back on other snapshots of living after loss and barely recognise myself. Many times over the last few months I have sobbed at my keyboard, crying for times lost, for times that will never be, and for the widow I was, but not for the woman I am now.

I will be forever thankful to every contributor to *Planet Grief.* Each comment, however brief, created a feeling of strength and solidarity as we tribe of bewildered souls struggled to form a new life from the ashes of our old one. I contacted 31 widows and widowers to ask for their blessing to use their words in this book, and I was overwhelmed by their support, how they hoped that their journey through bereavement might continue to provide hope, help and comfort to others. Many found it emotional. As Bonnie wrote back to me: 'I have to confess that your email took me straight back to those raw, early days. When I read my quotes I wept and wept, and I've thought of nothing else all week.'

There were two widows, 'Rose' and 'Sue G', that I was unable to track down, despite my best efforts. I hope that life is treating them well. I have changed their identifying details and trust that they are happy that their words are being used to help others claw their way back out from the pit of despair. I'd love to hear from them.

It was a joy to hear from men and women who, when I first 'met' them through the internet, were on their knees with grief. None of them have 'moved on' – they have all 'moved forward'. They have sailed the world, run marathons, started businesses, found new love, re-married, had babies, moved house, completed degrees, started new careers, relocated abroad or simply managed to go on holiday, sit in the garden or on the sofa without tears. As wonderful as it was learning about how their lives had changed from the days where even an hour felt like an eternity in Hell, the best news of all was learning that these men and women had reached a point in their life where they could say they were happy, even if as one widow confessed, '…sadness always bubbles just below the surface and is easily tapped into.' David, who thought being a fifty-year-old, fat, short and grey-haired widower with two children meant he was a lost cause is now living with another widow. Even Sam, suddenly widowed whilst walking to the first scan of her unborn child, says that life with her son is 'pretty good', an unthinkable statement not so long ago.

I said at the beginning of this book that if even you don't believe me that life will get better, just trust me. If you still don't trust me, trust the widows and widowers I contacted who wrote back to confirm that a good life after death is possible, such as Jules, who sent me this update when I contacted her. For me, Jules' words sum up everything I hope for anyone who despairs that bereavement has condemned them to a life of endless misery.

A postscript on me: I am now at 11 years (wow, can hardly believe that!). My children are now grown up, one working and one about to start university. They are happy and that pleases me. I worked really hard to keep their childhood 'normal'. I didn't want them to look back on their childhood and think: 'Everything was great until Dad died and then Mum was a blubbering mess in the corner'. I think I have managed to achieve this and that, for me, is a really big piece of happiness.

On a personal level, I did meet someone else. We met through mutual friends, we 'dated' (is that the right words for grown-ups?) slowly for a quite a few years and then he finally moved in with me. I too am happy.

I think of my husband every day at some point, just a passing thought or memory sometimes, sometimes more, but it is not with sadness any more. I loved him and he loved me. He would be so proud of me and our children. I no longer have tears and grief, but I do still have memories and thoughts, and love.

It will all be OK in the end.
We promise you.

THIS BOOK IS DEDICATED TO...

Whenever I had a book published and wondered to whom I should dedicate it, JS would urge me to think carefully about whose name I wanted in print alongside mine and remind me in a warning tone, 'Remember what my uncle said.'

JS's family was steeped in the book trade: his uncle, John Baker (known as JB), was a deeply respected and influential bookseller and publisher, latterly with Phoenix House (an imprint of JM Dent & Sons), as well his own eponymous publishing company. JS adored and admired his uncle, who along with his wife, Aunt Emmeline (who JB met when they both worked for Macmillan in the 1920s), lived with JS's family in Wimbledon. Although JB died in 1971, barely a day went by without some reference to him, and now JS is gone I find myself saying, 'As John's uncle used to say...'

One of the stories JS told was of an author John Baker published, and who dedicated his first book to his wife. By the time said book was published, husband and wife had separated. The author asked John Baker to change the dedication from his ex-wife to his current girlfriend (and cause of the divorce) on the next print run, an expensive and laborious task in the days of hand-set lettering. This was duly done, and the second edition published, only for the author to contact JB to say that he had a new girlfriend who was demanding that his ex-girlfriend's name be deleted and replaced with hers. The author was very sorry, but to save further tantrums, could JB change the dedication yet again? John Baker was a man not known for his tolerance; he told the author that a book dedication was earned, not demanded, and that until the author sorted out his love life, the ex-girlfriend's name would remain in print.

Every one of the people to whom this book is dedicated has earned their place in print. Rebuilding my life after JS's death has been a team effort – I call it Team HB – and what a Premiership-quality, Championship-winning side it has been. Some individuals who are named below are no longer in the current squad – we've drifted apart or gone our separate ways – but I will be forever grateful for the contribution they made at the bleakest time in my life. So with that in mind, this book is dedicated to:

Those on Treasure Beach on 27th February 2011, who plunged into the water in Paynes Bay, Barbados, and risked their lives to try to save JS: I don't know who you are, but your selfless bravery will never be forgotten. Thank you.

Valda Hamblion, who stepped out from the crowd. The phrase, 'Thank you,' doesn't seem enough for all that you did.

My brother, **John Bailey**, whom I used to call on a red toy phone from my bedroom to his ('This is Battersea Dogs Home!'), and 40 years later, was the first person I called from Barbados ('There's been a terrible accident'), and who took the earliest flight he could from London to be with me. John is one of life's truly great guys and a man I'm proud to call my brother. Love you, baby bro.

Tracey Stratton, the second person I spoke to, a woman who put her life on hold for me and managed to appear completely unfazed when I ran around the house screaming as I tried to escape from my own grief, even if she later admitted my behaviour freaked her out. Remember, whatever happens Trace, don't forget the diamonds.

JS's sister, **Sally Day**, and his niece and her husband, **Catherine** and **Chris Day**, who had their own immense grief to deal with, and who have continued to make me feel part of the Sinfield/Day clan in a way they have done since I first met them 25 years ago. I could not wish for better in-laws or tastier egg sandwiches.

Daniel & Jennie: Your father was so proud of you. So am I. Jennie: special love and thanks. xxx

The **Rev. Fraser Dyer**, my brother-in-law, who JS loved as much as I do, and who listened, counselled and supported me, *and* made fabulous soup.

Geoff & Corinne Ramskill: Strangers in the night who I wish I had met under different circumstances. Thank you for coming to my rescue and letting me pace in your bathroom.

Laney and Pam: You will both be forever in my heart. Laney: I still think I've won the bet.

Emma Sandalls: Wow! Look how far we've come since Gordon's Wine Bar. Proud of you, Thelma.

Kate Boydell: We've had our differences, but I owe you a great deal, as do all the widows and widowers who found comfort through your Merry Widow website. Thank you classmate.

To every reader of and contributor to *Planet Grief*: You helped so many people in the depths of despair, not just me. I award you all lifetime gold stars. ★★★

Shelley Whitehead: You are proof that the people you need most, come into your life at the time you need them most. As you often said to me, I'll always here for you, though I can't provide such delicious South African biscuits.

Jan Rochester: It wasn't supposed to turn out this way for either of us, was it? Thank goodness we have each other! Love you (but not your lippie). xxx

Robin & Rosalyn Browne: A calm and comforting eye in the storm of my hurricane of grief. Thank you for *everything*.

Mike Silver and Josephine Ruane: I often think of you, and the kindness you showed in Barbados and London.

Reneé Cooper; Karen Cotter; the late and very great Andrew Eliel; Helen English; Rob Francis; Murray and Joanne Fuller; David and Sue Glasser; Simone Green; Gwyn and Yvonne Headley; Helga Klausgraber not forgetting Lottie and Duke Church; Michael Leather; Terri Oosthuizen; Mark Riley; Sarah Sharp; Helen Webster; Leise Wilson and the Castle House ladies, Ruth and Diana; Mick Wells and Katherine Judge: I didn't always show it at the time, but for the dog-walking, the lunches, keeping an eye on Raglan Cottage, the blog techie stuff, the Ottolenghi ricotta tarts, the endless cups of tea, the phone calls which I often didn't answer or return, the invitations which I often turned down or ducked out of, for giving up your time to listen to me sobbing or ranting and for your patience, thank you.

Tony Hurley: JS used to say that he would trust you with his life; now I trust you with mine. The man at the top, and a top man. Thank you for knowing when to pass the tissues and when to tell me to stop sobbing and pull myself together.

David Johnson: Thank goodness for your 'l-ee-telle grey cells' and for your 'never give up' attitude. Poirot would be proud of you. I'm proud you're in my team.

Emily Thomas: Not just my editor, but a trusted friend who was consistently there for me throughout my darkest days. Emily, thank you for giving me the opportunity and confidence to write this book, for your sensitive shaping of the manuscript and for your good-natured patience when I dug my heels in over suggested edits.

The Stewart Family, Jamie and Oliver and Keith and Brenda, and the Bassingbourn gang, for being so welcoming to me under difficult circumstances.

JS: Just because you are gone, doesn't mean that you don't live on.

And finally, this book is dedicated to my Gorgeous Grey-Haired Widower, Ian Stewart: BB, I love you. You are my happy ending.

BIBLIOGRAPHY & RESOURCES

Frankl, Viktor E. 1946. *Man's Search for Meaning*. Reprint. London: Rider/Ebury Publishing, 2004.

Gilbert, Elizabeth. *Eat, Pray, Love*. London: Bloomsbury Publishing, 2006.

Green, John. *Paper Towns*. London: Bloomsbury Publishing, 2010.

Harper Neeld, Elizabeth. *Seven Choices: Finding Daylight After Loss Shatters Your World*. New York: Grand Central Publishing, 2008.

Maslin, Janet. *New York Times: Book of The Times* review of Joyce Carol Oates' *A Widow's Story*. February 13, 2011.

McCann, Kate. *Madeleine*. London: Bantam Press/Ebury, 2011.

Oates, Joyce Carol. *A Widow's Story*. London: Fourth Estate, 2011.

Tolle, Eckhart. 1999. *The Power of Now: A Guide to Spiritual Enlightenment*. Reprint. London: Hodder & Stoughton, 2005.

Turner, Elizabeth. *The Blue Skies of Autumn*. London: Simon & Schuster, 2011.

Cruse: Bereavement Care: www.cruse.org.uk

The Samaritans: www.samaritans.org

The Suzy Lamplugh Trust – Live Life Safe: www.suzylamplugh.org

WAY: Widowed and Young: www.widowedandyoung.org.uk

Every effort has been made to contact those whose words appear in this book and to obtain their blessing. If there are any errors or omissions, please do notify the publisher so that they can be corrected or incorporated in future reprints or editions.

ABOUT THE AUTHOR

Helen Bailey was born in Newcastle-upon-Tyne in 1964, and grew up in Ponteland, Northumberland. She spent more than three decades living and working in London, but since 2013 has lived in Royston, Hertfordshire, with her partner, his two sons, her dachshund, Boris, and a permanent sense of bewilderment as to how radically her life has changed since 27th February 2011, the date on which JS, her husband, drowned whilst they were on holiday in Barbados.

Further comfort, hope and help can be found at www.planetgrief.com

PLANET GRIEF